GOD HAS NO EDGES, DREAMS HAVE NO BOUNDARIES

Best Wishes

AWhm Bernard, Ph.D

GOD HAS NO EDGES,

DREAMS HAVE NO BOUNDARIES

Unlocking the Power of the Inner Mind

ARTHUR BERNARD

God Has No Edges, Dreams Have No Boundaries: Unlocking the Power of the Inner Mind

Illustrations by John Selleck.

All names have been changed to protect the privacy of the contributors.

Published by Wheatmark®
610 East Delano Street, Suite 104
Tucson, Arizona 85705 U.S.A.
www.wheatmark.com

International Standard Book Number: 978-1-60494-149-4
Library of Congress Control Number: 2008931644

CONTENTS

ACKNOWLEDGMENTS

My dreams were the primary inspiration for writing this book, so I thank my unconscious/superconscious mind for injecting me with wisdom and enlightenment. I don't know how or why I have had such unique adventures while asleep, but I can honestly say many of the most enduring and unique experiences of my life have come from this inner domain. They have opened my mind to the spiritual realm, revealed the inner healing dimensions of my cancer illness, led me into investments that have reimbursed me handsomely, and essentially helped me discover the real source of truth. I never would have thought of many of these ideas at the conscious level, and I felt an obligation to share much of what I have learned from my dreams so others would be stimulated to look for guidance in their dreams. Dreams can deepen your connection to the inner spirit, and awaken you to the great potential of knowledge that resides in your sleeping psyche.

There are many people to thank. First I would like to thank my beautiful and dedicated wife who has the most encompassing love I have ever experienced. She is my dream girl and has helped my dreams come true. With her intuitive insights, she has been the guiding beacon of my life. Whenever I need new dream material, she has been a constant provider. Her suggestion to move to California during our early married years sprang from her ability to listen to her inner spirit. This West Coast state was the home of her uncle, Jay Dunn, a gifted and inspiring Jungian analyst who ignited the dreaming mechanism in my soul and helped set me on a life path that got more and more spiritually bountiful. He made Jung proud. I thank you, Jay, for a job so well done, and I thank your beautiful wife, Esther, for encouraging and nurturing our California growth.

And what can I say about the great Jung who came to me in a dream and revealed a divine secret? A mind like his is a rare entity. His gifts to the world of science and the spirit are immeasurable, and his voluminous writings will endure forever.

I would also like to thank my two sons, Joshua and David, and the new addition to our family, Tim, who have all put up with my idiosyncrasies and filled my heart with love. David has kept me alert with his complex dreams, and Josh and Tim have given much support and encouragement to expand the dream seminars. The critical eyes of all three have been extremely helpful.

The writing of this book was greatly aided by one of my editors, Maude Adjarian. Thanks for your kind patience in laboring through this document a few times because of my additions. Tori DeAngelis, a writer in the Syracuse area, offered excellent suggestions and made significant contributions to my work. Susan Cohen's perceptive eye saw hidden gems that even I didn't know were there. Marilyn Forstot's sensitivity to the written word trimmed the excess down to essentials. John Selleck of Beverly Hills produced all the delightful drawings, which brought many of the dreams to life. Mr. Selleck's work is included in the National Watercolor Society's permanent collection, and he is an honorary member of Watercolor USA. His paint and collage works have been featured in *Watercolor Magic* and *American Artist* magazines, and he has won numerous awards in Collage Artists of America Exhibitions. Geraldine Stump created the epilogue poem, which could not have been more appropriate for my kite dream. I am especially thankful to Wheatmark book editor Susan Wenger, and publishing services specialist Kathryn Gautreaux. Their professional input and design talents were invaluable.

Special thanks to all of my personal clients and dream-seminar participants who were open to sharing their most intimate secrets and soul messages. Dream-workshop members were of great assistance in submitting so many dreams in so many categories. Space limited the number of dreams I could use, but the contribution of every dream played a major role in the creation of this book.

Extra thanks to Mark Sheron and Jack Blinzler for being such loyal and devoted friends. Our weekly telephone conversations for the past fourteen years have been inspirational. Your insights into my *acknowledgments*

dreams are soul-stirring and penetrating, often hitting the bull's-eye when I missed it. Your support during my cancer episode was a gift of life. My appreciation is also extended to Lesley Teitelbaum, who gave me immense support and kept my spirit nourished, and to Michael and Marsha Zaccaria for reading and commenting on segments of the book.

And lastly, I thank all of my friends and family for their continued interest, support, and love.

INTRODUCTION

Your vision will become clear only when you look into
your heart. Who looks outside, dreams. Who looks inside,
awakens.

Carl Jung

We Sleep to Awaken

This book is not only a how-to manual. It's a wake-up call full of
inner surprises. The first is illustrated in the title: *God Has No Edges,
Dreams Have No Boundaries.* A strong connection exists between its
two parts. Although the link may not be obvious at first glance, it will
be as this book unfolds. The second and probably the most significant
surprise is that this is a book that could bring another dimension to
personal quests for God. People who are suffering from the spiritual
hunger that traditional religion is not feeding can find substantial
nourishment within these pages.

You may not understand where your dreams come from or why
they come, but you have been granted this inner genius through a
natural inheritance, and great blessings await those of you who take
them seriously. Dreams can frequently exceed cognitive abilities and
conscious linear reasoning. Although the art of dream work is still
in its infancy, renewed interest in inner development is spawning
inspired inquiry into the complexity of human life. Throughout this
book, I offer examples of how dreams can heal serious illnesses, change
the course of history, contribute new discoveries to science, serve as
personal guides through emotional minefields, open up the spiritual
realm, foresee profitable financial investments, and reveal your hidden
talents and abilities. You may think of yourself as an average dreamer,
but you are capable of having extraordinary dreams and brilliant
insights that can reveal your unknown potential. Remarkably, all this

lies just on the other side of sleep. This book will show you step-by-step how to harness the power of this special gift. Make the most of it, and put it to good use helping yourself and others.

Leading educators recommend the Great Books series as if Plato, St. Augustine, Shakespeare, and Sartre are the most powerful instruments for personal growth. If you want a real, individually tailored education, however, your dreams can reveal the answers to many of your fundamental life issues and mysteries. Dreams teach you facts and truisms about yourself and the surrounding world. They furnish experiences that cannot be learned from books. Because of their symbolic nature, dreams do not address you straightforwardly. Rather, they take you into the heart of an inner universe that is pregnant with new potential and possibilities. A great living intelligence dreams inside you, knows who you are, and knows what you need—so listen, look, and transform yourself.

It's not by accident that the Bible and other sacred texts emphasize the importance of dreams in the search for truth. And while you may think that only the great biblical figures had awe-inspiring spiritual dreams, the truth is they happen today to ordinary people just like you and me. Gaps in thinking and ignorance about religious beliefs are besieged by new knowledge surfacing from the unconscious mind. Dreams are trying to guide the human race into creating a more aware and informed world. You may not realize what a crucial role you play in this drama, but your dreams do. If God himself thought it worthwhile to become one of us, we must be of great consequence.

Organized religion claims to have total knowledge of what God wants the individual to do. Its spokesmen declare they know the mind of God and therefore have the right to regulate your sex life, path to heaven, dietary habits, thoughts, marriage responsibilities, etc. These preacher-teachers have imprisoned and impoverished souls rather than liberated and enriched them. Sobering up time has arrived. If you are Christian, think Jesus is the answer, and that he's on his way back, dreams say think again. If you are a Muslim, believe that martyrdom is God's will, and that a reward of seventy-two virgins awaits you in heaven, dreams say think again. If you are Jewish and awaiting the arrival of the true Messiah who will inaugurate the new age of enlightenment and unity, dreams say think again.

Many different layers of discovery and revelation illuminate our lives. Microscopes gave humans the ability to see into the world of microbes to initiate the care, management, and perhaps the cure of deadly diseases. Pathologies are equally as pernicious today, but they are of a different order and more dangerous. Distorted and power-driven belief systems could wreak havoc in the world, and so current necessity demands opening minds to new avenues of truth.

There are many ways to expand the mind. Dreams are one of the best because they are natural. Dreaming occurs approximately two hours every night and produces an array of images with profound meanings for every level of the body, mind, and soul. One "big" dream can even alter the course of history, as proven by the Indian leader Gandhi in 1919. If acting upon a dream can alter nation building, it can also dramatically influence an individual life. Occasionally, a momentous, out-of-the-ordinary, high-energy dream full of puzzling images stimulates deep emotions and original thoughts. In chapter one, I share my initial experience with dreams, because the symbolism and message may relate to your journey and struggles on the spiritual path. When I was occupationally confused and spiritually lost, they set me on a course I had neither entertained nor anticipated. Dreams can do the same for you. They can even save your life.

Chapters two and three are replete with spiritual dreams of my private clients and seminar participants. Collectively, these dreams reveal that religion in the twenty-first century needs an injection of new knowledge, wisdom, and practices that can replace or be added to the established religions that have resisted basic change. The time is right to search for a more truthful and creative way to transform religion and the search for God.

There is no better place to seek spiritual authority than within the psyche. The dreams in these chapters span the human spectrum and have a message for everyone. Many of them describe the nature of God and the spiritual process and should be declared national treasures that are as valuable as shrines, battlefields, documents, and artifacts.

Chapter four takes you to the heart of your own healing temple. Healing has a double nature: the outer and inner. Outer remedies come from knowledge of the physical world, while inner remedies can manifest in dreams. Consulting the highly intuitive sense that pervades dreams is like consulting the wisest old-time family doctor who is aware of the most intimate workings of your body and mind and knows how to make and keep you healthy.

In the West, individuals have mainly relied on professionals to heal them through the splendid achievements of modern biomedicine. And most of the time, this method works, which is the way it should be. Because of its focus on the physical, however, much of the subtler inner causes of disease and distress are left largely untouched. Dreams not only help to fill in the gaps modern medicine leaves empty, but they also cover all aspects of the healing spectrum, from physical suffering to emotional distress and spiritual aching, all of which are caused by detachment from the deepest self.

Some of the healing dreams shared in chapter four will undoubtedly seem quite remarkable if you haven't had this unique experience. However, they will demonstrate that human minds have a data collection system full of health information that can be skillfully administered by the venerable healer who resides in the psyche. You will be introduced to the ancient Greek dream temples where Asklepios, the ancient Greek god of healing and the ideal physician appeared to dreamers and performed wondrous acts of healing. Although the symbols have changed and been updated through the centuries, the process dreamers follow to achieve such miracles remains precisely the same.

In chapter five, you will be taken step-by-step through a modern version of this ancient dream incubation practice. I personally used this technique when I had cancer, and the results were impressive. Petitioning your dreams for help with formidable problems could be one of the most important adventures on which you embark. This process greatly increases the probability that you will have a creative dream that could help you solve problems dealing with health, spiritual growth, weight control, addictions, financial gain, self-confidence, finding your true destiny, etc. What comes to you when you incubate a dream cannot just be taught but must also be experienced.

Chapter six provides you with several ways to penetrate the core meaning in dreams. Dream work is not a science; it is an art and should be approached with that in mind. Truth can be seen in a painting, a sculpture, a drawing, a poem, and a dream, as well as a mathematical formula. The pursuit of objectivity in this kind of work is an empty illusion. Results of dream work must be determined by their contributions to the dreamer's life. If they motivate action, deepen understanding, clarify a feeling, penetrate life's mysteries, or summon new and difficult questions, the work has great value. Who cares if it's unscientific?

Unraveling dreams starts with a simple approach and moves to a more complicated one. The group dream interpretation procedure goes beyond Jungian and Freudian psychology and takes the expertise of dream work out of the hands of professionals and places it in those of lay people. What is most extraordinary about this technique is that nonprofessionals can not only become skillful at understanding their own dreams, but can also help others grasp theirs.

The seventh chapter brings the two parts of the book title, *God Has No Edges, Dreams Have No Boundaries*, together. In the past, Newtonian physics perceived the universe as a great static machine with discrete bodies moving in space but separate from their surroundings. Today, the cosmos is envisioned as a great mind with unlimited creative power that is still expanding. Since your mind is connected to this divine mind, you are also more than your physical dimensions, and your mind has the capability to expand far beyond the limits of ego consciousness. You are a being of cosmic significance, and your life has a sacred meaning.

In the depths of your mind lives this endless imaginative divine force that seems to be most active in the sleep and dream state. Mental and emotional boundaries existing in the waking state can evaporate when the mind begins dreaming. People can be critical of others but not as diligent in assessing their own scruples, but the dreaming mind's brutal honesty can see through all protective smoke screens. Infatuation can obscure, but dreams penetrate the haze. Uncertainty about a career choice can vanish when dreams indicate destined careers. Creative ideas never consciously thought are unearthed in the dream state. Financial abundance can be based on dream guidance. Insurmountable problems can be figured out while dreaming. Dreams dissolve boundaries by seeing around corners, peeking into the future, breaking down time and space barriers, and connecting dreamers to the world of the spirit.

Chapter eight provides dream recall suggestions that will help overcome difficulties in remembering dreams. One of the most important motivating factors for recalling dreams is your desire. You've got to think and feel that your dreams can be of significant value. All of the examples shared in these pages demonstrate the power and wisdom of this slumbering giant that awakens when you sleep. Dreams are all for your benefit. You don't even have to pay for them! If you have any psychological or emotional blocks to shed, this chapter will help remove them. It's just like learning to drive your automobile. After a few lessons and a little experience, it becomes natural and easy.

The epilogue is my way of honoring dreams by visually presenting spirit as a living force. Although people may have anesthetized themselves to the message of dreams by the dazzle of the material world, spirit is alive and well and can be experienced and felt in the visions dreams bring. As John Gardner, President Lyndon Johnson's Secretary of Education, Health, and Welfare, so aptly put it, "You don't want to die with the music still in you."

This book is not a traditional or scholarly approach to understanding and using dreams. It is more of a personal and practical offering that seeks to help you gain access to a priceless underworld rich in usefulness and meaning.

Chapter 1

THE FOG CLEARS: AN INNER LANDSCAPE APPEARS

The eye sees a thing more clearly in dreams than the imagination awake.

Leonardo da Vinci

Dreams that Made a Difference

In the summer of 1938, Franz Jagerstatter, an Austrian farmer, had a vivid dream that later would play a major role in whether he would live or die: "I saw a beautiful shining railroad train with a huge German Swastika that circled around a mountain. Streams of children and adults—huge numbers—rushed toward the train to jump on. I thought I wanted to also get on but a voice said to me: 'This train is going right to hell.'"[1]

After Hitler annexed Austria, young men were conscripted into the German army. Because of his Christian religious training, Franz was unwilling to join the fight and kill another human being. When asked during his trial why he frowned upon serving the Third Reich, he shared his dream as part of his defense. Found guilty of treason for refusing to serve in Hitler's armed forces on August 9, 1943, he was publicly beheaded on the guillotine. His dream played a major role in his decision to not join the Nazi war effort and, in a sense, cost him his life.

J. Cannon Middleton, a successful and popular New York City businessman, became unaccountably depressed after booking passage on the *Titanic* on March 23, 1912. On April 3 and 4, he dreamt repeatedly that the *Titanic* capsized in midocean and that countless passengers were struggling in the icy waters. The following day he cabled his wife and several friends about his nightmare

1

and decided to reschedule his trip for a future date. His dream saved his life.[2]

In 1913, Carl Jung was extremely troubled over feelings of disorientation and intense inner pressure. These became so strong that he suspected a severe psychic disturbance within himself. He reviewed his life, thinking there may have been some childhood experience he was suppressing. In the autumn of 1913, he experienced the pressure as moving outward, as if something dark and sinister was about to happen in concrete reality.

In October 1913, he had a series of dreams and visions with the following theme: "All of Europe was covered by a monstrous flood which eventually turned to a sea of blood. A frightful catastrophe was progressing. Caught in the waves were drowned bodies of countless thousands and the floating rubble of civilization. An inner voice spoke. 'Look at it well; it is wholly real and it will be so.'"[3] He still thought it related to a potential psychosis within himself. Then, in June 1914, World War I erupted. His unconscious mind's antenna had picked up what was in the atmosphere and transmitted a dream of the devastation that lay ahead.

A lawyer who attended one of my dream seminars shared a dream about a case she thought would be impossible to win. Extremely worried the night before her brief was due, she dreamt she was presented with an argument she hadn't thought about and upon awakening knew it would win the case. She used the reasoning supplied by her dream in court and won.

Fourteen years ago when I was dealing with cancer, I had a series of dreams (which I discuss in greater detail in chapter four) that touched upon the diagnosis, treatment, final healing, and the underlying lesson to be learned from my illness. The sudden and succinct revelations from these dreams made a major contribution to my healing process.

And lastly, a very good friend of mine quit his accounting partnership to start a business in Poland that distributed a well-known lubricant that was made in England. In the first few years, the progress was so slow that he was at the point of giving up. Then he had the following dream. "A strange man asked me how my business worked. I begin explaining, and after a few moments he stepped back, gasped, and said, 'My God, you are sitting on a gold mine.'" Of course it renewed his confidence and proved to be prophetic.

Dreams Reveal the Mysteries within Our Minds

The above dreams are examples of the tremendous insight into the mysteries of our inner life. Franz Jaggerstatter's dream helped his community see the heroic nature of sticking to principles and showed that following the crowd can obliterate the moral compass of the individual mind. Mr. Middleton's dream demonstrated the unconscious ability we have to transcend space and time in our dreams. Jung's dream proved the profound effect society's atmosphere has on our psyche and to what extent our own inner experience coincides with the ambient environment in general. The lawyer's dream presented the creative potential we have that goes beyond the limited conscious mind. My dreams demonstrated the interconnection between the body and inner mind and how great distances between the known and unknown can be traversed by a brief dream. Future potential was revealed in my friend's dream, which demonstrates the dreaming mind's intuitive strength and reliability.

These are just a few examples of how dreams shape images that produce freshness and vitality. They are normal phenomena that can advise, correct, warn, diagnose and even heal impending physical ailments. They peel away illusions, reveal the truth, and increase coping ability in times of stress. They give birth to new creative possibilities, are a primary source of spiritual revelations, and can predict future events. They provide solutions to problems that seem insurmountable, present information that is way ahead of its time, and give us a glimpse into past lives. There seem to be no limitations to the inventive potential available in the dream state.

Knowledge that comes from inside you while you are sleeping and dreaming may be of equal and sometimes greater importance than knowledge acquired from outside sources. Your dreams are constantly trying to teach you what you don't know. It's easy to give credibility to conscious thoughts: now it's time to do the same to unconscious ones.

Famous Dreamers

Here is a small sample of recorded dreams from famous accomplished people. This list will give you an idea of how highly these prominent people valued their nocturnal messages and the way the mind expands during dreams:

- Shortly before he was killed, Abraham Lincoln dreamt of his own assassination.
- A dream led to Lyndon Johnson's decision not to seek a second term.
- Paul McCartney's song "Yesterday," voted the most popular song of the century by a BBC poll, came to him through a dream where he heard a classical string ensemble playing the melody.
- Mary Shelley wrote the novel *Frankenstein* when she was eighteen and revealed that she got the story from a dream, in which she saw "the hideous phantasm of a man stretched out, and then, on the working of some powerful engine, show signs of life, and stir with an uneasy, half vital motion." The story of Frankenstein's monster has inspired over fifty films.[4]
- Madame Walker, born to a former slave family, became the first self-made American female millionaire because a dream showed her how to cure baldness.
- Jack Nicklaus credits a dream he had in 1964 with improving his golf game and rescuing him from a bad slump.
- Albert Einstein had a dream that he said was the basis of his theory of relativity.[5]
- Sitting Bull claimed that a dream before the Battle of Little Big Horn encouraged him to attack because it assured him of victory.[6]
- Stephen King has stated that his dreams provide him with major ideas for many of his novels.

- Vincent Van Gogh wrote that "I dream my paintings, and then I paint my dreams."[7]

The Dreaming Mind

Scientists once thought that dreams were a rather rare experience probably caused by overeating, repressed aggressive or sexual feelings, or the stimulation of the sensory system during sleep. If science cannot explain the ultimate mystery of dreaming, it certainly can explain the biological activity when we do dream.

In 1952, Nathaniel Kleitman at the University of Chicago made the startling discovery that everyone dreams every night during four to six cycles of sleep. A person falls asleep and in approximately ninety minutes begins dreaming for about five to ten minutes. The dreaming is called REM sleep and is accompanied by rapid eye movement, loss of reflexes, and increased pulse rate and brain activity. The sleeper then sinks down into sleep for about another hour and a half and begins dreaming again, this time for ten to twenty minutes. That person sleeps again for another hour and a half, begins dreaming for a third time for twenty to thirty minutes, sleeps once more for ninety minutes, and has one final dream period that can last from thirty minutes to an hour. These dream and sleep sessions can vary greatly with an individual. The dreaming process is systematic, and so we may speculate that it takes place automatically. But *why* that process happens is scientific speculation. No one knows why dreams start, why they occur at regular, definite intervals, and why at other times of the night there are no disturbances in the regular sleep cycle. If, as Freud believed, dreams express repressed wishes, then why do they occur at such regular intervals? Do we have such constant repressed wishes? It's obviously a physiological stimulus that controls dreaming. Dreams occur the way they do because that's apparently nature's intention.

Great minds have speculated on the purposes and goals of dreams. Carl Gustav Jung, the Swiss psychiatrist, explored the dreaming mind through his own dreams and those of his countless clients. The work he produced on the subject is perhaps the most comprehensive and profound body of dream knowledge that has ever been brought to light. His penetrating eye saw the wisdom of the ages in dreams where most of us see just a blur. Some of Jung's major findings and thoughts about dreams are as follows:

- Often dreams may appear senseless, but it is the dreamers who lack the understanding and imagination to discern these enigmatic messages.
- Dreams are pure nature, arise spontaneously, and show the natural truth and reality of the dreamer.
- Dreams are autonomous and obey their own laws.
- Psychological balance is a primary function of the dreaming mind.
- The more one-sided the conscious attitude, the more possibility of vivid dreams that try to counterbalance this stance.
- Dreams are often anticipatory. They can produce unmistakable information about future possibilities and events.
- Dream symbols do not have fixed meanings. Each one has a special significance of its own.
- Dreams can show there is an inner symbolic connection between a physical illness and a psychological problem.
- Telepathy in dreams can no longer be disputed.
- Dreams are always a little bit ahead of the dreamer.
- The art of interpreting dreams can neither be learned from a book nor from theories.
- Understanding of dreams enriches consciousness.[8]

Jung made countless more observations, and I strongly recommend reading his works. The next chapter gives a more comprehensive view of how Jung connects spirituality and dreams.

There seems to be no limitation to the inventiveness of our dreams. There is an overall purpose and goal that dreams strive for: they want to unravel the nature of consciousness and make dreamers into complete and whole people.

Concealed in a little acorn is the map of the giant oak it can become. Many oaks look alike, but they are each unique. So are human beings. Their blueprint is hidden from conscious view but contains the soul's outstanding potential. The conscious mind may not see this unique path, but the inner eye does. Each person has a special task that belongs to that individual and that individual alone.

Dreams help us discover impediments to our wholeness and the means to overcome these roadblocks. Dreamers can cooperate with this process by becoming conscious of their dreams and then taking action on what dreams may ask. What occurs in the human system in its drive to wholeness is not so different from the new worldview that is emerging within the sciences. Physics has broken away from classical mechanics and now claims that the physical universe is unbroken wholeness. Biology has proven the interdependence and oneness of life. Modern astrophysicists are convinced that all stars and planets evolved from the same primordial substance. Humans all breathe the same air, travel in the same space, are warmed by the same sun and cooled by the same rain. Interconnectedness of the whole universe may be the fundamental reality. From ancient times to the present, humans have gone on quests to find this elusive knowledge. Few have succeeded. Today at this crucial moment in history, the prospects look even bleaker. Turmoil and fragmentation exist on all continents, as do ecological disasters.

What is urgently needed today is a major revolution in consciousness. In this country, I don't think it can come about through our mental health practices, which have gone the way of modern medicine. Technology, pharmacology, and managed care have helped heal the body but have deadened the spirit. Dreams are needed more than ever today. They are free. The self-help realm is a marketing mecca in America: CDs guarantee out-of-body experiences, books offer enlightenment from self-proclaimed gurus, retreats promise deeper soul connections, and seminars propose insight into past lives. But dreams don't cost anything, and they are available every night. All these self-help modes would be nonexistent if people were not deeply yearning to be whole. There isn't anyone I know who hasn't felt an existential emptiness at times. Something is missing.

Without an awareness of our suffering as a problem of spirit, attempted solutions will be shallow and useless. You can flit from church to church, drug to drug, store to store, casino to casino, eat more and more to distract yourself or ease the pain. Most mistake this emptiness for a psychological problem. It is not. A secularized world cannot identify the void as spiritual emptiness. Even though what is missing is not easily recognizable, dreams can illuminate the underlying dynamics and open up a new path to heal the soul. Dreams summon dreamers to a deeper existence.

I know because it happened to me. I was a spiritually deprived person, unaware that my soul was hungry and that I wasn't feeding it the right food. Attempting to sustain myself on the big three values in America—money, power, and sex—filled me with the wrong food. And then one day, the nourishment I needed came in a dream.

An Early Midlife Crisis

For most people the classic midlife crisis begins around age forty. But I started early. At twenty-four, I felt like a lost soul in the middle of a full-blown identity crisis. The opening lines of Dante Alleghieri's *The Divine Comedy* sums up my feelings: "Midway through the path of life that men pursue I found me in a darkling wood astray, For the direct way had been lost from view."[9]

These lines, written in the early fourteenth century, begin one of the most famous spiritual pilgrimages in Western literature. My own spiritual pilgrimage began in the late 1950s. As soon as I graduated from college, I was drafted into the army and sent to Europe. After a few months, I returned to the States to marry the girl of my dreams, Sondra, and we spent the next year and a half living in a small German town about ninety miles south of Frankfurt. Secretly, I was thrilled when I was drafted because it meant I could postpone planning my uncertain future. I taught poorly educated enlisted men basic math and English skills, and we were living on a king's ransom—private first class pay of $180 a month—which was more than adequate to satisfy our needs. God was the farthest thing from my mind.

When we returned to the States, virtually nothing had changed to clarify my direction. I had a BA degree in sociology and anthropology—a pretty unmarketable credential—and several envelopes of cash I'd stuffed into my pockets during our wedding reception. I was a young man wandering adrift in what seemed a bewildering and challenging world, and I wasn't up to the task. Having a conscious mind that was uncertain and aimless was not a great asset for career building, but fortunately I was about to discover a concealed directional finder. My dreaming mind was about to demonstrate how deep human life can be—a notion that ran counter to my conscious conviction.

Sondy and I talked a lot about our future, and then one day she came up with what seemed like the perfect solution to my existential angst: "Let's go to California!" Both of us had family there, and her father gave us additional encouragement: "If I were your age, that's what I would do." So we packed up my new father-in-law's gift, a Ford station wagon, and traveled west. Even as we enjoyed the adventure, the question of what to do with my life clanged in the back of my mind like an old church bell that wouldn't stop ringing.

My wife and I arrived in Los Angeles in November 1958. I was sure we'd landed in paradise. Palm trees swayed, beaches invited us to take long walks, and Christmastime enchanted us with its bathwater temperatures and blissful absence of snow and ice. During the late 1950s, Los Angeles was indeed a magical place. It was new, colorful, open, and friendly and had an adventurous spirit that seemed to say, "You can try anything here."

Predictably, though, all of my problems came with me. But my wife demonstrated more wisdom than I. My motive for leaving the East Coast was to run away, and so was hers—though with an important difference. One reason Sondy suggested we travel west was to meet with her uncle, a well-known Jungian analyst, Dr. Jay Dunn, who lived in LA. Sondra correctly surmised that he could help me find my way. For me, he was not unlike Dante's guide, whose intelligence helped transform the poet's life.

A Veil to the Inner World Is Lifted

Cures for deep-seated ills don't necessarily come easily, especially when the patient is as resistant as I was. When I met my wife's uncle, I sensed a powerful, intuitive presence. He was extremely kind, exuded a natural wisdom, and had an uncanny ability to focus on the person at hand, probably not unlike his own analyst, Jung himself. I wondered what would happen to me when he offered to take me on as a patient. I was both eager and apprehensive, especially at the thought that there was something truly wrong with me. Would my work in therapy uncover the pathology I knew was lurking just below the surface?

I'm often asked how I became interested in dreams. Until my first therapy session, I don't recall ever having had one, and I had even less of an idea what dreams might mean. I lacked a sense of the internal workings of my conscious mind, much less my unconscious one. If Socrates was right that an unexamined life isn't worth living, I was in sorry shape indeed.

My first therapy session with Dr. Dunn was the beginning of a major change for me. It transported me into another world where the messages in dreams seemed more compelling than those of my waking life. The rules of the subconscious, I soon learned, were radically different from those of the conscious mind. Initially, what seemed of immense value in my dreams appeared to hold little value in the waking world and vice versa. As the first meeting was ending, Dr. Dunn asked if I recalled my dreams. I said I didn't. But surprisingly, his question triggered the memory of a dream I'd had when I was five or six years old. I asked him why it was important to remember dreams. He then related a remarkable story about his first pressing case. Its message became the catalyst for my lifelong interest in dreams.

His patient was a young man who had been drafted into the army as a chaplain during World War II. Chaplains were not expected to fight in combat. Toward the end of the war, he was sent into what was supposed to be a secure military locality but which quickly became a combat zone when the Germans launched a surprise offensive. The chaplain found himself in the thick of battle and had to defend himself when two German soldiers attacked him. His survival instinct kicked in, and he killed them both, one with a rifle, the other with his bare hands.

When he regained his normal awareness and realized what he had done, his mind snapped. The army sent him back to the States to undergo treatment for "battle fatigue," but military psychiatrists could not help him. His symptoms included difficulty concentrating, an overwhelming sense of guilt, despair, and depression that led to an inability to hold down a job. Unfortunately, the Post Traumatic Stress Disorder (PTSD) diagnosis had not been conceived yet. Several years after the incident, he still couldn't stay employed, experienced traumatic flashbacks, and was consumed with anxiety and an overpowering sense of self-condemnation and stagnation. He was also plagued by a recurring nightmare but dismissed it in the same way the army physicians did. For him, it was nothing more than a mental reenactment of the killings but otherwise held no inherent meaning. Finally, a friend suggested that the man consult Dr. Dunn because of his specialty in understanding dreams. After describing the experience that led to his breakdown, he shared his nightmare:

> I am back on the battlefield in Europe sitting on the ground. In front of me is a large strawberry shortcake, my favorite dessert! Slightly beyond that are the bodies of the two dead German soldiers I killed. Their eyes are empty sockets—they have been gouged out. Other dead soldiers lie strewn around the battlefield, and destroyed vehicles are still smoldering. Acrid smoke permeates the air. I feel okay with what I see. As I reach down and scoop up a large piece of cake, I notice to my horror that the strawberries are not the fruit but the eyeballs of the dead German soldiers. I know I must eat them; I have no choice. Squeamishly, I bite into the cake and feel the eyeballs hit the roof of my mouth. I awaken horrified, retching uncontrollably.

The man asked Dunn what the strange dream meant. Dunn was quiet for a moment. He knew this tortured soul had been suffering for seven years and that he needed drastic action to help him. He stood up, pointed a finger at his client, and said, "You, my man, are a murderer, a killer, and furthermore, there's a side of you that loved it!" The patient jumped out of his seat, screamed, and bolted out the door, ran down the stairway, crossed the street to his car, and sped away. Dunn was deeply concerned. His intuition had led him to this dramatic interpretation, but he hadn't expected such an extreme reaction. He tried calling the client later that day but couldn't reach him, and his wife said she hadn't heard from him. The next day, the patient called back and asked to schedule another appointment. When the former chaplain arrived at Dunn's office, he shook the analyst's hand profusely, gave him a big hug, and thanked him for his profound and accurate interpretation. He told Dunn he wasn't sure why, but a great burden had been lifted from his soul. How could the analyst have arrived at such a blunt conclusion, he asked, and why had he delivered it in such an accusatory manner?

Dunn explained his logic. He knew the chaplain had been tormented with guilt since the killings and that he came from a strong religious background that emphasized charity, patience, and brotherly love. In the war zone, he was forced to temporarily abandon those principles by committing the ultimate unthinkable act: murder. He had broken the sixth commandment, "Thou shalt not kill." The client's unconscious reaction was ironic: his conscious mind was in torment over his actions, yet in the dream, he was eating his ideal dessert. How and why had these divergent symbols met to produce such intense feelings? How could his mind equate the violence of killing with the decadence of a delicious dessert?

As we will soon see, the unconscious mind never tries to fool our conscious awareness. It is not a trickster. Its aim is to inform, instruct, and change attitudes. It does so in the only way it knows: through direct symbolic experience. To the dreamer, strawberry shortcake was a delightful indulgence, although he couldn't swallow it because of the gouged-out eyes. Yet he had to "eat" it. What couldn't he digest? The part of him that actually savored the kill, Dunn explained. It made him feel powerful, an uncommon feeling for this gentle man. Under life-or-death circumstances, Dunn said, we can all be murderers; moreover, part of us may actually enjoy it. As a therapist who counseled Vietnam veterans, I can attest to this fact. For some of these soldiers, jungle warfare with its stealth and the excitement of the hunt and kill was a thrill. With all of this intense emotion, they were marinating in their own hormones, making their addiction all the stronger. In fact, after a nine-month tour of duty, some of them found civilian life too boring and they reenlisted for another stint in Vietnam. For Dunn's client, the strawberry shortcake was his unconscious revelation that he found some perverse satisfaction in his deed. Once he could accept that part of himself, he could begin resolving his turmoil and start on the road to recovery.

As Dr. Dunn finished telling this story, he said he felt this man needed a dramatic confrontation with the unconscious to jolt him out of his guilt-ridden conflict. I was impressed. Understanding a dream could start a person on the road to recovery! Dreams could heal! To me, this was a profound possibility, one I would never have considered before this session.

I wondered if I, too, could experience such remarkable dreams and whether they could shed light on my troubled life. That same night, I awoke from a dream that astonished me with its imagery and touched me deeply. I still see it as one of the most memorable experiences of my life, though, at the time, I had no idea what it was trying to convey. It was like hearing the sounds of a rare instrument whose strings had not been plucked for years.

Inner Treasure and the Sacrifice

I am walking through the streets of Winthrop Beach, Massachusetts, a seaside town that was my childhood home. There are no buildings, vegetation, or people, only asphalt streets and sidewalks made of liquid gold. They have the consistency of quicksand, and I know if I tried walking on them, I would sink to my death. Feeling so uncomfortable near these walkways, I decide to stroll up the street to the beach, my most cherished realm since childhood.

The day is beautiful, with clear skies, a light breeze, and comfortable temperatures. Standing on the shore with small waves lapping at my feet, I look out to sea. For some inexplicable reason, I turn around to look at the sea wall. Much to my surprise, I see a large, imposing, modern home situated on top of a huge rock. I have never seen this house before. In fact, no home had ever been built on the ocean side of the beach because of the severe tides that wracked the area during Northeastern storms. Carved in the rock below the house is a spiral staircase that leads up to the structure.

As I put my foot on the first step to walk up, Dr. Dunn appears, puts his arm around my shoulders, and says, "Come, I'll go up with you." When we reach the top of the stairs, we stop in front of an expansive living room window that spans the width of the house. Just inside the glass is a pedestal, about three feet high, covered with a velvet cloth. On top is a rough stone about the size of a big fist. It has many jagged edges with light and dark surfaces. Deeply chiseled into the surface is a cross—just a plain and simple cross. I sense that the stone has a great power, a magic force, and contains the answer to many mysteries—in particular, the secret keys to the purpose and meaning of my life. Waves of energy emanate from the surface like heat ripples that rise from hot pavement. My desire to possess it is intense. If I could own it, I would need nothing else because I would know the meaning and purpose of my life. It is the most valuable object I could ever hope to possess. I look for a door into the room, but there is none visible, so I stare longingly at the stone and feel its great power with a deep reverence.

Looking beyond the pedestal into the right corner of the room, I see a man in the shadows and immediately sense he is the keeper of the stone. He walks forward and stops next to the pedestal. Dressed in a plain-colored robe, he is approximately sixty-five years of age, short, bald, and stocky, with a large head and a thick, powerful neck. He has the air of a monk or priest. Although we communicate, no words are expressed; only our minds speak to each other. "I want that stone," I say. He laughs and replies, "You can't have that stone unless you sacrifice something for it." I am baffled, so I turn to Dr. Dunn (who has been standing inconspicuously by me the whole time) for help. He reaches into his pocket and pulls out a fork and spoon, places them in the shape of a Christian cross, binds them tightly at the joining point with a thin strip of leather, then hands the object to me. I know that this cross can be exchanged for the stone. Feeling rescued, I reach for it, and I awaken—fully awake and alert as if I had never slept.

Feelings of surprise, reverence, and bewilderment surged through me.

Trying to Unravel What It All Means

I had absolutely no idea what this dream was trying to convey to me, although I did sense its holiness. Sacredness was a rare feeling for me, yet *this experience* was the initial driving force behind my spiritual interest and journey. It was the first in a series of reverential dreams that would span more than forty-five years of my life, and which still occur occasionally, especially when I forget my life purpose and allow my mind to wander off the path.

At some point in life, most people have experienced an unusually intense, vivid dream or vision that seems to flood their consciousness. Although I knew nothing about dreams, I did sense that something universal had been touched and that entwined in the symbolism of my dream was some profound idea that was attempting to connect my inner and outer worlds. This internal adventure had the earmarks of a small religious experience that definitely brought a change of attitude about what was real. Later in life, I would know with certainty that these powerful symbols expressed the innermost needs of my soul. Up to that point, however, no other external object or event ever had as much meaning as this subjective experience. These dream symbols were living entities that wanted to transform my conscious attitudes. What a mystery! To think that I didn't personally manufacture these images and that they were products of spontaneous internal combustion was astonishing.

Unfortunately, I didn't work on this dream in therapy. When I brought it to my analyst, he validated its importance but suggested we put it on the back burner because I had so many other problems to tackle. At the end of the session, he made the prescient statement that I would have to spend much time wading through a lot of childhood issues and that my life would take a major turn when I hit middle age. Many of my dreams seemed to point to a late development, and they were as accurate as the analyst. I stayed in therapy for two years and then decided to take a break. Although I didn't work with the dream on a conscious level until I left therapy, I think it began working on me. It must have permeated my consciousness because I became interested in New Age explorations such as transcendental meditation, psychic healing, and aura reading. In the forty-five years since, not a week has gone by that I haven't reflected on the spiritual meaning of those unforgettable symbols.

I emphasize again at that stage of my life, I knew nothing about psychology or the dreaming mind. My conscious mind could not have concocted this scenario given my limited state of awareness at the time. Was I giving this message to myself? It felt as if some energy or intelligent power, an age-old forgotten wisdom outside the range of my conscious mind, was trying to awaken me to another reality. This spirit force knew me, and I wasn't aware that it did until this dream. I don't think I dreamt this dream. It felt like this dream dreamt me.

Perhaps another way of saying this is that many of us seek God, but in actuality what may be going on is that God is seeking us. Some dreams bear the imprint of an inner celestial power, and this was one of them. When I dreamt it, I had no interest in religious or spiritual issues. Yet this dream addressed them in spades. Whatever we consciously undervalue is often given extraordinary value in dreams.

Over the years I have come to believe that this superconscious part of mind plays a major role in steering us to our destiny.[10] Spirit was seeking me in this first act of revelation just as spirit is seeking you to lift the veil from your eyes to illuminate the mysteries that surpass personal interests. Sacred dreams have a goal, and I believe their purpose is the same for everyone—to bring awareness of the divine within. There's an unconscious force available to all that can suggest radically different paths from those consciously pursued in daily life. These paths are always for our highest good. Many modern dream theorists say dreams are primarily a reaction to conscious thoughts and what is going on at that time, but it was Jung's contention that some dreams emerge seemingly from out of the blue to impress dreamers with a deeply felt sense of mystery. They want individuals to enter the mystery of their minds, explore the unknown, and become adventurers in the inner landscape of the soul. Life is so much more soul stirring than we realize. Jung believed that many modern ills were due to the loss of connection to religious roots and therefore, to meaning. Reconnecting to this spiritual reality can act as a transforming and renewing power; dogma is not enough, and teachings from books or the pulpit fall far short. What comes directly from the psyche is the refreshing spiritual water that revitalizes. Such was the case with my dream.

Because of the central role this dream played for me, I will share my thoughts on what it was trying to tell me. Doing so will, I hope, offer a better sense of how dreams evolve over time and help shape lives, especially if their messages are heeded. Even though my dream applies to me personally, it also expresses a universal problem everyone can relate to. It took many years for the inner meaning of this dream to unfold. Even after forty-five years, I still make new connections. The great Jung admitted there are some "big" dreams of his that took him three to five years to understand.

A Troubled Background

I was born during the Depression, and my father contracted pneumonia and died six months before my birth. My mother had to move back to her parents' home for their help in raising my older brother and myself. She went to work, and my grandmother essentially raised us. I had a strong dislike for her and she for me. I was told by a family member that she suggested my mother have an abortion when she was pregnant with me. I felt unwanted and unloved, except for my grandfather, who was my father figure—a kind soul whom I loved dearly. In later years after I became a therapist, it was bittersweet to hear stories of how certain clients felt the greatest fondness for the person who loved them the most: their grandmother. They could do no wrong in Grandma's eyes. In my case, I thought I could do no *right*!

Although my family life was filled with conflict and turmoil, once I stepped outdoors, life became an exciting adventure. My street was a block from the beach and filled with boys my age. I was thrilled to be with my neighborhood friends in an environment with endless places to explore. It was joyful to live in what I saw as a coastal paradise, though it was really a working-class community. When I was twelve, my mother remarried, and my brother and I had to leave the area. I, however, took every opportunity I could to return. Winthrop Beach was my womb, and I never wanted to leave it. Perhaps it was my search for the security and nurturance (which I did not get as a child) that kept bringing me back.

My Winthrop Beach dream took me to a completely different space. It was now an inner landscape that pointed to a new discovery in familiar terrain, as well as to a future action of psychological and spiritual importance. What was once a familiar landscape had now become a barren land, and what I sought there could now only be found in myself. It was time to begin seeing my home of origin in a different light.

In my home growing up, I remember the great value my mom placed on money and using people to accumulate it. My mother would frequently say that in the pursuit of money, it isn't what you know; it's who you know. Make the right connections and use others to help you make your fortune. I think the gold sidewalks in my dream symbolized the material wealth so many of us spend our lives pursuing, but my dream told me they were too unstable and lacked the solidity to support me. They were definitely made of real gold but seemed ominously dangerous. If I had attempted to walk on them, my life would have slipped away, and no one would have been there to rescue me. By contrast, the stone cliff had a firm foundation and a permanency, which supported life. It reminded me of Jesus's injunction to Simon Peter: "And I say also unto thee, That thou art Peter, and upon this rock I will build my church; and the gates of hell shall not prevail against it" (Matt. 16:18—all biblical quotes drawn from the King James Version of the Bible). The house embodied a new state of awareness, one that commanded a higher view of life, rested on a foundation of truth, and was close to the source of all life—the ocean.

The spiral stone stairwell symbolized my inner desire to move up in the world, raising my consciousness to a higher level. Obviously, the analyst was a positive symbol of a person who was willing to join me on my adventure. I can honestly say he was the only male figure I had ever met that I wanted to pattern my life after.

But the most compelling symbol of all was the stone. If a rock could speak, this one did. It had such a mystical power—the feeling of a living force. If I saw this same stone through the eyes of my conscious mind, it would have appeared as worthless as a handful of beach pebbles. But as a living symbol in my dream, it was a priceless treasure. There is a permanency about stone, which is billions of years old and doesn't decompose like vegetation. Moses received the Ten Commandments on tablets of stone, and the people of ancient Egypt worshipped stone statues of their Pharaohs because they were thought to preserve the kings' indestructible souls. In the New Testament, the rock is a symbol of Christ, who is described as a "living stone." In my dream, I think the stone symbolized my wholeness, my completeness and solidity. Although it was far from perfectly smooth and symmetrically uniform, it contained all the opposites in balance. It was both jagged and smooth, light and dark, flat and uneven, pointed and blunt—a finished product harmonious in its opposing forces, a sign of some future potential where the opposing forces within me would stop warring with each other and live calmly and peacefully. I think this stone was my Holy Grail. My conscious mind certainly wasn't searching for it, but my unconscious mind, this invisible guide, was leading me onward.

Everyone is on a quest. Some know it, but most don't. People search for financial security, the perfect mate, health, status, the ideal job, fame, and happiness, but they neglect their spiritual development—the very thing that gives true meaning to life. Some great inner truth lives inside me, and I must fathom it.

Beneath it all, the Grail has a spiritual origin. According to legend, it always resides in a castle and has divine powers and an enormous effect on people. Legend has it that when the Grail's power is not present, nature no longer re-creates and the power of knights diminishes. But whoever recognizes the Grail is showered with good fortune. The inner meaning of the Grail is very much alive today, and the search for it is the spiritual journey for all pilgrims seeking their truth. There are many paths to the Grail, all valid and all individually unique: no one right way exists for everybody.

The Philosopher's Stone

Another interesting connection I discovered in my search for the meaning of the stone: during twelfth century Europe, there was a flourishing of alchemy, which was a pseudo science or art aimed at transmuting base metals into gold. Alchemists proposed the existence of the philosopher's stone, a mysterious, unknown substance that they believed was the key to converting common inexpensive metals such as lead into gold. This "stone" was thought to cure illness, create spiritual renewal, and lengthen life. Various confusing descriptions portray the philosopher's stone, but it was often described as a common substance that could be discovered everywhere but was almost always unrecognized and unappreciated. Jung's in-depth study of alchemy brought him to conclude that alchemists were unconsciously projecting onto the conversion of base metals into gold a spiritual quest— the search for enlightenment, wisdom, wholeness, and health of the human psyche. In other words, the search for alchemical gold was really an attempt to discover their true spiritual nature.[11]

Like the Holy Grail, the philosopher's stone resides in everyone. Whoever glimpses the stone catches sight of the truth, which is the noblest of treasures. My ego-centeredness was probably the major contributor to distancing myself from this inner world. This dream taught me there was something inside myself that couldn't shine its radiance because I didn't know how to uncover it. It was like a diamond in its natural state: dull and rough until processed to bring out its true luminosity.

Some Deeper Thoughts on My Symbolism

In my dream, the custodian of the stone reminded me of the keeper of the treasure in legends where spiritual power and wealth must be protected against hostile forces or intrusion by the unworthy. He was fully mindful of what I needed to give up before I could receive the knowledge and power contained in the stone symbol.

The cross in the stone was perhaps symbolic of the sacrifice I needed to make. What puzzled me about this dream was the Christian symbolism. I'm Jewish, but most of my big dreams have had Christian imagery. I dream of crosses, churches, and Jesus, rather than synagogues, rabbis, or tallises. I guess in my soul, Christianity speaks more to me than Judaism, although portions of Christianity have always puzzled me. I could never grasp the idea that Jesus died for our sins and that belief in him would eradicate not only our sins but the sins of the whole world. I have met many Christians who accept Jesus Christ as Savior but are still plagued by internal suffering and guilt. Although I have asked many Christians to explain this, either they cannot, or their explanations leave me in the dark. What I have extrapolated from the crucifixion is that cross bearing is inevitable. All people in all religions must bear the burdens of life. They are not called upon to endure Jesus's cross but are destined to shoulder their own hardships and grief to fulfill the purpose of their lives, which hopefully leads to salvation. This was my truth, and it was set in stone.

Most puzzling were the fork and spoon representing the sacrifice I needed to make. Why these symbols? Dreams do not make mistakes. The unconscious chooses symbols that best represent what the soul world needs to say to the dreamer. I had such a strong emotional reaction when I saw the utensils in the form of a cross that I later realized they were alive with meaning. One of my personal vices is gluttony, eating and drinking too much. Sacrificing appetite gratification could certainly be one of the main messages of this dream, but that explanation just didn't seem to be enough. I knew the symbol was trying to communicate something much more vital.

As the years progressed, I had other dreams that were also connected to the theme of my big dream. When I had bladder cancer, I asked my dreams what I had to learn from this experience. What they delivered related back to my "sacrifice" dream. Quite clearly, it was in the spiritual realm where the surrender needed to take place. I had to stop feeding my ego and my tendency to self-centeredness in order to grow as a spiritual human being. For the first time, I understood why I did so many TV interviews, had my own radio show, and gave dream seminars. It was for my ego—my need to be popular, recognized, and important. I was trying to impress people with what I knew and what I had accomplished. What needed to be crucified was my self-absorption and selfishness in general. Humility and gratitude were now a necessity. Egotism turns individuals into their own worst enemies. As Pogo once famously said, "We have met the enemy, and it is us."[12] The ego is not something that needs to be eradicated; it just needs to stop being nourished so it doesn't get inflated. What an eye opener!

We Often Don't Know What We Need, but Dreams Do

This initial dream tried to clue me in on what my lifetime search was all about. I was in the dark and didn't know what I needed, but obviously something inside me did. Some spiritual practitioners would say it was God. I didn't think it was the "big" God, but maybe it was a little God, a God in the making. Is there someone watching over sleepers, some kind of attendant that helps produce these remarkable messages? Is it a guardian angel? How does the unconscious deliver the exact message that needs to be heard? There are so many questions I have no specific answers for, and maybe that's the way it's supposed to be. The mystery needs to be kept intact. But the one thing I am certain of and that readers can count on is the importance of maintaining faith in the unseen courier who will often deliver truth in symbolic form. Something is looking out for individual welfare and improvement, even if that something can never be known.

A Basic Cause of Unhappiness

When I was practicing as a therapist, probably my unhappiest clients were those who had everything they wanted materially but could not understand why they were still so miserable. All the ego entrapments, which are not lasting sources of joy, permeated their lives. Pleasure, power, money, popularity, and excitement need to be replenished over and over because their effect is short lived.

I know that Christianity is based on the idea that you have to live your life for Christ. From what I have seen, the Christian church has become an end in itself. It has lost sight of its main purpose—to elevate human nature instead of magnifying the power of its own establishment. What my dream taught me didn't come from dogma, the pulpit, or the Bible, and I don't think it came as a product of my personal history. It came from the spiritual universe, which is in all of us. The greatest Bible ever written is within the marrow of our bones and preaches individual messages every evening. Evangelists can quote John, Luke, or Mark, but only the inner preacher knows what he is talking about when he comes to you.

Individuals always have choices, and at the time that I had the dream about the stone, one of my major conflicts was either to be a servant of the higher self (the stone and cross) or a slave to my lower one (the fork and spoon). Transforming the lower qualities into higher ones is one of the main purposes of the world's great religions. There's a lot more to the dream, but the essence to me is clear: life demands sacrifice, and the spiritual life demands a particular sacrifice of the ego as the center of the personality.

I will never forget my Winthrop Beach thought-provoking dream; it is one that needs to be shared. In *The Psychology of the Unconscious*, Jung noted that he considered it the duty of anyone undertaking a spiritual path to share one's findings on this journey of discovery, whether it's refreshing spiritual water or a barren desert of error. The one aids, the other warns.[13] Even though my dream applied to me personally, it also expressed a universal problem everyone could relate to.

People all over the world believe dreams are real while they are dreaming. When they awaken, the process seems to be reversed— the sensory world becomes real, and the dream world becomes an illusion. But both worlds can be authentic. If dreams can have such validity, why can't people value them more?

Western Culture Puts Little Value on Dreams

Western culture attributes little importance to dreams. In my family of origin and community, I don't recall anyone ever mentioning dreams or their importance. Children were reared without being taught the value of dreams. If a nightmare was brought up, the typical response was "Forget about it. It's only a dream." When souls are cut off from their instincts, fearful dreams are often nature's way of reconnecting dreamers to their roots. Dreams bring to light the neglected and unknown. An opportunity for grasping the underlying dynamics of life itself is lost when dreams are not examined. The unconscious mind can produce dreams that depict the straightforward inner truth even when conscious intelligence is obscured and inept.

Empirical science and the rational mind have taken human beings to limits not thought possible a hundred years ago. Since the conscious mind's reasoning powers have limitations, however, nature provides a unique supermind that is resourceful, innovative, and above all, individually tailored to suit personal needs. Logic and reason can accomplish great works, but living things get fed by roots—things that aren't seen with the naked eye but exist below ground. What often makes a difference in life is what can't be seen. Dreams help people observe the roots that form part of the unseen life that dreams them. Often undervalued by traditional religion, human souls are the direct link to the dimensions of the spiritual world. The conscious mind rests on the invisible shoulders of giants and geniuses, and this colossal intelligence is often brought to light through dreams. As you will see in the next chapter, many lives have been opened to this realm of knowledge that has always been part of the human makeup.

Chapter 2

GOD HAS NO EDGES: A NEW/OLD VISION

Dreams are like stars—you can never touch them but if you
follow them they can lead to your destiny.

Anonymous

Wake-Up Calls

If you slumber through life, you will definitely get a wake-up
call, even if you didn't realize you were unconscious at the wheel. You
cannot be immunized from these subpoenas that are served from the
Highest Court in your inner landscape. Religious people may say
these summonses are God's punishment for past wrongdoings. They
are not. They are reminders that your compass requires realignment
to what is vital and in need of urgent navigation. Wake-up calls can
bring your life to a shut down, demanding immediate attention to
something significant that has been neglected. These awakenings are
commands to appear before your inner truth. Books, expert authori-
ties, and life formulas are available to all of us. But the keys for new
life sources and changes inevitably come from within.

Wake-up calls come in many forms: some are severe, while others
are more benign. Health can suddenly fail, or other catastrophic
incidents such as job loss, financial crisis, or emotional upheaval can
occur. Then there are the gentler ways—the right word at the right
moment, a sudden vision, or a powerful earthshaking dream. Yes, you
can just fall asleep and observe how your soul is trying to orchestrate
change. This was how my spiritual wake-up call came seven years
after I had quit my teaching job and started a private psychotherapy
practice.

You Don't Know Who God Is

It's nighttime. I am walking down a pitch-black hallway in a strange and unfamiliar building. A female voice calls me by my last name. "Bernard, come in this room; I need to talk to you." I sense it is important because the voice sounds sincere and honest. I follow the source of the sound since it is too dark to see. I stop at an open door that leads into a plain, bare room, dimly lit at one end. Two glowing candles on a desk illuminate the withered face of an ancient woman. Deep furrows line her face. Her light blue eyes, however, are youthful and seem incongruous in her aged face. These eyes know things, deep things. She looks up at me and says, "Bernard, come closer, I want to tell you something very important." Eagerly, I walk up to the desk and peer into her venerable face. She raises her arm, points her finger at me, and says, "I could help you become a superb therapist, but I am not going to help you."

Stunned and deeply disappointed, I ask, "Why not?"

"Because you do not know who God is—yet." Her strong implication is that God exists, but my ignorance keeps me in the dark. I awaken.

When I was a young man, religion and spirituality were not subjects of great interest to me. I was much more interested in climbing the ladder of success. After several years as a public school teacher in Los Angeles, I left teaching to become a psychotherapist.

I was happily married to Sondra and had two great sons, Joshua and David, but I felt a lot of anxiety about my professional and financial future. Teaching had been a secure job. Building a private practice and seminar business had no certainties or assurances, let alone the consistency of the weekly paycheck upon which I had come to depend.

The Winthrop Beach dream I described in the previous chapter attempted to jump-start me into exploring the inner world for answers to nagging and complex spiritual issues. My internal resistances were strong. Daily life was a struggle, and finances were a constant issue. My concept of God was vague and impersonal: some colossal bearded old man to pray to when I felt threatened, helpless, or in need of something. If my prayers weren't immediately answered, I assumed it meant that God didn't like me, that my prayers were not sincere enough or weren't that important to God, or that there wasn't anyone there to listen. A desire to know about God was the furthest thing from my mind, and the idea that it had to do with my success as a therapist seemed even more remote. I resented that idea partly because I knew many atheists and agnostics who were successful and had risen to the heights of their professions. Obviously one can live life without God and do quite well. So why was this obstacle put in my path? Was destiny playing a role in my life? If it was, it seemed like a huge challenge. I knew I had the choice to pursue this invitation or decline it. After all, we live in a free-will universe. With some resistance then, I accepted the offer made by the wise old woman in my dream and sought the answer to an issue that has plagued humankind since the dawn of civilization. My search took me down a path where dreams once again were the gateway to enlightenment.

The Dreaming Mind's Agenda

This dream taught me that the inner mind has its own agenda and goals and is not just a feedback system for the conscious mind. Dreams can react to conscious choices and actions, just as they can take the lead through initiating autonomous ideas. Humans are complex and multidimensional entities rather than the simple, uncomplicated ones described by cognitive and behavioral psychologists. Powerful forces in the unconscious mind attempt to direct people toward future growth. The ego likes to think the conscious mind is the author of all our major endeavors, insights, and motivations. It is not! Life works better when the conscious mind becomes the servant of this inner voice. The unconscious mind sees correctly even when conscious reason is ignorant, blocked, and ineffective.

For one brief moment in my life, a veil was lifted and a crack of light momentarily illuminated this inner kingdom. The ancient feminine wisdom spoke words that would have challenged even the most intense rationalist or nonbeliever. I must admit if someone had told me in the waking world that I needed to know who God was to become a successful therapist, I would have dismissed those words instantly. But this woman in my dream was someone special, a figure of biblical proportions who commanded my attention because of her intense spirituality.

Spiritual Crisis

Apparently, my inner mind was telling me I was in a spiritual crisis I knew nothing about. The dream envelope was opened, and I had received my orders, so it was time to depart on a personal quest for God. This was the real beginning of my spiritual education and reminded me of another lesson I had learned several years before this ancient-woman dream. An old Hopi Indian introduced me to the spiritual crisis of his tribe that drove right to the heart of twentieth-century religion's barren landscape. In a few simple sentences, this elder from the Black Mesa illuminated the religious dilemma of his Hopi people and our times. The old religious structures and rituals that once had magic power to influence faith, behavior, and events were losing their vitality.

My wife and I were standing on the roof of a Hopi house waiting for the start of the annual snake dance in which Hopi Indians dance with live rattlesnakes in their mouths. The snake dance is actually a rain dance dating back many thousands of years in an agricultural region where precipitation is marginal, and nothing is more important than the timely arrival of summer rain. We had heard about this ceremony from an Indian trader in Farmington, New Mexico, who insisted that we needed to immediately drive three hundred miles to see it. We arrived a few hours before the start of the ceremony, which took place at Shungopavi Mesa on the Hopi Indian Reservation.

Rattlesnakes are the emissaries to the Rain Powers and are held sacred by the Indians. The dance takes place in a plaza, which is surrounded by homes connected with flat roofs. Visitors climb onto the roofs to observe the dance. No cameras or recorders are allowed. The day my wife and I witnessed the ceremony was brutally hot.

A venerable old-timer sitting on a box next to me offered to share his seat. He explained the intent of the dance and then surprised me with the following comments: "I have been coming here for over sixty years, and the truth of the matter is it always rained during the ceremony, after the ceremony, that evening, or by the next day—until 1942. Then it all stopped. The Great War had begun and military trucks with their gasoline vapors came onto our unspoiled land. The army came and our world started changing. Since then, the dance doesn't work anymore. Our ceremony fails us: we can't make the rain come. But you know what? Even though our religion doesn't work anymore, we still go through the motions." Then he added, "Just like your religion doesn't work anymore. Still you, too, go through the motions."

His simple words told me their myth had died. The soul went out of it and his gods didn't seem to work anymore. Maybe most people's gods don't work anymore. Perhaps the old gods have died and the new ones haven't arrived yet. Many people in traditional religions are no longer willing to simply go through the motions because they want to genuinely feel reconnected to the roots of the divine. Church bells don't seem to chime loudly now. It's ironic that while churches are failing to meet congregant needs, interest in spiritual matters of all kinds, especially personal experience, has never been greater.

An article in the January 9, 2006, issue of *USA Today* entitled, "Is God Dead in Europe? Many Signs Suggest Yes," seems to prove that organized religion is failing the masses.. This impressive article on European religious trends indicates the practice of traditional religion is in free fall. In Czechoslovakia, alcoholics outnumber practicing Christians, and more Czechs believe in UFOs than God. In most European countries, there has been a 40 percent decline in church attendance and religious practices since 1970. Cultural leaders and the ruling classes are antireligious and Christophobic. Court decisions have banned school prayer, dismantled nativity scenes from public squares, and legalized gay marriages. After two world wars and countless centuries of religious conflicts and persecution, old beliefs are dying; but only time will tell if new ones evolve.[1]

In the United Sates, where religious belief is extremely strong, that faith is also going through dramatic changes. The U.S. Religious Landscape Survey released in February, 2008, by the Pew Forum on Religion and Public Life interviewed more than 35,000 American adults to discover significant changes occurring in this country's religious life. Some of the important findings were: atheists made up less than 2 percent of the total population; 82 percent claimed religion was an important component in their lives; and 44 percent have swapped their original religion for another. Americans are jumping the religious fence into what they hope will be greener pastures. Some aren't jumping at all and prefer no religious affiliation. More than one quarter of younger Americans (ages eighteen to twenty-nine) report no religious connection. They firmly believe in God but can't conceive of any organized traditional religion revealing the profound secrets of the divine. Preferring not to call themselves religious, they refer to their status as spiritual and are searching for something new that touches their spirit. They may be the forerunners of a new religion where individuals realize secrets sought outside of self are really contained within each human being. The old gods are undergoing a major transformation.[2]

History shows that gods die all the time. Zeus and his entourage of Greek Gods fell off Mount Olympus. Osiris, Ra, and Set faded away in Egypt, as have the gods of the Romans and the Norse people. The great temples of the ancient world and the majestic cathedrals of the Middle Ages are mostly reminders of a divine grandeur whose vitality has ebbed. And primitive peoples' gods carved in stone and wood are spread out in museum display cases worshipped by avid folk-art collectors.

Where did all these gods come from? Zeus and his entourage came from our minds. They were projections from within our psyche to help us understand a puzzling world, to gain control over natural events that could overwhelm us, and to satisfy our material and emotional needs. Outside the mind, these mythological beings are nonexistent.

Where have all the gods gone? Science has explained many out of existence, but there has been a price to pay. Perhaps past civilizations had more certainty when people knew where they stood. The collective mind and beliefs held sway over the individual, but today individuals don't have that certainty. Spiritual life can't compete with the intense interaction that takes place across America's major bridge— economics. Financial opportunities that create movement away from home are commonplace, resulting in lost contact with family, old friends, and community. People are too busy. This lifestyle toward which Americans have migrated creates enormous emotional stresses. Prescription drugs may be the new gods we depend on for relief.

However, belief systems that created this lifestyle are under bombardment. People think everything can be explained away rationally, and scientific achievements convince them they are masters of the earthly plane. However, there is a limit to human reason and comprehension: it's incapable of grasping that which is beyond its borders. Modern men and women have forgotten how to wonder—how to imagine and stay aware of the greatness, the vastness, and the majesty of our remarkable cosmos. A growing number of Americans are beginning to realize they are in a spiritual crisis and in need of renewal. The inner life has been neglected for too long. These conditions are fertile ground for the inner self to rebel, to demand recognition and a chance to be heard. All extremes bring their opposite into focus.

Dreams Reveal Truth at Any Age

Pursuing an inner life can mean many things: cultivating a closer relationship to God or spiritual discipline; tranquility and peace of mind; or finding connection to the spirit. Basically, though, it's searching for the inner truth, which is within and can rear its head at any age. In *Memories, Dreams and Reflections,* C. G. Jung shares a precocious spiritual crisis that occurred when he was eleven or twelve. One summer day, he walked out of school and went to the cathedral square. Brilliant sunshine lit a glorious blue sky, and the cathedral roof glittered in the sun. He thought the world and the cathedral were beautiful and that God who sat on a golden throne far above it made it all. This was the cathedral where his father was a Protestant minister.

Then a dark thought tried to enter his mind, but he shut it out with great trepidation. If he had allowed himself to think the thought, he would be committing the most awful of sins—a sin against the Holy Ghost—that could not be forgiven. Committing that kind of sin would damn him to hell for all eternity. Struggling with this inner torment for three days, Jung forced himself to think it through. He reasoned that some Higher Power wanted him to think the very thoughts he didn't want to know. He remembered that Adam and Eve were parentless and created directly by God. And God only creates perfection. Yet they committed the first sin by doing what God told them not to do. But God had placed them in the garden and had arranged everything so they would have to sin. God's intention was that they should sin. These thoughts had somehow liberated Jung from his worst torment, and he believed that God had placed him in this situation to arrange a decisive test—that everything depended on Jung understanding him correctly. So he gathered all his courage and allowed the thought to come through. Jung saw the cathedral and blue sky beneath where God sat on his Golden throne high above the world. "From under the throne comes an enormous turd that falls upon the sparkling new roof, shatters it and breaks the walls of the cathedral asunder." He immediately felt an enormous and indescribable relief. Instead of being damned, he felt that grace had been bestowed on him, a feeling of bliss that he had never before experienced. A feeling of illumination helped him understand things he had not previously known. These were things he thought were still unclear to his father, a man whom he believed had never experienced the will of God and thus, the miracle of grace, which made everything discernible.[3]

His father had believed in God as the Bible proclaimed and as his forefathers had taught him. "But he did not know the immediate living God who stands above his Bible and his church, and who calls on man to partake of his freedom."[4] One must utterly abandon to God; nothing matters but fulfilling his will. Otherwise, all is folly.

A spiritual crisis and awakening can come at any age. The following dream comes from a woman in her forties who was disenchanted with the spiritual content of her church. Her pastor was controlling and opposed to new ideas and philosophies. This in turn resulted in a dwindling membership. The church board consisted of people who

32

had been members for decades, who only paid lip service to change and were opposed to studying other religions. The woman also was in a book club studying Tao Buddhism, which contributed to her Christian spiritual growth. To her, the pastor was an unfriendly presence in the community who stifled spiritual growth.

Her dream illuminates an issue that many church-going people face—how church leaders can neglect an individual's real spiritual needs and be unaware they're doing it.

I am in the lobby of an unfamiliar Church building. An older couple is also there, and they seem familiar to me although their faces are not clear. They appear to be very responsible people, the kind the church can always count on. As I talk with them, we notice a soft spot on the outer wall. Going closer to inspect it, we realize the wall is soft and flaky. The scene changes, and I am in the same church in a room adjacent to the lobby talking with Reverend Beatrice. I ask her if she has seen the soft spot on the lobby wall; she responds that she has not been aware of it. I take her into the lobby to show her, and now there are several soft spots. As we continue to look, they grow larger and larger. The wall starts to bulge, and I realize it is going to fall on us. Horrified, we run toward the sanctuary where several faceless people are also panicked. There is a radiant, colored stained-glass skylight in the chapel, and bright sunlight is shining through it. The cha-pel is large and spacious with no pews. I feel the inevitability of being killed by these walls smashing in on us, but still the light is there. I am just beginning to scream when I wake up.

This dream brings to the dreamer's attention several points she hadn't clearly recognized. Her church had become unfamiliar. The type of members she met were old timers who just accepted what they were taught and could be counted on to assume responsible roles. They were not deep-thinking people who would query what the church was presenting to its members. For them, taking an individual path would be out of the question regardless of what the church taught. The reverend was unaware that her church was collapsing. Walls, which support the structure, were getting soft, and the whole building was in danger of collapsing. Even the sanctuary wasn't safe. But the one saving grace was the bright sun, the source of light, which was outside this church. The dreamer was in danger of a spiritual death if she continued her membership. In the wake of her revelation, she left and joined another church she hoped would satisfy her spiritual needs.

An Episcopalian minister in his late forties who had left the ministry had the following inner experience. This dream for him was a spiritual earthquake that resulted in his spiritual emancipation:

I am playing poker with three other men. It's draw poker and I am shocked to realize that the fourth hand is God. He's just an ordinary-looking man dressed in a plain business suit and tie. I can't believe that God is at my table and looks like any other middle-aged man. The cards are dealt, and God asks for three cards on the draw. Then God proceeds to tell an original joke. It's so funny that I start laughing in uncontrollable hysteria. I am laughing so hard that I wake myself up laughing deliriously.

The dreamer was deeply puzzled by his dream. His concept of God was of some kind Being who was far removed from humans and unknowable because he existed on a plane separate from his creation. Yet his dream showed exactly the opposite. Not only was God just an ordinary guy, he was sitting at his table and involved in the dreamer's personal affairs. This thought really shook him to the foundation of his belief system by trying to persuade the dreamer to start thinking differently about the nature of the creative force and maybe to take life a little more lightly.

The truth of life is hidden within your own self, but people keep searching for it in the outer world. Your inner self holds the solutions to many of your major life issues and is the key to grasping reality. The earlier you understand this, the greater will be your opportunities for growth. You don't have to wait for middle age to be enlightened. Because children are closer to their instincts and the unconscious mind, their dreams can frequently address spiritual issues. Between the ages of five and six, I had a spiritual dream that emphasized that I am a soul and not just a physical being. Of course I didn't understand the ultimate message of this dream until later in life. Perhaps coming to an understanding of your memorable childhood dreams will contribute to you being a healthier adult.

I am a baby that was born high in the sky, up in the heavens, approximately four to five months old and wearing diapers. I am lying on a cloud, just drifting and floating, when suddenly I fall through it and plummet to earth. My speed increases as I accelerate downward, and when I see the earth rushing up to greet me, I awaken, startled at my close call with death.

The Search for God

I didn't have a god that worked or didn't work. What I had learned from my Jewish upbringing was quite vague and had almost no impact on my daily life. Major Jewish holidays occurred several times a year, and I always felt my conscience trying to goad me into going to temple. Guilt and my wife's prodding to set an example for the children won out. I had put very little energy into studying my religion, Hebrew school and temple services were boring and painful experiences, and the best relief was a brief nap during responsive reading and sermons. Walking on the beach and exploring tide pools was what I considered a religious experience. But my dream of the ancient woman who refused to help me become a superb therapist because of my ignorance of God told me it was time to look for the divine.

Thinking that maybe books could convey the true inner experience of the divine, I decided to start reading. Until that time, I was unaware of what an important role dreams played in the origin and evolution of the world's religions. In the course of my research, I read of the following:

- In a dream, God made a covenant with Abraham and promised a great future for his descendants. So dreams helped create a special relationship between God and Israel.
- Jacob dreamt of a great ladder extending from earth to heaven. Angels ascended and descended. God made his presence known and assured Jacob that the land he was on would belong to him and his progeny after he had scattered them to the ends of the earth.
- Joseph, a master dream interpreter, revealed to Pharaoh that his dreams of corn and cows predicted seasons of plenty followed by those of famine. After he presented Pharaoh with a plan to avoid future starvation, Joseph was put in charge of a massive public works campaign to store food for the famine and eventually became the second most powerful man in Egypt. Joseph validated the Hebrew belief that God can send mighty messages in dreams.
- In the New Testament, Joseph was told the truth of Mary's pregnancy by an angel in a dream. Not only was he instructed not to cast her out but was also told what to name the child.
- The life of Jesus was saved by dreams of Joseph and the three wise men.

- Mohammed, the founder of Islam, had his divine mission and a portion of the Koran laid out in his dreams.
- Joseph Smith, founder of the Mormons, had revelations and instructions for creating a church come to him in his dreams.
- Beginning at the age of nine, Don Bosco was directed by God through dreams to enter the priesthood and create a religious order. He founded the Salesians, who became influential throughout Europe and sent missionaries around the world.
- Native Americans were long known to revere dreams as the avenue to spiritual indoctrination and growth.

My readings revealed that there were many religions in which dreams played a formative role. Myriad details and two years later, I was no closer to knowing God than I was the morning I had awakened from my dream of the ancient woman who had sent me on my search. However, I did make the following observations about the major religions I studied:

- Generally, followers of a particular religion have no doubt their beliefs and ideas are true and divinely inspired.
- Intolerance for other religions is rampant and can lead to violence, imprisonment, and murder. This rage will remain as long as religions are antagonistic toward each other.
- Religious beliefs have an enormous impact on an individual's daily life.
- People of faith do not need rational proof of even their wildest convictions.
- Church beliefs are taken as the highest authority.
- Fundamentalists have no conscious doubt that the Bible is the incontestable word of God.
- God watches and punishes us for evil deeds and rewards us for good ones.
- The dreaming mind is almost totally ignored in churches and temples.
- Some traditional religions try to improve people through fear, shame, and guilt.

The list could go on ad infinitum, but I did also see a positive side to religion. Churches and religious organizations do much honorable work to help the less fortunate, strengthen communal bonds, and provide a community setting to meet social needs. They do very little beyond what secular organizations can also do.

What I had hoped to find was a connection to God that was personal and touched me emotionally, one that made my heart pound and my spirit sing. Traditional religion didn't convince me it could provide this. From my studies, there seemed to be no general consensus about the validity of any of the various concepts of God. It was then I realized I was on my own. My task was clear but not so simple. My success centered on personally knowing and experiencing who or what God was, and I still was groping in the dark.

I kept coming back to my dream of the old woman. What did she mean? Where did she come from? What was this journey she sent me on? I couldn't find the answers outside myself. I couldn't find what I was looking for by reading a book, hearing a sermon, watching a television evangelist, or listening to theologians discuss the nature of God. I remember reading that God hid himself in the least likely place humans would think of looking—inside every individual. One could search the globe and come up empty-handed.

C. G. Jung and the God Within

Nothing I had read about the various religions penetrated to any deep level, but what did strike many inner chords were the writings and thoughts of C. G. Jung. I consider this founder of analytic psychology one of the great minds of the twentieth century. His penetrating insights were revolutionary and far ahead of his time, as was his dogma-free spirituality. As suggested in his book, *Psychological Reflections,* Jung believed religion was a fundamental activity of the human mind, and religious belief was not an adequate substitute for inner experience. In other words, no matter your religious affiliation, if blind allegiance is your sole practice, it becomes impossible to personally experience the God within. Regardless of what the world thinks about religious experience, the one who has experienced it has a great treasure stored inside that becomes a source of life, beauty, and wonder. Not only does that experience give new meaning to life, it also helps a person live more completely and provides a sense of majesty. There are no criteria that can invalidate this experience, especially if it helps you live a richer life.[5]

Jung was the first modern psychiatrist to say he felt he could not heal a neurotic patient unless that patient reconnected to a spiritual source within. For Jung, the spiritual was an instinct trying to connect us to our souls. Religions are great psychotherapeutic systems. The magnificent images that evolve from them represent recognition of the soul and its attendant struggles to grasp life's meaning. This universal foundation unites humankind, and once an individual has lost connection to the source, he or she becomes emotionally unstable.

Contrast this with the more rational approach—that humans created religion to lessen their anxiety about their own mortality and the power of the universe. This is a lot different than Jung's idea that we are born with a religious impulse to help reconnect us to the creative force in the universe.

Jung's belief in the healing power of a religious experience played a crucial role in the founding of Alcoholics Anonymous. In the early 1930s, Rowland H., a successful American businessman, went to see Jung after failing to find a cure for his alcoholism. After a year of therapy, he became relatively sober. Upon his return to the United States, he relapsed and went back to Switzerland again to seek treatment from Jung. But Jung respectfully told him that what he had to offer would be of no avail for a permanent cure; he was beyond medical or psychiatric help. Jung suggested that his only hope lay in seeking a spiritual or religious experience—a genuine conversion. He also needed to throw himself into some religious organization— it didn't matter which one—surrender himself to God, pray for a miracle, and hope for the best. There was no need for dogma or creed: only an experience. Jung had seen recovery in some who had done this.

Rowland returned to the States, followed Jung's advice, and eventually recovered. He shared his experience with friends who also followed a similar path to sobriety. Eventually Bill Wilson, the founder of AA, was told of the "miracle that worked." He was an atheist and found the whole idea of surrendering to God repulsive. Since he was both addicted and had a physical allergy to alcohol, his prognosis was dim—psychosis and death. But in one of his blackest depressions, he beseeched God to show himself because he was ready to do anything, even believe. He saw a blinding white light and felt a great wind. A boundless peace enveloped him, and his obsession to drink was snapped off instantly. He then envisioned a chain reaction among alcoholics, one carrying the good news to another. This spiritual experience was the foundation of an organization that has been of great help to millions of alcoholics everywhere.[6]

Jung and the God-Image

In the introduction of *Memories, Dreams and Reflection*, Aniela Jaffe, Jung's editor, collaborator, and confidante, mentions that this book was the only place in his extensive writings where Jung spoke of God and his personal experience with him. For Jung, God could only be experienced firsthand. Where religion was concerned, he believed people could not truly understand something until they had experienced it internally. The psyche, especially the unconscious portion, spontaneously produces images with a religious content. So by its very nature, it is "religious." The human intellect can never answer questions of God nor give any proof of God's existence.

In his scientific works, Jung seldom speaks of God. There, he is very careful to use the term "the God-image" in the human psyche. In his autobiography, however, Jung's language is subjective because he elaborates on his personal experiences, but in his professional writings as a psychiatrist, the language is more in line with scientific inquiry. He was very sensitive to criticism, especially because of his openness and honesty in revealing his religious experiences and thoughts. According to Jung, the psyche contains the whole personality, both the conscious and unconscious mind, with all their attendant thoughts and feelings. Using the analogy of the sun as the center of the solar system, he called the primary organizing principle in the psyche the "self." In a way, it could be called a model God that is imprinted in all humans. The conscious personality side of the psyche has the ego as its center. This is what gets individuals into trouble because in the extreme, the ego tends to be self-centered and self-absorbed, has an insatiable need for recognition, demands attention, can be overly competitive, and wants its own way regardless of the needs of others.

If the individual is to become a whole and complete person, he or she must sacrifice the ego's position to the highest authority within—the self—which is actually the archetype of God. This image of the God within is there at birth and generally unfolds over a long period of time. If the ego cooperates, it realizes there is something greater than it. Discovering and experiencing the self is the goal of existence. Said another way, finding the God within is the purpose of life. It keeps the individual balanced, centered, and open to its creative power. When a person finally achieves this, he or she realizes that something bigger than the ego—an original and resourceful power—is offering guidance through a divine blueprint.

The primary way the self communicates to us is through dreams and other psychic experiences. Archetypal symbols that represent the self in dreams can be the Christ, a mandala (balanced geometric design usually with four quadrants, symbolic of the universe), a circle, a divine child, fire, wind, a flaming torch, fiery chariot, penetrating light, lightning, water, the sun, a star, a magic stone, a messenger. Dreams contain many powerful forces that could symbolize the psychic inner energies that nature has granted all people. Fall in love and you are possessed by an energy that can transform and overwhelm you. Venus has struck. Get enraged and Mars is ready to do battle. Gods with human form live inside everyone.

C. G. Jung—The Messenger from Beyond

Since my original dream posed the problem of knowing God, I began to assume this same source could also disclose the answer. And it happened! After two years of reading, studying, and looking for God, Jung himself appeared in my dreams, delivering in clear and simple words the truth I had been searching for. This revelatory dream introduced me to an idea about God that I had never consciously entertained. This dream occurred approximately fifteen years after Jung died. I had never met Jung but had seen a movie about him, read many of his writings, and even had access to privately distributed works that weren't released to the public. My memory does not recall the statement he makes in my dream as coming from anything I had read by Jung. There are, of course, numerous writings I have not read, and he very well *could have* stated what he does here:

I am walking by a round table in a spacious cafeteria where Jung and another man are seated. The other man is a stranger I do not recognize, but I am astounded at seeing Jung. Oh, my gosh! I am thrilled that the great man is here in my presence. As I pass the table, he calls out to me, "Bernard, sit down, I want to tell you who God is."

I stop, step back from the table quite astonished at his request, and reply, "Oh, Dr. Jung, that's all right, no need to do that because I have been studying, and I know who God is!" He reacts, "Oh, no you don't. Sit down." I again insist, "Yes I do." His next response is much more emphatic. In fact, he raises his voice and says, "No, you still don't know who God is, so sit down and listen."

Now, I would have thought it a great honor to have polished his shoes, carried his briefcase, or cleaned his office. When this master speaks in such strong tones, you obey. I did.

He looks me straight in the eyes and says: "Listen, Bernard, God is neither a man nor a being with a long white beard sitting on a throne dispensing wisdom. That's not God. God is the life force. It is the spirit that creates and animates all of life."

I awakened wide-eyed and lost in wonder. One of the first thoughts that came to me was the lines of a John Lennon song: "You may say I'm a dreamer, but I'm not the only one. I hope someday you will join us, and the world will live as one."

I had never thought about God that way. Probably at some level, I thought of God as the Big Patrolman in the sky, waiting to punish us for some wrongdoing. As mentioned in the description of my dream, Jung emphasized that God was not a great parental figure, ensconced on a throne waiting to dole out his infinite intelligence or send out his angelic messengers in answer to human prayers.

The notion of God is the mystery of mysteries, and to define the Almighty is difficult and puzzling. God means so many different things to so many people. I personally don't think the conscious mind is capable of giving a clear picture of the Supreme Being. The conscious mind is very limited, and we do not possess perfect knowledge. Human belief systems have to fill in the blanks. In so doing, our minds can easily create delusions that understanding is perfect and complete. In many theologies, the ideas move into more and more remote zones of abstraction. When religious groups start accepting these myths as truths, reason is thrown out the window, and the capacity for potential harm to humankind increases.

Some people have no doubt that God was a special white man who was born of a virgin. Others use hyperbolic adjectives to define who and what God is: eternal, all-loving, omnipresent, omniscient, omnipotent, and morally perfect. To go to war over competing mythologies strikes me as groundless and absurd. But people have destroyed and murdered each other over contending notions about God and have left a legacy of intense hatred and a fierce desire for retaliation.

What Jung presented in my dream seems so much more benign. If God is the deepest and most profound force within, all people must have a great deal of internal undiscovered potential. It could be well worth our best effort to find out what that means. If God is this life force within, maybe we don't have to risk our necks, take drugs, or harm people to feel alive.

I felt that some special teaching had been revealed to me. As mentioned, I do not know if Jung ever claimed what he did in my dream during his lifetime, and I cannot recall reading this statement in any of Jung's works that I had read. As much as I could understand, for Jung, God was a great paradox, a great mystery.

Several years after this dream, I called the librarian at the Jung Institute in San Francisco, because a Jungian analyst told me she had read everything Jung ever wrote and would know if what he had told me in the dream was a statement I had read. She responded to my question with an emphatic "No," but then resoundingly added, "I'm sure it's something he believed!"

I thought about my dream of Jung for a long time. It was one of those dreams that seems so wise, so moving and soul-stirring that it is a feast for the mind and heart and may take years to reveal its true essence. It's like having a special gourmet meal that one can feast on eternally and experience subtle new tastes and textures.

God is unknowable. But for Jung, he is also one of the most certain and immediate experiences. What Jung meant by an experience was that there is a force in the world that functions independently and unforeseeably in human life, almost like a power that has its own intention—a fate—that people cannot control. Maybe God lies beyond the limit of human conscious understanding, but the unconscious mind spontaneously sends dreams that plant ideas about the divine that demand harvesting and examination.

In a letter he wrote to a young woman in August 1957, Jung said God is the ultimate mystery. And when he spoke of God, he meant the image that humans make of him. No one knows what God is like, or that person would be a God himself.[7] For Jung, the unconscious was the medium through which religious experience flows. The archetypal symbols of God, which arise primarily in the collective unconscious, could symbolize the Creator but could also be expressions of the life force that lies within and represents potential wholeness and creative power. God doesn't care what he is called: Jehovah, Allah, Wankan Tonka, Brahma, Tonto, or Yahweh. It's all the same, because God resides in all human bodies.

For most people, raising the deeper secrets that lie within is a difficult task. Literal and rational training and religious education in dogmas have walled minds off from the internal sage. Fortunately, human souls are endowed with a transparent window that offers a view of an inner realm. Powerful religious or spiritual dreams were thought to be the domain of biblical characters or people of great fame, but they are really within the jurisdiction of all who seek them. Everyone has the capability of contacting this hallowed dimension in dreams.

The Bible has two consistent images associated with God. The first is an anthropomorphic one of an old man with a beard and long flowing hair as white as snow who converses with people, responds to their prayers, and has similar emotions as his creations. The second is more spiritual. It communicates a different message: that a unifying spiritual intelligence is manifested at every level of creation. That intelligence is like a spiritual DNA that is the hereditary material in humans and all other organisms. This God-image seems to be more consistent with the recent findings of science. Human beings live in an unfolding, expanding universe where consciousness is moving toward greater complexity.

My main lesson from this dream was that this creative force is everywhere and in everything. The force that created the universe, that makes hearts beat, causes tulips to bloom, giant oaks to grow, and salmon to swim upstream is everywhere and in everything. There is a oneness that connects all things, a creative energy that is the basic foundation and building block of all life. All people have the living spirit of God within them—the life force that creates and animates their lives. The energy that created the cosmos and shaped the universe is the same power we use to mold our lives.

Humans have trillions of cells in their bodies that come together in an extraordinary cooperative endeavor. The whole system has remarkable potential that far outstrips any one cell, because each individual cell is dedicated to the health of the whole system. Ecosystems undergo the same process to maintain health. What Jung told me in my dream promotes the idea of this planet as an interconnected community in which everyone is responsible for making it healthier.

What would human experience be like in a "oneness universe"? On the external level, a oneness universe can already be seen in the globalization trend and technological revolution. For the first time in the whole of human experience, electronic breakthroughs give men and women the outer experience of potentially connecting to millions on the planet. Although there is a deepening economic interconnection between countries, globalization isn't just about economics; it's even more about the need for a paradigm shift in consciousness. Humanity has long been divided by external differences such as race, religion, gender, and nationality, none of which should threaten or diminish us. What may well be the most celebrated accomplishment of the twenty-first century is the recognition that the human community is one—bound together as a single giant congregation needing to consciously realize it has a common God and a common destiny. Our purpose is to evolve by recognizing we are all part of this enormous family, obligated to cooperate with each other so the next generations can have a better future.

What Jung told me could be one of humanity's primary wake-up calls. This is essentially what my dreams and those of many others are trying to impress upon the conscious mind.

Human experience on the inner level stresses the linking of people without any conscious effort. Many individuals have had mystical experiences that give the feeling of being one with the universe, realizing the underlying connectedness and unity of all things on the planet and beyond. For example, over half the attendees in my dream seminars have had the experience of receiving a call from someone they were thinking about only moments before. Or perhaps they felt deep love surface regarding a family member and later find out that person was having similar thoughts and feelings about them at the same time. Psi experiments[8] have produced results far beyond chance in the areas of telepathy, clairvoyance, precognition, and psychokinesis. It has been suggested by quantum theory that matter and consciousness interpenetrate. This could mean that humans share a common heritage and that the separation between nature and people is an illusion.

This is not a new idea. The Pantheists assume that the essence of God is in all things. Nature religions, including many American Indian and African religions believe in the dynamic unity of all life. In Vedanta, a philosophy taught by the Vedas, the most ancient scriptures of India, the basic teaching is that the real nature of humanity is divine and God is the innermost Self. Religion is therefore a search for self, a search for God within. The great Hindu sage Sri Rama Krishna stated, "Seekest thou God? Then seek Him in man! His Divinity is manifest more in man than in any other object. Man is the greatest manifestation of God."[9] At worst, we are unaware of our true nature.

"There is a world of 'hungry people' looking for a deeper relationship with God."[10] This statement by Father Thomas Keating, the abbot of St. Joseph's Abbey in Massachusetts, appeared in the September 5, 2005, *Newsweek* special article on spirituality in America. The God is Dead era of the 1960s was partly based on the assumption that if science can't explain it, then what can't be known (by scientific methods) seems unrewarding. But the rational theology of that era has been replaced by a passion for an immediate, transcendent experience of God.

Newsweek set out to chart the varying paths Americans have taken on their spiritual journey to find God. Journalists visited storefront churches in Brooklyn, mosques in Los Angeles, Christian activists in West Virginia, a Catholic college in Ohio. They observed Americans of all creeds and practices: Pentecostals hollering God's name, Catholics contemplating the Eucharist, Jews seeking God in the Kabbalah, Pagan religions seeking God in nature, Zen Buddhists seeking enlightenment in meditation, and Muslims praying to create a more God-centered Islam.[11]

People are waking up, and what they are looking for is communion with the divine. Knowledge about God is not good enough. Knowing God by reason or faith lacks a dynamic principle. Individuals can be ultra orthodox and well versed in theology, but the real question is have they experienced God within themselves? This is the real issue for seekers today, not the fundamentalist goals of teaching intelligent design in the schools or appointing another conservative to the Supreme Court.

A 2005 *Newsweek* poll found that 80 percent of the people surveyed believed that more than one faith could be a path to salvation, which is most likely not what they were taught in Sunday school.[12] This quest for spiritual union with God is as old as mankind. So many ancient cultures believed that God spoke to people in dreams. If God spoke in dreams to the ancient patriarchs, why wouldn't the divine reach out to ordinary men and women?

Maybe God is looking for us but finds it hard to get through when we're awake and are so preoccupied with religious minutiae. Almost all the ancient patriarchs in the Old Testament received their instructions from God in their dreams. Many ancient cultures believed certain dreams were communications from God. There are countless examples of people making contact with inner spiritual realms without the help of a church or formal religion. People don't need the sacraments of the church to be saved. Of course, Christians who believe in the rapture have no need for dreams that open into the spiritual world. For them, life on the earth plane is a halfway house, a pause on the way to heaven. But according to dreams, people don't have to wait to experience God until they get to heaven—wherever that is.

The following is a dream about the nature of God to demonstrate how the unconscious attempts to bring a particular theological viewpoint to awareness. I think this dream is a first cousin to what Jung told me in my dream and thus adds another piece to the puzzle.

John Dunne, a well-known aeronautical designer and theoretician on the nature of time, dreamt it. In *The Still Good Hand of God*, Dunne shares a dream in which he was sitting on a hill overlooking the River Jordan in Israel. On the other side of the river, he could see a large number of people who represented all of humanity. The whole of that side was covered in shadow.

The deep shadow was contrasted so strongly with the brilliant sunshine in which I sat, and ended so abruptly at the water's edge, that I became puzzled as to what might be the cause thereof. Then

it dawned upon me that, about 100 yards to my left and slightly behind me, God was sitting working with bent head at something of which I was ignorant. I did not see Him because I could not turn my head. I merely knew He was there. The whole scene was as silent as a picture. And the shadow, which lay upon the world, was the shadow of God. It was everywhere—on people and between people.

I was deeply puzzled about one thing. God's shadow was lying over the whole world. Then why did those blind fools not see it? As I asked myself this, I became abruptly aware that two yards to my left and just behind the limit of my field of sight, there was standing an allegorical angel. I don't know what the angel looked like, and that is quite unimportant. It symbolized something that could be questioned.

And I fitted him with an allegorical make-up that would be in keeping with the rest of the vision. I made him a conventional angel, tall, dark, beardless and attired in a long white garment. But I was not interested in him. Wild curiosity held me in its grip. I called to him and pointed. "Look! Look!" I cried, "God's shadow! It's everywhere! It's all around them! Why don't they see it?"

I had expected the reply to be something conventional like being too much absorbed in their own worldly affairs; but if that answer had come I would have discredited it; for my sympathies were with these people, and I knew that many of them were searching everywhere for evidence of God's existence.

The answer that came—came immediately in five, short decisive words—which was completely unexpected. "Because God has no edges," said the angel.

He awoke and carefully memorized every detail of the dream. He concluded it was psychologically impossible to be aware of anything that "has no edges." Obviously there was no place in the whole world where God was absent. God had world-filling properties; consequently, it would be useless to search anywhere for evidence of God.[13]

It is a remarkable fact that billions of people worship a God who is invisible to the human eye. This may make it difficult to remember that the life force He represents is present in all things. But not being seen does not mean nonexistent or unknowable. God can be experienced. The wind can't be seen, but it can be felt. Atoms or white blood cells can't be noticed with the naked eye, but microscopes prove they exist. The roots of plants can't be directly observed, but everyone knows they sustain growing things. Perhaps it is time to recognize that something earth-shaking is happening in the human psyche that is manifesting in books, workshops, and radio and television programs. What has been sealed up in human psyches for centuries has burst out into conscious awareness. I don't think anything can stop this forward progress of consciousness. But backlashes have occurred.

The secularization of religion has produced angry reactions in the United States from fundamentalist elements in Christianity. These constituents are demonizing the present as a period of moral decay and suggesting that only belief in a fundamentalist God can restore ethical community life, attendance at church, and more responsible sexuality. Abroad, fundamentalist Muslims see progress as a major threat to an ancient way of life. And so these religious elements attempt to bring back the past. Humanity finds itself involved in murderous conflicts over competing revelations, dogmatic purity, and divine responsibility. It seems impossible that in this day, theological ideas can incite passions that leave behind ruined communities and countries. Western men and women thought politics could be separated from religion. How wrong could they be? Millions will pursue the age-old quest to bring all of human life under their version of God's sovereignty. Listening to Ahmadinejad, the president of Iran, one realizes the mind of the Middle Ages is very much alive and well. Ahmadinejad thinks he knows what God wants. Probably most fundamentalists—whether Western or Middle Eastern—think they know God's will. That's a dangerous position. Muslims believe God has revealed a comprehensive law that governs all human affairs. When people speak about what God thinks and wants, it's their own experience and interpretation. Thinking God's hand was guiding history, individuals and whole nations rushed into WWI and WWII.

Complete religious certainty is what is really unholy and blasphemous. Here in the United States, we have some of the biggest and loudest churches in the world. Preachers have free rein and infiltrate television to deliver shameful sermons. The latest "star" in the Christian world is Joel Osteen, pastor of nondenominational Lakewood Church in Houston. He has stated that one of God's top priorities is to shower blessings on Christians in his lifetime. God loves you and wants you to be rich—not broke! Members now have a heavenly ATM machine with no limit. And tithing pastor Osteen's church will bring even grander jackpots. Clearly, the Christian community has not learned from the scandals of Jim and Tammy Bakker, Jimmy Swaggert, and Catholic priests.

Moral Majority founder Jerry Falwell was certain that 9/11 resulted from God removing his protection from America because of abortion and immorality. John Hagee, CEO of John Hagee Ministries, has stated that God has a foreign policy for Israel and war is part of God's plan. Seven Hundred Club founder Pat Robertson has claimed Israeli Prime Minister Ariel Sharon's stroke was divine punishment for dividing God's land, and AIDS was God's punishment for homosexuals. More than twenty years ago, Oral Roberts said he was reading a spy novel when God appeared to him and commanded that he raise $8 million for Robert's university or else he would be "called home." He raised it! God can do wonders! Now his son and current president of the university, Richard Roberts, says that God is speaking again, insisting that Richard deny lawsuit allegations that imperil the forty-four-year-old Bible belt college's integrity.[14] It's a good thing God has sound legal sense! (He has since resigned because of God's command.)

Dreams are like bones. Bones don't lie. Religions have many skeletons in the closet. Exposure of Catholic sexual skeletons has a long history, and it makes us wonder—does religion make people better or worse?

Fundamentalist minds are certain about their convictions, and I'm sure their dreams are just as conclusive about their truths. I would love to know what the current Pope Benedict dreams. Consciously, if your moral sense insists on something different from the Pope's teachings, your sense of right and wrong is inaccurate. Instead of having courage and principles, you have sin. The Pope's stand on women's roles, homosexuality, and abortion are autocratic. Catholicism is a monarchy, and its only real commodity is moral authority. Look what happened to Galileo when he challenged the biblical view that the earth rather than the sun was the center of our solar system. He was persecuted for an indisputable truth. Yet, if the Bible says it, that settles it. Galileo's punishment was mild compared to the banishment, torture, and execution of other alleged heretics in Christian Europe during medieval times.

Religion does not have the answer for everyone. In the following dream submitted to me by a fundamentalist Christian, it is evident how dreams persuade a one-sided attitude that the "gospel" truth is alive and well in the unconscious mind. This compelling and impressive message attempts to straighten out a perverted and twisted sense of religious exclusivity that assumes a monopoly on advanced tickets for passage through the heavenly gates:

I have died. A surrey-like carriage driven by my former pastor who recently died appears out of the sky. He steps down from the carriage, takes my hand, and helps me to board the vehicle. There are several others on board I know who have also recently died. We travel upward into the sky and arrive at the outskirts of heaven.

As a newcomer, I am introduced to a guide who will be with me as I prepare for what is to come. There seem to be many different spaces or areas before me. Each area has to do with unlearning one of the lies that we as humans believed on earth. In the initial area, the first lie I unlearned was that fear has power over me. I no longer see myself as a victim. It is the first time I ever experienced being without anxiety or fear.

We leave this area and go past a place where many who considered themselves Christians on earth are laughing at their own past prejudices and opinions. They are discussing the zoo of heaven where there is a different animal to represent each of God's truths on earth. One of them is talking about the Mormon creature that represents a truth that was given only to the Mormons. All the "Christians" were embarrassed that they had so discounted God's truth because of their prejudices and beliefs that God could only manifest in certain ways. The dream continues from space to space, and at the end with each undoing of a lie, a light that was present from the beginning gets brighter and brighter, and the dreamer knows she is getting closer and closer to the truth of God.

Religious conflicts go on and on and on. If the world's religions are not fighting amongst themselves about heaven, they are fighting about hell. Many Catholics, Protestants, Muslims, and Jews think those of other faiths are misguided. Fundamentalist Muslims even believe "infidels" deserve to die. Why do these religions care so much about what other people believe? It is time people moved beyond the religious ideas that evolved during the Bronze Age and the twelfth century. History has demonstrated that religion hasn't drawn people together but instead pushed them apart. If religion in general has not been a force for unity, what within the human psyche can begin promoting this idea of harmony?

There are ideas that are currently surfacing from the depths of humanity's unconscious minds that tell us we must take on a new responsibility for creating this unity. The scientific mind has slipped weapons of devastating destructive ability into our hands, and we can no longer remain unenlightened. Knowledge of God's nature is essential for survival and peace. What might be most astonishing about dreams is that they clearly reveal humans are linked together in ways they have yet to grasp. As the next chapter will show, the unconscious mind is prodding men and women everywhere to take full measure of what rightly belongs to them.

Chapter 3

WE ARE ALL THE ANOINTED ONES: THE NEW MESSIAHS!

> To believe in God or in a guiding force because someone tells you to is the height of stupidity. We are given senses to receive our information within. With our own eyes we see, and with our own skin we feel. With our intelligence, it is intended that we understand. But each person must puzzle it out for himself or herself.
>
> *Sophie Burnham*

There is no need to delve deeper into the destructive aspects of religion. Sam Harris, author of *The End of Faith*,[1] and Christopher Hitchens, author of *God is Not Great*,[2] have done more than an adequate job in describing how religion can warp minds and lead to turmoil and destruction of life. They have helped open people's eyes to the dangers and absurdities of organized religion. Their much-needed criticism has permeated the insular walls erected by religious fundamentalists. My hope is that what they say wakes people up and stimulates them to move religious ideas into a new evolutionary phase. Religion will never disappear, because it's an instinct. What is demanded of human beings is to continue the evolutionary advancement of the species, especially in consciousness and awareness of ourselves as the second creators of the world. We are essential for the completion of creation. Unless we grasp this thought, the current world spiritual crisis will either stagnate or worsen.

The Time Is Ripe for Change

"We are living in unprecedented times," writes Jung in *The Undiscovered Self*. It is a time of *kairos*, which in ancient Greek means "the right or opportune moment; a moment in time when an opening appears and something special happens; or a time for a metamorphosis of the Gods."[3] The unimaginable has happened in the world. Weapons of mass destruction are in the hands of radicals or being sought by them. As a result, religious leaders now warn that the "end times" are imminent. There seems to be no one on the horizon who can lead humanity out of this quagmire. Looking for a savior from the political realm or religious institutions can be discouraging and depressing.

With constant threats and saber rattling hovering over our heads, individuals seem to be on their own. The time for change is long overdue, and encouraging signs of a tremendous upsurge of spiritual unfolding are manifesting everywhere. The choice for change does not lie with God. It lies with the human community. Whether people continue on the spiral downward toward the eventual destruction of humankind or take a new route to peace, fellowship and open-mindedness depend on all of us. As you will see, redeemers are individuals, and they are closer to home than we realize.

Dreams Can Be a Primary Source for Change

Dreams have extraordinary views on this subject. Many ideas that most have forgotten are crucial to personal well-being and evolution as well as planetary harmony. Concealed in the subliminal mind is the single-most important and forgotten piece of truth. This chapter aims to remind readers of what it is to prompt thinking men and women to grasp this sacred knowledge. Dreams are trying to convert us to an old belief system—something known in the distant past but that time, change, and neglect have allowed to slip away. This conversion attempt is not done in the spirit of televangelism, which tries to influence and reshape religious beliefs. People are born into membership of this inner church, and the congregation is the human race. There are no monetary obligations or proselytizing. When the conscious mind can't interfere, the inner mind, which is infinitely more powerful and intelligent, sends dreams that strive to correct belief systems that miss the mark.

The dramatic insights that are presented in the next few dreams are intended to ignite the abundant creative potential lying dormant in your psyche, just waiting to be harvested and ingested. This is what happened to me because I was open to my dreams. I don't know why these messages came through me at that particular time—maybe it was grace. Good things happen to people, and we don't know why. They come spontaneously from that portion of the psyche that functions autonomously and whose ideas and thoughts contradict, challenge, and astound the ego with its novel way of expression.

Approximately twenty years ago, I had the following dream:

I am again at Winthrop Beach in Massachusetts, the area of my childhood. Standing at the shore, dressed in a simple off-white robe, I look out to sea, and for some unknown reason, I stride out, thinking I can walk on water, and I do. With each step, I get further and further from the shore, heading for the breakwater about a half mile out. I realize this is not an extraordinary accomplishment, because the surface of the ocean feels like it is composed of a thin layer of a transparent rubbery material—perhaps a thin sheet of clear plastic that can support my weight. I know that as long as I keep moving to deeper water, the surface will support me. As soon as I stop, though, I know I will break through and fall into the water. When I'm slightly beyond the breakwater, I think, "What am I doing out here?" With that thought, I notice a sandbar that leads to a narrow, box-shaped wooden boathouse. The ocean's surface has returned to its natural state. I walk onto the shoal and open the door of this plain, simple structure. Inside is a beautifully hand-carved, intricately designed, one-man Eskimo kayak. I hear a voice say to me, "Get in the kayak and paddle out to the middle of the ocean, and there wait until the Great Fish rises from its depth." In my mind I picture the biggest and grandest fish in the sea, much larger than a whale. I start paddling out to sea, and then I wake up.

The ocean is a symbol for the source of all life. There are many mysteries in its depths, and my dream is trying to get me to go far from the shore, out into the watery vastness. Some secret is waiting to reveal itself if I can find the center of this vast body of water. Symbolically, the center seems to indicate an organizing principle—a point around which something revolves or rotates. A Hindu doctrine states that God resides in the center, where the radii of a wheel meet at the axis. Metaphorically, the center has a strong spiritual connotation and suggests identification with the supreme principle of the universe.

When it comes to walking on water, I certainly don't equate any of my abilities with those of Jesus. There has been only one Master. He was the first and last person who could walk on water. In fact, walking on water was a small, almost insignificant part of the dream—except that it enabled me to keep moving to deeper water. As long as I kept advancing, kept heading for the ocean depths, I wouldn't break the surface and drown. To me, the essence of my dream was the kayak and the command to paddle out to the middle of the ocean to wait for the Great Fish. This small, one-man boat indicated that I had to go alone. At the time, I think I had been trying to find a group situation that would help me on my spiritual journey. But this dream indicated that in my case, the great mysteries of life could be revealed only to those seekers who follow their own inner compass—not from the safety of the crowd in a conventional setting, but from trekking the unique individual path whose signposts may be obscured but whose directional finder is true. Light from my own candle would have to illuminate my path.

Initially, I had no idea what the Great Fish meant. The best I could do was to anticipate some big idea, perhaps the biggest in my life that would emerge from my unconscious if I was patient and centered. Then I researched the Great Fish in the *Dictionary of all*

Scriptures and Myths.[4] I learned it was a symbol of the higher self and primordial truth. In the dictionary was an interesting quote from the book *Qabbalah.* According to the *Zohar,* a classic of Jewish mysticism, "He (God) had his dwelling in the Great Sea and was a fish therein." Myth also has it that the Hindu creator God, Brahma; the Hindu preserver God, Vishnu; and the Egyptian God of light, Horus, appeared in fish form.[5]

The Path to the Grail Is Unique and Individual

Joseph Campbell's story of King Arthur and the Knights of the Round Table is a marvelous tale that illustrates the need to take an original path. The king and his knights had to find the Holy Grail in the woods that were beyond the borders of Camelot. This seemed simple enough, so they rode out together in a group. But they got lost and ended up where they had started. After many similar beginnings with the same results, someone came up with a new idea. Each knight should find his own entry into the woods; no more mass entries. The way to the Grail was now decided on an individual basis. Only the knights who paved their own paths found the Grail. Knights did not live separate and secluded lives. Companionship and sharing exploits were enjoyed, but each had to discover his sole route to the Grail.

It's no different today. Everyone has a one-person kayak and must find a personal light to illuminate the path to the divine within. Often, at appointed places on this journey, an individual will share with other pilgrims on the path. But each individual map is the ultimate guide, and it unfailingly leads to the next step on the journey. This doesn't mean you should not participate in an organized religion. Sharing common beliefs and being involved in community services and activities can be helpful and healing. The congregation, the rabbi, the priest, or society may assist in guiding, but the final decision will always rest with the individual. However, churches and temples have their own agendas, and personal spiritual growth may not be their top priority.

Many church leaders distrust and fear mystical experiences and are skeptical of people who have them. I have personally shared some of my esoteric experiences and "big" dreams with a rabbi and had them dismissed as being meaningless or "just products of my imagination." It's ironic that this same rabbi could give a sermon on mystical experiences of well-known biblical figures. Congregants of mainline churches are hungry for transcendent experiences but find church emphasis on functional routine. Many church leaders may be selected on the basis of their managerial and organizational skills and are probably not asked about their spiritual growth or connecting to the divine through encounters that transcend normal human experience.

We Are All the Anointed Ones

There was some great message that wanted to come through in my fish dream, but I wasn't getting the complete picture. For many months, not a day went by without my reflecting on the images. But I needed more enlightenment. I had an intellectual understanding of the dream, but what I needed was an inner personal experience that revealed the essence of the Great Fish. My unconscious knew it and sent me a response some years later in an amazing dream.

I am standing on the shore of Winthrop Beach (at approximately the same location of the Great Fish dream). I enter the water to
about hip level. A small wave rolls in, just about two feet high,
and I brace myself for a gentle jolt. This mild surge jostles me just
enough to jar an idea loose. Unexpectedly, I recall the dream of
the past, and the meaning flows into my mind when a loud voice
speaks, "You are the anointed one! You are the anointed one!" In
an instant, I understand that the Great Fish has surfaced, and the
viewpoint that it represents is the single biggest idea of my life. I am
so excited that I run out of the water looking for my wife, yelling,
"Sondy, I am the anointed one! I am the anointed one!" And as I
am coming up out of the dream, I realize and even keep repeating,
"We are all the anointed ones!"

I was astounded and felt honored and blessed that the spirit had
granted me this revelation. It took several days for me to come down
off my high so I could examine the dream in greater detail and reflect
on what it meant. In its most basic sense, this dream was telling me
that a divine influence is inherent in all human beings—but most
don't realize it. My dream is not just for me; it's for everybody. Even
Jesus said, "Ye are Gods" (John 10:34, KJV). Could this be the "New
Religion?" The old ones aren't working too well. They seem to be a
breeding ground for making enemies. Some of the world's biggest lies
have been spun in the churches, temples, and mosques of organized
religion. Clearly, my dream was trying to turn me on to my own
divinity and encourage others to do the same.

Believing the divine is within everyone is not a new idea; in fact
it's rather old. The *Bhagavad-Gita* is a sacred Hindu text written
between 500 and 50 BCE. Its main point is that all things are each
a part of the One Creative Force and that human beings, along with
all creations are but manifestations of this One Divine Spirit. The
Church of Divine Science's basic foundation for truth is that God is
present everywhere, therefore God is here. Thomas Aquinas (1225–
1274), Catholicism's ultimate theologian, concluded through logical
argument that God must be present in all things. Just by being born,
people become anointed ones. Meister Johannes Eckhart, a thirteenth-
century Christian mystic, was convinced God is infinite, everywhere,

and the essence of all things. Plato, Walt Whitman, Emerson, and Beethoven were similar believers.

If someone in a temple or church had told me I was born with a divine nature, I would have dismissed and forgotten the thought. But when it came through my dream, it was like a horse kick to the chest. I classify this type of dream as an inner *revelation*, which according to *Webster's Dictionary* is an act of revealing or communicating a divine truth—an enlightening or astonishing disclosure.

My inner mind already possessed the truth when I had the original dream of the Great Fish, but I couldn't grasp the essence of this evocative symbol until its inner secret was revealed in my dream. From this direct experience, I have begun more and more to rely upon the inner light, the presence of this creative force in my own soul, to navigate me into the truth. God is not in some far-off heavenly and unreachable place, but in the nucleus of my body and my soul. I consider myself an ordinary guy. There is nothing special about me except that I am taller than the average person and for some unknown reason have what I consider to be unique dreams every once in a while. And this is the main point. There is something exceptional in all people. According to Solomon Almoli, a sixteenth-century rabbi, judge, and lawyer, "Every person has approximately one great thing to say to the world in his lifetime, while the remainder of his ideas are merely echoes of other people's thoughts."[6] With the divine force bestowed upon us at birth, we are the directors of our own drama. People are not puppets—no one is pulling the strings but the individuals themselves. The world is waiting for humanity to actualize its own nobility.

In remote times, human intellectual capacity was immature, and consciousness was projected into mountains, rivers, trees, animals, and all the other forces of nature. As the universe unfolded and human understanding became more complex, conscious knowing slowly developed a scientific approach. Projections began to be withdrawn and the world became despiritualized. The gods of antiquity lost their potency and abdicated their thrones. In modern times, projections (when people see in others qualities that they themselves possess) haven't disappeared; they've just become more unconscious. Everyday life abounds with them.

A pantheon of celebrities who are literally worshiped all over the world has replaced the old gods. These modern gods are not confined to nature's realms but are visible in movie theatres, on television screens, and in publications. Publicists create myths about molding them into high-level public personalities. Just like the gods of old, they are presented as living grandiose lifestyles, which makes them worthy of our adoration and worship. Fortunately, their sordid sides also get exposed. In many ways they resemble the average person—they can be just as unhappy, depressed, frightened, and miserable. They, too, get addicted to drugs, can't make their marriages work, have uncontrollable tempers, or are inadequate parents. When their scandalous stories hit the news, these star-gods lose luster and become demystified. Outer veneers dissolve rapidly. Inner-world messages are the crucial ones. Dreams want to make clear that the real gods live inside us and that they are what create feelings of authentic human nobility.

The Greek word *Christ* means the "anointed one." The word *Messiah* is the English rendering of the Hebrew "anointed one." Fundamentally, a human who is anointed is bestowed with the Spirit of Truth and with the primary purpose to help others discern what is true and what is not. In ancient Hebrew culture, *anointed* meant to be selected as the legitimate inheritor of leadership, whether as king, priest, or prophet. Elaborate rituals were conducted to sanctify the ceremony, especially pouring oil on the head as a sign of God's special favor. That doesn't happen now. Ordainment is part of natural human inheritance. The main mission of the biblical Messiah is to restore the relationship between man and God and usher in the kingdom of peace and truth. According to the prophet Jeremiah (Jeremiah 23:3–6), the Messiah, the legendary long-awaited notable, would come and reign as king and deal wisely and do what is right and just in the land. But the truth is, humans are the true Messiahs, the rightful kings and queens.

Hallowed and complicated sacraments are unnecessary for induction into this exclusive club. Many dreams in this chapter dreamt by ordinary people emphasize humankind's divine nature. The Holy Spirit has impregnated all, and when people come to realize it, they shall give birth to their own unique version of God as manifested in humans.

"We the people" are going to save the world, not some politi-
cian or fundamentalist medicine men and their religious organizations that conceal their own self-interest while preaching gibberish to
the masses. Just as Christ knew his place in the drama of life, dreams
help dreamers see where spirit is trying to guide consciousness into the
future so people can discover their true nature, which is essential for
human ennoblement. Spirit is not some vague theological notion. It's
a living reality. According to Christian belief, the Holy Spirit impregnated Mary's womb. This is not just a Christian myth but also a fundamental metaphor for the incarnation of many beings. Hundreds of
virgin-birth myths existed in pagan religions around the same time
Christianity appeared. The idea behind these births was that gods and
semigods lived on earth in the likeness of men, such as Buddha, Plato,
Hercules, Quetzalcoatl, Alexander the Great, and the Pharaohs.

These concepts that come from dreams represent a new paradigm
in religious understanding. The old way of thinking about religion
creates more problems and hostilities than it solves. As Jung mentioned, society is living in a time of *kairos*—a time of change. And
this change has the capacity to revolutionize the way humans think
about the purpose of their lives. At the core of this new spiritual
paradigm is a staggering conviction; on the soul level, people have
been immaculately conceived, and a great adventure awaits each individual who desires to discover what this means to him or her. Accepting divinity amplifies human capacities. Dreams help those who heed
them push beyond the usual limits of the conscious mind. Just like
Christ accepted his life with all its challenges, so, too, must each of us
take full responsibility for our lives.

The Messiah is anyone and everyone. Rabbi Arthur Green says
it best: "The actual effort to redeem the world is turned to us in
history, and is done by all of us, day by day. Messiah has been waiting
on the periphery since the very beginning of history, ready to come
forth when the time is right. According to one legend, he sits among
the lepers at the gates of Rome—today we would likely find him
in an AIDS hospice—tending to wounds. Only when redemption
is about to be completed will messiah be allowed to arrive. Rather
than messiah redeeming us, we redeem messiah."[7] Maybe the time for
deliverance is now.

Our Fundamental Nature—Big and Little Messiahs

Discovering our fundamental nature seems to be the cardinal point in grasping who and what we are in this world. Human beings are all consecrated, and the list of anointed ones is long. Some messiahs among us are better known than others. Oprah Winfrey is a savior to thousands of children in her Angel Network, which is dedicated to inspiring people to make a difference in the lives of others. The network has funded over sixty schools in thirteen countries. Bill and Melinda Gates are messiahs. Their foundation has announced the funding of forty-three research projects that will receive $436 million to implement radical proposals for confronting world health problems. Perhaps Oprah, Bill, and Melinda have started an epidemic of charitable giving among billionaires. In June 2007, Peter Peterson, cofounder of the Blackstone group, became an instant billionaire when his company went public. He has chosen to put the billion dollars and much of his remaining estate into trying to preserve the American dream for generations to come.

Countless other messiahs are offering portions of their wealth to treat cancer, preserve African wildlife, create jobs, care for the environment, support human rights, assist natural-disaster victims, create children's charities, and so on. Many medical-doctor messiahs donate their services. Doctors without Borders (DWB), an independent international medical humanitarian organization, delivers emergency aid to people who are excluded from health care in more than seventy countries. Each year, medical and nonmedical professionals depart on more than 4,700 aid assignments. When a DWB ophthalmologist restores sight to a blind child in some remote village, that doctor has been elevated to messianic stature.

Messiahs come in all sizes, shapes, ethnicity, sexes, and ages. If we think necessary changes needed in the world will come from politics, we should think again. Nicholas D. Kristof, a *New York Times* columnist, wrote a stimulating article that examines the upsurge in numbers of young people willing to do the job themselves. Nicholas calls them "social engineers," the twenty-first-century counterparts to the student protestors of the 1960s. During a visit to Thailand, Andrew Klaber, a twenty-six-year-old Harvard Business and Law

School student was appalled at the number of teenage girls forced into prostitution because their parents had died of AIDS. So he founded Orphans Against AIDS, an organization that provides funding for academic scholarships. Every cent raised goes to the children, because he and his friends pay administrative costs from their own money. Soraya Salti, a young Jordanian woman is attempting to revitalize the Arab world by teaching entrepreneurship. Her organization, Injaz, is currently training 100,000 Arab students in twelve Arab countries to initiate businesses and sustain them.[8]

And then there are the Messiahs whose good deeds are never celebrated but who nevertheless uplift the lives of others. The nurse who saves lives in the emergency operating room; the neighbor you can count on to take you shopping; young people who perform community services; soldiers who risk their lives to save their friends; people who collect food and feed the homeless; teachers who bring light to the mentally and physically challenged: they, too, are Messiahs. Messiahs are everywhere, in all communities around the globe, and more committed souls are adding their names to the list each day. The human community doesn't have to wait thousands of years to be saved by some obscure Savior. Spiritual growth is not measured by how individuals look in a holy robe or by the number of days spent fasting or sitting in a meditative position. Spiritual progress and "Messiahship" are granted to those who consider problems of others equally as important as their own. There is even an added benefit. In *The Healing Power of Doing Good*, Allan Luks describes a study he conducted regarding the positive effects of helping strangers. He observed that dramatic improvements in health began with a rush of good feeling and continued into a sharp stress reduction and release of painkilling endorphins. This, in turn, resulted in long-lasting feelings of emotional well-being. Messiahs, it seems, stay healthier.[9]

Why Humanity Is Flawed

Maybe one of the major reasons human beings feel imperfect and are frequently depressed is because they have forgotten their divine nature. Many religions and psychologists attribute human defects to ignorance, disobeying God, conflicts between the id and superego, and being born into sin. But maybe the primary cause of discontent is thinking of ourselves as mere mortals, separate ego-centered beings struggling in a hostile world facing inevitable death rather than listening to what our dreams are trying to tell us—that divinity is our essential quality. Perhaps we will always perceive life as an ordeal with pain, heartache, and suffering until we accept that at our deepest core we have an extraordinary self that is unbounded and akin to the creative force itself.

What does all this mean? It means that individuals are not victims of current conditions but messengers and builders of a new world that can correct the imbalances and chaos of our present state. It means people can find greatness by applying their talents and abilities in the service of others. Great people are ordinary people who do the simple, yet extraordinary thing—serve other people. The way to success is to know what special talents and abilities lie within, develop them with love, unite them with your humanitarian impulse, and give them to the world with love. It can be in the business world, the marriage and parenting world, or whatever worlds you touch.

This thought could prove stunning, especially to the Christian mind. Many Christians have made the erroneous assumption that only the great biblical characters were anointed. But according to my dream, all human beings are anointed. Everyone has received consecration just by being born into this world.

The Second Coming of the Messiah

The Jews believe their Messiah's reign lies far in the future and Jesus was not the true Messiah because he did not usher in world peace. The Jewish Messiah will be a human being without overtones of divinity and will bring about certain changes in the world; but he must fill many criteria before he is acknowledged. Muslims believe in Jesus, but their Messiah, the Mahdi, will supplant him and transform the world into a perfect Islamic Society. Many Christians believe in the second coming of Jesus Christ to fulfill prophecies that God made in the Bible. He will not come as he did in the first—the suffering servant of humble origin. Rather, he will come on the clouds of the sky with power and glory. The armies of heaven will be under his command, and he will rule for a thousand years.

Of course no one knows when this will happen, "not even the

angels in heaven, nor the Son, but only the Father" (Matt. 24:36). I don't know if there is any other event in history that is more anticipated than the Second Coming. But I don't think we can wait around for this grand life-saving happening. Alarming events that are occurring now at a rapid pace could lead to global devastation. Indeed, there seems to be great doubt in humanity's ability to find solutions to problems that appear unsolvable.

It would be heartening to see Jesus thundering down on a white horse, but perhaps this impending arrival may be examined another way. After all, the First Coming ended up in a crucifixion and a few thousand years of continuous religious wars.

The Second Coming Is Here

Is there another possible meaning for the Second Coming? Before responding to this question, I will offer a few short dreams that were shared at my dream seminars. They will shed light on my dream of the Great Fish and will once again stress that dreams are a powerful source of religious experience and higher intelligence.

The following was a simple short dream of a nine-year-old as shared by her mother:

I am in church and ask the minister the following question: Reverend, what does God look like? And she looks right at me and replies: Why, God looks just like you.

Sometimes it's unfortunate that adults can't see with the same simplicity and freshness as children. Children ask questions adults have difficulty answering. Why is the sky blue? What does God look like? Who created God? But the unconsciousness of a child has spiritual clarity. According to this dream, meeting God in heaven after physical death is not a prerequisite for this encounter.

This dream theme emphasizes the God force within and tells us that every time we look in the mirror, we see it.

This next dream comes from a young woman.

I am standing outside a room that has a sign at the door entry. It says, "God lives here!" I open the door, and in the middle of this large, bare room is an empty chair. I surmise that God is not in yet, so I leave and return later. Again I open the door and see a similar scene and think God has still not arrived. When I return for a third time and open the door, I see a written note lying on the seat. I enter, walk to the chair, and pick up the note, which reads, "We were waiting for you to sit in the chair."

The following quote of St. Francis expresses the same idea more succinctly: "What you are looking for is what is looking!" People are looking for their true selves. The unconscious of the young female dreamer refreshes her memory with a reminder to be conscious of her divine status. I see many people who have dreams similar to this. The unconscious mind is trying to bring about a collective awakening, a major, sweeping shift in consciousness. Again, this unseen life dreams the individual, not the other way around.

God Can Only Be Felt

Jessica had one of those spontaneous dream experiences that can't be planned for but that generates powerful images that become life-long treasures.

I met God in a dream for the first time! Although surrounded by a penetrating brightness that was intensely white, my eyes were not affected. Beautiful voices could be heard, which created a feeling of extreme joy. I don't know what they were singing nor could I see them, yet I knew they were there. The feeling of love was so intense I did not want to wake up and be removed from it. No one spoke, but I had a deep understanding from that moment on that would be a gift for life. I knew that I would never accept and know God cognitively but only through the fullness of my heart. What I had tasted was pure love.

Destroy the God

Paula had quite a remarkable dream that enabled her to see how a false God outside herself had to be demolished so she could awaken to the inner deity.

I was in a temple as the leader of an ancient tribe. We were in danger because an enemy tribe of barbarians and murderers was on its way to kill us, and we were severely outnumbered. Near us in the temple was a huge stone medallion with an ancient transcript inscribed on the surface. To save our lives, it needed to be read, and I was the one that had to decipher it. I was having difficulty and feeling desperate because the killers were almost on us, and my tribe was yelling at me to hurry. Finally, I decoded it, and the message was, "Destroy the God." I started yelling, "It says, 'Destroy the God.'" We began scrambling around looking for a statue of the God, but there was none. Suddenly I realized that the medallion with the inscription was the God. I picked up a sledgehammer and broke it. An escape route appeared. I thought we had to run, but instead I realized that by breaking the stone, I had unleashed a wall of water that drowned the enemy. They were strewn all about, dead on their black horses. The unleashed water had gone about four blocks from the temple to ensure all the assailants were dead.

This was a really transformative dream for Paula. She expresses its impact on her life in her own words: "I was hesitant about taking action in the dream by myself, thinking that some hero type would save us. A person would appear who was wiser, stronger, and more competent than me to step up and do what had to be done, just like a Superman or an Einstein. But I realized I was the leader and that just standing in front of the statue and praying wouldn't give us the power to defeat the enemy. Our tribe needed a way out. When I stepped up and broke the sacred symbol to protect and free my tribe, it unleashed a power to wash away this evil force. The stone symbol of God must be emblematic of the imaginary strong person—God force—outside of myself that would save the day. My spirit was trying to tell me that mighty force was I, and that my connection to the power of the God force wasn't a symbol outside myself. The real God lived inside me and gave me the true power to wash those negative forces out of my life."

False gods made of clay, stone, and wood have been worshipped throughout history. So much personal power is projected into these objects, and they are given credit for successes where none is due.

Waking Up to the Holy Spirit Within

The last dream awakened the dreamer to the real God who lived inside her. Could this last dream be another potent meaning for the Second Coming? The New Testament describes Jesus as being very unlike and superior to ordinary human beings, but as he said and as the previous dreams emphasize, all living souls can achieve higher levels of awareness. The universal power of God is within, so there is much we can do to access our own majesty and grandeur and bring unity and stability to our hectic lives and our communities. I know there are many biblical scholars who subscribe to the Second Coming as doomsday, a time of calamity and the possible demise of the world. Are the evangelicals leading us down a path to self-destruction? Are they supporting the End Times as a fast track to heaven? Maybe these apocalyptic visions are trying to suggest the time is ripe for change. The dreams mentioned in this chapter insist that we have the formidable creative power to transform our consciousness. What may be fading away is ignorance of our true nature and the divisions created by this unconsciousness. Perhaps a crucial aspect of the God within is consciousness. What many of these dreams say is that God is not an isolated Supreme Being residing in a far-off place, overseeing human dealings and then casting judgment on human conduct. Since God resides in each and every person, he illuminates individual minds with this divine consciousness. Jesus is the perfect example of this. Divine consciousness can shine forth in both waking and dreaming states. It radiates on everyone and embraces one and all.

I like the analogy that Dr. Brian Weiss uses in *Many Masters—Many Lives*. From his experience as a psychiatrist, he has concluded that everyone has a huge and valuable diamond within. Everyone has the same diamond, which makes every inner jewel equal to each other. Many facets are covered with dirt and tar, so the soul's responsibility is to clean each facet, because only when the surface is brilliant can it reflect rainbow colors. Some have cleaned many of the facets, others have done the same with just a few and so they don't sparkle like they could. A brilliant diamond sits in everyone's breast, and the only difference between diamonds is the number of facets cleaned.[10]

We Are the Cocreators in the Universe

Since the God force is equivalent to creative power, people help fashion the universe and have the responsibility of designing their subjective and objective reality. Along with God, we are cocreators of the universe. We are essential for the completion of creation. This is a most dramatic idea—much different than the one that suggests the God in heaven has all the responsibility for running the universe and is the Divine Judge who determines entry into his heavenly kingdom. But a God who has a plan for us to become him is a completely different issue. Now the responsibility falls on mortal shoulders. Humans become the center of the universe and can make the evolutionary leap with commitment and hard work. Individuals are their own hope and are also the conduits that can create love where it did not exist before and to help fellow humans achieve higher levels of awareness. There are no preset formulas to accomplish this. Praying five times a day on hands and knees, saying five hail Mary's, fasting, seeing a priest regularly, or going to church faithfully may not be the "way." An entire lifetime can be spent following the teachings and beliefs of others without finding the true path. We have to pick our own way through the distinctive features of our own life experiences, talents, and abilities. It is a mysterious process; you never know when an inner connection to the Holy Grail of the soul will be made. If anything is for certain, everyone has inner potential that may seem just out of reach because we have not been taught how to harness it.

This is not to say we should be reluctant to engage in organized religion. There are many benefits of sharing common beliefs and participating in worthwhile community services. People who belong to an organized religious group in general improve their state of mind and health. The jury is out on whether this is due to their religious beliefs or ongoing involvement and connection to congregation members. Organized religion has improved the lives of many people, but adherents shouldn't assume that their religion is the end-all of truth. We must look outside our religions to our dreams and other belief systems in order to become more spiritually well-rounded individuals.

Our Minds Can Play Tricks

Nature loves variety. No two stones are the same. No two trees are the same. No two people are the same. No two waves are the same. The true destiny of everything is to be itself. People become unique individuals through mental faculties, intuitive abilities, and action systems. Determining the course of human events lies within human power, but there is a great propensity for deception in this process because religious leaders claim to know what an invisible creator wants. Individuals will know God when they know themselves! People may often assume that it is God they believe in when in reality, it may be their own concerns and power drives shaping their God perspective. Christopher Hitchens in *God is Not Great* hits the mark when he says God did not create man in His own image; man created God in his image.[11]

If it was the way the Bible says, people should be very wary of a God that destroys and supports mass murder. In Belfast, Ireland, Hitchens saw rival religious death squads burn down neighborhoods, torture, and kill members of another Christian sect. Not long ago in Bosnia, towns were looted and inhabitants massacred under the guise of an ethnic cleansing that was really religious purging. In 1988, Ayatollah Khomeini, the then religious leader and dictator of Iran, issued a religious edict to assassinate a novelist who had insulted Islam. Khomeini publicly offered money in his own name as a bounty. In more recent times, Shiite and Sunni Muslims are murdering each other in Iraq. As Anne Lamott said, "You can safely assume that you've created God in your own image when it turns out that God hates all the same people you do."[12]

Leonard Pitts, a columnist for the *Miami Herald*, wrote an article that addressed the issue of hate and learning to live together. He reminded us of the logical, inevitable result of the refusal to accept that some racial, sexual, religious, or cultural fraction of the population must live outside the circle of human compassion. The Nazis institutionalized hatred and wed technology to it so that six million Jews and five million more "undesirables" could be efficiently put to death. Hitler's regime didn't invent racial hatred. It's as ancient as Cain and Abel and as widespread as a common cold. Deuteronomy explicitly encourages the faithful to slay anyone who gives allegiance to foreign gods. It seems people never learn. Dead Jews become dead Serbs become dead Rwandans become dead Muslims, yet pious hatreds are expressed by some religions because they think their hatreds are just. It seems that even history can't wake some people up. But everybody doesn't have to wake up: a few will be enough to start a major shift in consciousness. Humanity doesn't have to destroy itself.[13] Closed minds can be opened, and dreams are able to accomplish that.

I remember a client who was a very devout Catholic and a firm believer in Jesus. He taught Sunday school and emphasized his frequent church attendance and pious behavior. The dream he shared concerned a bully menacing people and bossing them around. He went up to the bully and told him he shouldn't treat people so harshly. His unenlightened intellect made absolutely no personal connection to this abusive symbol until his wife and son came to one of his sessions and explained how he intimidated his family and students. It's so easy to be blind to your own faults, but dreams open eyes. They do not miss the target.

The Mind Is the Key

Edgar Cayce, the great Christian seer, emphasized over and over that human minds build human lives. Since God is the light of consciousness that sparkles in the mind of every person, the mind has a great deal of power and influence. In the *Holographic Universe*, Michael Talbot gives countless examples of how images created by the mind can have an extremely powerful effect on the human body by altering the immune system, replicating the effects of powerful drugs, and healing wounds with astonishing speed.[14]

Talbot cites a study done by Carl Simonton, a radiation oncologist, in which 159 patients with cancers considered medically incurable were taught mental-imaging techniques. Expected survival time for such patients was twelve months. Sixty-three patients were alive after four years. Fourteen showed no evidence of the disease, and the cancers regressed in twelve patients. The average survival time of the group as a whole was 24.4 months, clearly demonstrating that images formed in the mind can have a dramatic effect on an incurable cancer.

Talbot emphasizes the mind's power by describing a number of placebo experiments that further demonstrate how the mind's thoughts influence the body. For example, a physician at the Sloan-Kettering Cancer Center in New York regularly rid his patients of warts by painting a harmless purple dye on them. Another study cited found that placebos were 56 percent as effective as morphine in relieving pain. In a 1962 experiment, test subjects were told they would be participating in a study on the effects of LSD. Instead they were given a placebo, and within thirty minutes after taking it, they experienced symptoms of the actual drug—loss of control and profound insight into life's essence. In *Love, Medicine and Miracles*, Connecticut surgeon Bernie Siegel claims diseases originate, to some extent, within the mind. So if the mind has the ability to originate disease, it conversely must have the power to generate health. The mind is a potent force.[15]

All of the above examples, coupled with the dreams mentioned earlier, emphasize that people are a medium for the force that has created the universe. According to one ancient Greek aphorism, one of the best ways to know God is to "know thyself." This saying is attributed to Socrates and is inscribed in golden letters at the beam of the entrance to the Temple of Apollo at Delphi. Self-understanding is as important to human development as $E=mc^2$ is to physics.

The old tradition of seeking religious authority through biblical expertise or a spiritual guru is in the process of being replaced by the consciousness of self-reliance. Individuals must find their own truth and path. For thousands of years, the wisdom and authority of the past was the customary route, but today traditional religious practice and dogma may not work for many true seekers. People everywhere are searching the world for a personal experience of God. Dreams have shown many that this living creative force is so close; in fact, it is inside everyone.

The Dark Side

"Knowing thyself" means to be conscious of all the qualities within—the favorable, creative, novel, ugly, and evil, the dark and the light: all flaws, blemishes, weaknesses, and failings as well as all that ennobles. What I want to avoid here is a theological discussion of the nature of evil and how religions perceive this darkness in the world. I don't have the slightest idea if God is all good or a mixture of good and evil or why he allows good people to suffer. Does he intervene and shape earthly events? Does he take sides in wars? I don't know. These issues are for theologians to discuss. Natural disasters kill thousands. How could a good God permit this? Earth changes occur naturally. Rain can be excessive. The earth shifts and moves. How can a God be loved when he allows so much suffering and pain in the world? What kind of a God could allow the Holocaust? There are Jewish people who have given up on God because of the six million who were exterminated. Genocide continues to happen today. Maybe God is beyond good and evil. But it seems to me that God isn't the problem: man is.

One can justify any action, even murder, by attributing the deed to God's will. If individuals sincerely believe the Rain God won't bring rainstorms unless a virgin is sacrificed, then the offering is made. If warriors are convinced that the God of their tribe has made them bulletproof, they charge directly into a hail of fire. According to radical Muslims, Allah approves of slaughtering people by driving bomb-laden vehicles into crowded marketplaces as long as the correct people are killed. Male Muslim suicide bombers believe they are going straight to heaven where they will be offered a harem of seventy-two virgins. These beliefs have appeal because they suggest life can be simplified. Independent thinking is not a high priority for those who unswervingly follow their leaders.

Religious people who serve in Iraq frequently ask themselves this question: How could God allow anyone to go through this? What does God have to do with this war? I say, "Nothing." Man is the creator and the stimulus for its continuance. In May 2007, *Newsweek* ran a special on the war's impact on chaplains. Close to 30 percent now have grave doubts about trying to develop a spiritual orientation toward their work. They find it extremely difficult to reconcile the war with a good and loving God. One chaplain had repetitive nightmares of throwing up little flag-draped caskets. He was finding it difficult to stomach his belief system with the carnage and death. Many GIs ask, "If I'm a child of God, why isn't he protecting me?" Some stop believing; others end up hating God. Many become sick of religion and believe people make God into what they need at the moment. They even end up hating those who try to explain God but really don't know what they are talking about. Maybe what they hate is the fantasy they have been taught about God. The human intellect by itself is incapable of grasping the complete issue of the dark side of existence. It needs some help. I prefer to demonstrate how dreams can illuminate our understanding of this issue with greater impact— and leave a lasting impression.

God Lies

Envisioning only a God that is all good and loving can produce dreams that attempt to round out your outlook and give a more complete picture of divine wholeness. Missing pieces presented can be shocking. A dreamer in one of my workshops had this stunning example of a dream attempting to remedy a distorted viewpoint about God:

I am attending a seminar in a small classroom with others who have no identifying characteristics, and we are all eagerly awaiting the instructor. She enters and stands in front of the class. Her hair is snow white and luminescent.

Clothed in a very plain dress, she has holes in her face where her eyes should be. She is old, blind, and speaks a single monotone statement: "Sometimes God lies." I am astounded and feel a mix of bewilderment and exhilaration.

The dreamer's reaction to his experience follows: "I have been seeking to learn more about my feminine side, and there I am, at an educational function, being taught by an archetypal wise old woman. What she teaches leaves me shocked and dismayed but also exhilarated. I thought that my dear, psychologically naïve mother spoke for God when she taught me to follow the teachings of the church. By being a good boy, I would find my life increasingly blessed, as I got older. The wise old woman in my dream with deep insight (represented by her blindness) released me from my conflicts about disbelieving my mother or God. This acceptance produced the exhilaration in my dream that continues to energize my individual quest to discover the divine." This dream emphasizes God is not primarily an ethical God. Until his dream, evil was split off from God. By trivializing this aspect of human nature and attempting to deny its reality, all hell can break loose, and nobody seems to be responsible.

Another dream seminar participant shared the following dream that had an enduring impact on her and illuminated deep issues surrounding the dark side of human nature.

I am standing in my living room, having a pleasant talk with a friend. I turn to look into my backyard, which is beautifully landscaped with a variety of plants and flowers. I notice one small ugly black plant, and I focus my attention on it. As I do, it begins to grow. I keep looking at it, and it keeps growing to the point where it begins blocking out the sunlight, and the other plants start drooping from lack of light. I turn back to my friend, enjoy talking to her for a few moments, and then look back into the yard. The ugly little plant has shrunken back to its original size. I focus on it and again it starts growing. But this time, I stare longer, and it starts to take over the whole backyard. It is black, ugly, and hairy with a slimy mucous. The flowers begin dying from lack of light, as do the other plants deprived of sunlight. I turn away and again talk to my friend. After a few moments, I turn to look at the small black plant, and again it has shriveled back to its original size. I repeat this scenario several times in the dream and awaken.

The dark plant is a fact of nature. Watch children at play and notice the jealousy, self-centeredness, anger, and possessiveness they demonstrate. Every human is created with a dark side. It's not an accident. Evil exists. Spell *evil* backward and you get *live*. Evil is what tries to destroy life and is opposed to the creative force that attempts to bring imaginative patterns into existence as it elevates consciousness. In this dream, there is a special message: "What the mind focuses on grows." Direct your thinking toward losing, and you lose. Dwell on never finding an ideal mate, and it happens. Focus on never being able to be happy, and you end up on antidepressants. Since mind is the builder, giving intense focus to something makes it become a reality. The Bible states in Proverbs 23:7, "For as he thinketh in his heart, so is he." Like positive thoughts, negative ones are selected, and they can be dismissed by perseverance and a shift in focus. It may not happen the first or even the tenth time, but it's worth the struggle.

Both light and dark components are our inheritance. Individuals united into families, communities, and nations choose which force they express. Will it be resentment, anger, and hate, or will it be compassion? The God force is like electricity. Plug into it and run a toaster, or use it to electrocute someone. People can broaden their life or restrict it. They can be generous or stingy; it is a matter of choice.

The Power of the Mind

Joan had been feeling overwhelmed and fearful as a newly single parent when she had this dream that demonstrated the power of the human mind.

I was at an outside picnic area with my young son. Suddenly, a tornado appeared and everyone scattered. Picking up my son, I ran for safety, but the tornado followed me wherever I went. Infuriated, I finally turned around to face it and then demanded that the tornado leave us alone. It quickly headed in another direction. My life changed after this dream. I felt a lot more confident, and I knew I could handle my problems successfully.

Intense, threatening storms often represent mental and emotional turmoil. Joan had to cope with the responsibility of bringing up a child as a single parent coupled with the uncertainty of the future. The dream captures a sense of imminent danger, but this dreamer found a quality in her mind that showed great courage. She looked fear right in the face, stood up to it, and did the thing she thought she couldn't do. These actions in dreams are like rehearsals that have a carry-over effect in waking life.

We Have Rules and Choices

If the universe has rules, why shouldn't we? The sun rises every morning, and we don't spin out into space. Jets fly to their destinations. Electricity illuminates homes. Bridges don't collapse. The laws of thermodynamics, electricity, gravity, hydraulics, aerodynamics, and planetary motion keep balance in the universe. There are also universal laws that help us comprehend the life process. Bruce McArthur's *Your Life* gives a comprehensive explanation of the universal laws at work in our lives: like begets like, as you sow, so shall you reap, the law of expectancy and the law of attraction. The dream of The Black Plant demonstrates the law of attraction by showing how thinking creates reality.[16]

To a large degree, spiritual growth and life itself are dependent on choice. Humans are adept at denial, but it seems clear in the tornado dream the responsibility for what the mind focuses on is left to the individual. Evil doesn't overwhelm unless it is allowed to do so. Life is more than just a conditioning process. It would be convenient if evil did not exist, but since it does, choice becomes crucial for spiritual unfolding and higher consciousness. Evil is confronted in the following dream of a forty-five-year-old female brought up as a Catholic. She challenges Satan with remarkable results.

I am walking down a long dark passageway and notice I am dressed like a man from another century— perhaps the 1800s. Walking beside me is an androgynous creature of another century with blond hair and a blue shirt (mine is black). Although we don't acknowledge names, somehow I know he is the angel Gabriel. We approach a door, and he insists I open and enter. I refuse because a great fear overtakes me. The angel insists that I must go through the door alone. I enter the room, and a man wearing gray clothes is reclining on a sofa. It's Satan, and he seems complacent. He stands and shouts, "I have been waiting to meet you." He comes close and exhales fire at me. I'm terrified and open my mouth to scream for help. Much to my surprise, I'm also able to exhale fire, which quickly repels Satan. I grew fire from fighting fire. When I again call for help, Satan disappears, and at the same time the angel envelops me in his arms and says, "You are safe." I wake up.

As a child, this woman totally accepted Christian doctrine. At the time of the dream, she had gone far beyond accepting the dogma connected to Satan. For many, the idea of a real devil seems to be the obsolete residue of archaic superstition, but some religions have accepted the belief that Satan is the archenemy of God and is an evil power in the spiritual world. In the New Testament, Satan afflicts people, fights against the work of God, and is a murderer and liar. In the Koran, Satan compels people to sin, drives them to madness, and causes Muslims to be cowardly.

The dreamer understood Satan in a much more modern light. When she had the dream, the most troubling aspect in her conscious life was a strong passivity—she was just waiting for things to happen and had opted to take the easy route in life. She was a slug. Even Satan had an apathetic quality about him, making him a sort of "lazy devil." This slothfulness was her devil within. The angel Gabriel prodded her into confronting this inertia. Historically, Gabriel is a symbol for the messenger of the higher plane who brings good tidings—a sense of joy at discovering new potential within the soul. This dream had a lasting effect in helping her recognize she had the capacity to overcome her self-made obstacles.

Sally was a middle-age female priest at a large church who oversaw a multitude of ministries. Responsibilities included sermon preparation, pastoral appointments, staff meetings, and coordination of goals and visions with leaders of the many ministries that supported the church's mission. Her life was a whir of people and activities. This dream occurred approximately one month before she went on a three-month sabbatical.

> I am standing alone in the middle of a large field and am very busy taking care of my tasks for many people. Although I am so active, I sense there is barrenness all around. I am doing all this work for God, but God comes and whispers in my ear, "Sally, don't you know I would rather dance?"

This dream is so simple, yet so reflective. She stated that the dream allowed her to let go and enjoy her time off without guilt. She didn't see God in the dream; she just felt a personal presence. She knew it was God, felt his total love and his desire for her to make a course correction in her life. Sometimes it is difficult to see things a different way. When individuals are unable to make the mental shift on their own, help comes from deep within. Here again we see the real vitality of a living religion, a divine presence of a higher consciousness within that is very much aware of our needs. In Sally's case, that sacred presence let her know her ministry needed to temporarily be put aside. This force wanted her attention to create greater balance in her life—it was time to play. Her final words regarding the dream were: "I believe that God comes into our lives and 'kisses' us in a variety of ways. Mine was a sweet whisper in my ear. It has caused my spirit to dance."

As can be seen from some of these inner phenomena, the discovery and the experience of the enduring connection with the divine can radically change lives. Sometimes it occurs out of the blue for seemingly no reason. Awakening from a powerful, uplifting dream can have a lifelong effect. A person could be walking in the mountains, meditating by a lake, watching a loved one die, praying, or being silent when the psyche is spontaneously overwhelmed by images, feelings, a vision, or a penetrating luminosity—and that individual is never quite the same again. Why does this happen? Religious people say this is God's grace, but who really knows?

Connecting to the Spirit

Spiritual experiences are not uncommon: I have had them, and I'm sure many of you have done likewise. A spiritual experience is unique, personal, and can have a great aftereffect. It can include out-of-body events, visions, seeing white light, near-death experiences, speaking in tongues, a profound sense of being connected to all things, seeing angels, and so forth. Of course, you can get enlightened from these experiences for a brief period, but trying to maintain it in everyday living is another issue, and maybe that's the way it should be. The psyche gets animated. After a quick glimpse of transcendence, that brief look dissolves. But it whets the appetite, and we try to reproduce it. That's why there are so many self-help books. The authors may not recognize the underlying dynamic, but I see most of them as trying to help us develop this internal God force. Our spiritual riches and wholeness exist within, and connecting to this inner divine heaven may be the journey's end.

How do we secure this heaven within? What are the ways to claim and maintain it? Every time we make progress, another goal appears. I do not have a definitive answer, because I struggle with the same dilemma. My suggestion is to decide on a few practices and do them diligently on a daily basis. Your dreams will help monitor your progress and let you know when you've arrived. If an experience or a dream creates bliss, you know the path is true, especially if it persists for a while and immunizes you from shifting mood swings.

It isn't the scope of this book to offer counsel on the many and diverse ways to connect to God. What I have tried to demonstrate is how dreams are one of the primary mediums that the spirit uses to make strong connections and recharge spiritual batteries. From my experience and those of my clients, I would also like to offer other conscious ways that can lead to a union with the life force:

- Meditate.
- Listen to inspirational music.
- Visit someone confined to a hospital when you don't feel like it.
- Strive to create good in the world by doing a random kind deed.
- Pray alone or with others.
- Practice yoga.
- Go to a secluded place and talk to God in a loud voice.
- Convert a negative emotion into a positive force: anger, for example, can fill you with the power to achieve.
- Develop a new relationship.
- Eat healthy food in a very conscious manner.
- Go walking alone and try to sense the spirit within.
- Join a hiking group.
- If you are a loner, force yourself to spend time with others.
- If you can't stand being alone, push yourself to spend solitary time.
- Practice silence: the ancient Greeks believed stillness was the abode of God.
- Do not interrupt others when they are talking.

Everyone is unique and animated in distinctive ways. Be vigilant about what is going on when endeavoring to contact the sacred inwardly. Don't get bogged down in dogmas. Find your individual path up the mountain, because all paths lead to the top. Share personal experiences with others to help them on their journey.

The Protective Coat of Humility

I need to caution you about the idea that we are all "the anointed ones." In democratizing the creative force in the universe, there is a danger of feeling self-important to the point of becoming a bloated savior. If you notice yourself having brilliant discussions with world leaders on how to ensure peace, or begin to think what a profoundly wise person you are, beware. In the extreme, it can be a pathological condition. Inflated by power, some leaders have delusions of grandeur and imagine that God speaks through them. Just because someone hears inner voices doesn't mean those utterances come from God. People follow such leaders because they have an innate need to be led and have others make decisions for them.

Grandiosity is the ego speaking as it fools the mind. It can be dangerous for survival. Hitler was grandiose in the extreme, and he ended up in flames. Throughout history, church officials have used the name of God to sanction rules focusing on sin and guilt while stressing the differences of other religions. It's been two thousand years since Christ came to earth with the promise of peace and brotherly love, yet not so long ago followers of Christ were burning people at the stake, damning them to hell, and warring in the name of God. The way religion has been practiced has not brought the peace the world desperately needs. The problem is not organized religion; it's the dogmatic authority figures who run those religions. According to the saying of Jesus, evil is in the eye of the beholder, so if one sees sin and evil around every corner and in people of different religions, the real problem is with the one doing the seeing. Great spiritual leaders and teachers preach unconditional love and abstention from violence. Their major characteristic is humility.

The primary condition for spiritual growth is humility. Humility is always the best shelter against being perverted by power. Anyone bloated by his or her inflated sense of self-importance is off the spiritual map. People who are truly humble are realistic about their sense of self, are grateful for what they have as gifts of the spirit, and find joy in helping the community. They accept their limitations and realize that needing others is not only a virtue but also a source of learning. We are all holy, and by ennobling each other, we honor God.

People who have an exaggerated sense of self-importance have dreams that try to bring them back to reality. A successful minister who was puffed up by his own haughtiness dreamt he was a retarded midget with no personal power. A female supervisor who considered herself a model of kindness and consideration dreamt she was combative and greedy. She had a one-sided perfect image of herself and needed to be taken down a peg. In the next chapter, I will explain in more detail how the dreaming mind offers equilibrium when individuals get too caught up in themselves.

Chapter 4

IS THERE A DOCTOR IN YOUR HOUSE? YES!

The first wealth is health.

Ralph Waldo Emerson

C. G. Jung believed that when we sleep, we come in contact with a healing force that is not as available during waking hours. This is quite an uncommon statement in light of modern beliefs in the restorative power of modern medicine. But Jung's statement came to life when it was authenticated in one of my dream seminars. Part of the all-day dream workshop I led included a dream incubation and induction that prepared people to have a meaningful dream that evening on any life issue or problem that was resistant to resolution. As usual, a high percent of the participants fell asleep during the induction and several of those remembered a helping dream. (The incubation is a technique for asking a dream for an answer to a specific question, and the induction is a guided imagery with deep contemplation that brings about a problem-solving dream, usually listened to before going to sleep—see order form at the back of the book.)

Healing Can Occur in the Dream State

One young lady had a foot neuropathy that had been troubling her for two years. She had tried numerous medicines and procedures, but nothing worked.

The following is a transcription of her exact words concerning the healing dream and its aftermath.

Nothing was as pressing as the throbbing pain in my foot. Did I think it would work? No! But I was in so much pain I thought I would give it a try. A psychologist had told me years earlier that I couldn't relax enough for hypnotherapy and terminated my "quit smoking" sessions. Whenever I was in a training presentation on visualization, meditation, or relaxation, I would scoff silently at these techniques because I thought they were silly and useless. I think what made the difference this time was that the dream induction took place halfway through the seminar. By that time, there was a very peaceful environment, and the material was so interesting, credible, and thought-provoking.

Her dream follows:

I saw an image of my foot, and I could see through it like I had x-ray eyes. Suddenly, a bright light scanned and enveloped my foot, penetrating into the interior. I sensed and knew it was a healing light. When I came out of the induction, I was pain free.

I think I remembered everything, and it feels great to be pain free. Oh! One other thing—I did have some moments of doubt after I had my healing dream, and every time I had those doubts, the pain would return. I expressed this to a woman sitting next to me, and she said, "Keep believing and hold fast to your healing." She was right. When the doubt went away, the pain would go away. It happened a few more times during the following weeks, but I remembered what she said and have held fast to my healing.

I checked with her nine months after this experience, and she was still pain free. The inner and outer features of this curing experience point out the dual nature of the healing route we can often take. When these two forces come together according to an individual's needs, they can become a powerful wonder drug.

Inner Healing and Traditional Medicine

One could call this a mystical experience and a mystifying cure:

being healed by a small sun that lives in the depths of the unconscious mind. This certainly is an unscientific idea, so it's easy to see why people have neglected to think in these terms. Living in a culture that diminishes the esoteric and often excludes it in religious and formal education discourages exploring this natural tendency of the unconscious mind to communicate in mystical terms. I believe these uncommon types of cures are more frequent than appears but are not publicly talked about, because the medical profession lacks an explanation and might consider them a threat to traditional health care. There seems to be some powerful fast-healing force that can be contacted in this realm of the unconscious. Under certain conditions during the sleep state, it appears to be as effective as conventional therapy.

There is a doctor in the house—your house, my house, and everyone's house. This inner healer is invaluable to our health and is always available as the vital partner of any other physician you may consult. Enacted below the threshold of consciousness, the very brief healing drama in my seminar participant's foot dream brought an immediate cure. The key is learning the art of how, when, and where to visit the exclusive personal physician that practices within.

The Doctor Within Heals a Sex Problem

Loretta was a divorced woman in her early forties who sought sex therapy for being nonorgasmic. Her condition was primary, meaning she had never had an orgasm regardless of the methods she employed. From masturbation to intercourse, nothing worked for her. One of my parameters for sexual counseling was to work with couples only. I generally referred unmarried people to a sex therapist. When I offered to refer her to a female sex therapist, she decided not to focus on that issue with me but rather to explore her shyness, emotional suppression, and insecurities.

She was a very active dreamer, and after a few months of therapy I suggested she could learn how to program her dreams for any problem that was unresolved. A short time after I taught her how to do this, she came to a session in extremely high spirits coupled with a beaming smile that lit up my office. Her adeptness at programming dreams culminated in the following dream experience:

89

> I lie nude on an examination table in a doctor's office with a plain white sheet covering my body. When the doctor enters, I notice his advanced age, perhaps in his late seventies. His white coat is blotched with mustard and ketchup stains, and his gray beard is somewhat disheveled. He reaches under the sheet and begins fondling me, which immediately turns me on sexually. We make passionate love, and during intercourse I experience a magnificent orgasm. I awaken very excited.

From that moment on, she experienced orgasms with her current boyfriend during intercourse. I was curious about why her unconscious had chosen such an elderly man. She revealed that when she married in her early twenties, she had a sexual affair with the next-door neighbor who was in his seventies. It was the best sex she had experienced up to that point in her life, even though an orgasm did not occur. Explanations cannot do justice to this inner adventure. I am not sure of the dynamics behind her breakthrough. Perhaps the driving force that generated this healing dream was a combination of her optimism, expectations, and intense desire.

For many women, sexual issues are still fraught with secrecy and are considered lewd and immoral, even in this so-called age of sexual freedom and open-mindedness. This breakthrough dream bypassed the need for sex education, self-awareness exercises, communication skills, medication, and behavioral techniques. Of course, there was much follow-up on the possible origin of her difficulty, but the sexual blockage was permanently removed. This was one of those dreams that provided an impressive experience, which was inspirational because it healed what was lacking. Probably, most of our difficulties come from losing contact with our instincts. And where can we often get in touch with the force that knows how to reconnect our energies? In our dreams.

Ancient Cultures Knew the Secret

Many ancient cultures knew the secret, because they took healing dreams for granted. The ancient Greeks believed dreams were "real" experiences. Thus, they created conditions that would induce specific dreams that could heal, reveal a dreamer's current and future health status, or provide guidance toward effective treatments. Not only did they experience dreams as real, they also perceived their gods as real. Ancient Greek gods took on human form, displayed emotions of human beings, resided in human society, and intervened in human affairs. With this fusion of god and dream reality, powerful inner forces were unleashed, creating an art of healing that to us seems miraculous.

In many ways, the Greeks were like you and me. When ill, they visited traditional doctors. If that didn't work, they consulted alternative medicine. Today people go to acupuncturists, herbalists, nutritionists, hypnotherapists, massage therapists, and psychic healers. For the Greeks, the choices were less extensive and usually involved traveling to a dream temple to be healed while in the dream state.

Although this may sound like a fairy tale, it is not. Being ill is serious business. The sick and disabled sought cures in the holy sites of dream temples and would travel great distances, seeking to have their bodies repaired. There were no automobiles, trains, airplanes, or buses in those days, so most people walked. The rich and poor came, as did the famous and the unknown. Everyone was welcome. All sought cures in the dream state from the same inner physician, Asklepios, who appeared to those who sought him.

The "cult" of the Greek healing god Asklepios successfully flourished for a thousand years. More than three hundred temples were built from the end of the sixth century BC until the end of the fifth century AD. Something very special happened in these holy places. The dreams people sought and the healings that resulted are etched in stone and attest to cures we would call miracles today, because they are inexplicable.

According to Greek legend, Asklepios was born to the sun god, Apollo, who impregnated a human woman named Coronis, whose name means "crowlike." And so their son was believed to be a combination of his father's celestial splendor and his mother's earthlike blackness. Asklepios, therefore, was "destined" to rule both the heavenly and dark powers of the earth. The most popular version of this myth claims that because Coronis betrayed her god-lover Apollo by marrying a human, Apollo's sister slew her and placed the corpse on top of a funeral pyre. However, as the flames roared around her,

Coronis gave birth to Asklepios before dying, and Apollo snatched the newborn from the flames. Apollo surrendered the infant to Chiron, a centaur, who raised Asklepios and taught him the skills and secrets of medicine. Soon Asklepios surpassed his teacher and became so miraculously adept as a healer that he could even raise the dead! Such "godly" behavior evoked the anger of Zeus, who killed Asklepios with a mighty thunderbolt. Then, surprisingly, Zeus raised Asklepios to the divine rank of a "healing god." Zeus honored Asklepios by sending him into the heavens as the constellation Orion.[1]

In reality, Asklepios was once an extraordinary but very human physician. He was such an astonishing healer, however, that he became greatly revered, and the mantle of a god was eventually conferred upon him, because no one could believe that a mere human would have such skills. Thus, the myth of Asklepios was born and endured throughout the ages. Priests and followers of Asklepios constructed dream temples where the sick could directly seek health guidance and healing—*in their dreams!* Because dreams were already widely accepted and greatly valued as sacred revealers of information and truth, the establishing of dream temples was a logical occurrence.

From primitive societies to the more sophisticated Greek and Roman civilizations, human beings relied on their gods to aid them in everything from the weather to war and to healing—all the things they assumed a human being could not directly control. Since they believed so much of their lives was a gift of the gods, the idea of Asklepios as a healing god they could seek in a sacred dream temple was easily welcomed.

I had the privilege of visiting the ruins of the most famous and celebrated healing centers at Epidaurus, located on the plains of the Argolid west of Athens. This sacred site had a magical sense of beauty, harmony, and tranquility. What struck me initially was the total silence that enveloped the area. So many of these venerated healing centers were located in remote areas—on mountaintops, in deep valleys and isolated plains, places that were not easily accessible—because the Greeks believed the gods lived in silence. Modern men and women are addicted to noise, which offers a kind of amnesia from feeling isolated and lonely. For many, silence feels frightening. Psalm 46:10: "Be still, and know that I am God." When people sleep, the sounds of the world are silenced, and then the inner world comes to life, connecting souls to the healer within.

During the height of ancient Greek civilization, "incubants" would brave the hardships of travel and make pilgrimages to those beautiful dream temples. After their arrival, certain rites of purification were performed. Water played an important role in the preparation process, which could take weeks or even months. Bathing not only cleansed the body, but also purified and freed the soul from contamination by the physical, setting it free for communion with the god. Praying, chanting, discussing dreams, and attending theatrical performances were a few of the sacred rituals necessary for proper preparation. The mind had to be optimistic and focused.

Finally, with the help of priests, they would enter into the *abaton*, the innermost chamber where their sacred "temple sleep" would hopefully induce successful healing dreams. The "right" dream brought the patient an instantaneous cure. A healing always took place if Asklepios appeared in the dream and performed his treatment, or if his mascots—a snake and a dog—appeared and licked or touched the ill portion of the body. The snake symbolized the power of rejuvenation because shedding its skin meant a rebirth into a new body free of illness. Dogs are man's best friend and a symbol of devotion and unconditional love. Even today, dogs have been known to heal people using their paws or their entire bodies to send life-force energy.[2]

Asklepios was a daring surgeon. In the dream state, he would perform complex operations that far exceeded the medical capability of those times. He opened the skull for brain surgery, performed open-heart operations, and even took eyes out of the sockets of the blind and returned them for vision restoration. It is unlikely any of these patients would have survived if the surgeries were done in the waking world.

If a healing dream did not occur, the dreamer did not doubt the incubation and induction dream rituals or the actual accessibility of the healing god but concluded that more extensive preparation for the divine visitation was necessary. Generally, the dreamer's belief in the healing power of the dream state was absolute because of the intense mental and physical preparation and awareness of the temple's success rate. This is why these practices were so successful.

When Asklepios did appear, he often took different forms, such as an old wizened figure, sometimes with a beard sometimes without, carrying a rustic wooden staff. Alternately, he appeared as a radiantly beautiful youth who was quick-witted and had sparkling eyes. His appearances were many and various. Actually, each dreamer depicted the qualities of godliness and divine power through a physical image that was believable to that dreamer. That same phenomenon is true today. The healing force likely to appear in the dream state would be appropriate for today's context and would probably look more like a modern physician. But the curative power can take any form such as food, a beam of light, a growing plant, an animal, a child, water, dancing, and so on.

Once the incubant experienced the healing dream, recording its contents and results by inscribing them onto stone tablets at the temple was necessary to affirm the experience. Cured patients were obligated to pay a fee that was comfortable within that person's economic status. It could be paid anytime within a year. All the tablets at the dream temples represented a kind of temple diary, much the same as a dream diary chronicles one's dream experiences. Most of the tablets were destroyed during wars, but approximately one hundred remained intact. Since much of this ancient dream healing process information comes from these testimonials, a small sample will suggest what is possible. The tablets cited below are drawn from *Asklepios, A Collection and Interpretation of the Testimonies*. The translations are accounts that bring to life what was etched in stone so many centuries ago.

The most direct and immediate cures were those of instant healing from direct contact with Asklepios in a dream.

- Alcetis of Halieses suffered from blindness. When he dreamt, the god came to him and with his fingers opened up his eyes. At first he saw the trees in the sanctuary. At daybreak he walked out sound.
- In battle, Gorgias of Heracleia had been wounded by an arrow in the lung and for a year and a half had suppurated so badly that he had filled many basins with pus. While sleeping in the temple, he had a dream. It seemed to him that the god extracted the arrow point from his lung. When day came, he walked out sound.

A divine kiss had an even more dramatic effect:

- Proclus experienced great pain from arthritis. Fearful about having a future with such a dreaded disease, he implored the god. When he fell asleep, he saw, so he thought, the god bend over his legs and kiss them. And Proclus lived his whole life unconcerned about this disease and arrived at a ripe old age without experiencing such an ailment.

- Cleimenes of Argus was paralyzed in body. He came to the abaton and slept there and saw a dream. It seemed to him that the god wound red woolen strips of material around his body and led him for a bath a short distance away from the temple to a lake, the water of which was extremely cold. When he behaved in a frightened manner, Asklepios said he would not heal people who were faint-hearted and lacked faith. But those who came into his temple full of hope would be sent away well. When he woke up, he took a cold bath and walked out healed.

Asklepios generally appeared to everyone who sought his counsel and help. Occasionally, he did not proffer healing in the dream, but rather focused on the bad habits that caused incurable health problems. For example:

- A young Assyrian came to Asklepios dying from dropsy—an abnormal swelling of the joints and body cavities due to the build-up of clear watery fluid. He lived a life of luxury and was continually drunk. Because he refused to give up his alcoholism, Asklepios "took no care of him" and did not visit him even in a dream. When the youth grumbled about this, the god finally appeared and told him he only gave healing to those who really desired it: "but you do things that aggravate your disease, for you give yourself up to luxury, and you accumulate luxurious meals upon your water-logged and worn out stomach and, as it were, choke water with a flood of mud."[3]

For several centuries, no medical treatment was given nor were dream interpreters necessary. You were either healed or you were not. Upon awakening from a healing dream, organic changes had occurred.

Only the god of healing knew the remedies and performed the essential curative measure in a dream. Asklepios was not only interested in the physical healing but also spiritual and moral healing.

Clearly, the ancient Greeks knew that humans are much more than their bodies. For a person too ill to be moved, another could sleep in proxy and gain valuable healing information. Responsibility was shifted to the substitute who could have valid dreams for the sick person. This is a common phenomenon in dreams where accurate information about those close to us is revealed. Aristotle was convinced that precognitive dreams about friends and loved ones occur because of a dreamer's deep personal involvement with them. With knowledge about their values and attitudes, the unconscious can reach definite trends and conclusions about their behavior.

While many of the temple dreamers experienced spontaneous healing, many were prescribed treatments, medicines, and diets. Oftentimes, Asklepios's advice was directly contrary to that of physicians of that era. For example, he would prescribe rigorous exercise where a patient's earthly doctor had instead prescribed total bed rest. And Asklepios's treatment would inevitably work!

Cures at Epidaurus Are Not Rational

In *Healing Dream and Ritual*, C. A. Meier, cofounder of the Jung Institute in Zurich, brilliantly expounds on the suprapersonal aspects of illness and how dreams reveal a transcendental path to healing. He suggests that the cures at Epidaurus will always be regarded as ambiguous and controversial. Meier warns that single cases may be impressive but lack statistical significance; and because of their miraculous qualities, they can be easily overvalued. Ancient medicine or a physician played a secondary role in the healing process. The primary source of recovery from illness was a divine doctor named Asklepios. Cures for illnesses came from the inner spiritual realm. Our dreaming mind cannot only see our bodily condition; it can also become the medium of the healing process. It's a complete hygienic system. These dreamers must have had a great faith in the irrational nature of life.[4]

Were Asklepios's interventions "miracle healings"? Do they differ from miracle healings that occurred in medieval churches and still continue in sacred spaces today? Possibly. I tend to think the dreamer made a profound contact with his innermost self—the self that not only knows how to create physical, mental, emotional, and spiritual harmony, but that also has its divine connection to the healer god within. It is this inner self that becomes the internal doctor when needed. This self exists within the psyche, and the ancients created conditions so dreamers could make the connection. What was done at these dream temples is still being done today. I call it natural healing through incubation and induction rituals that give birth to healing dreams. Journeying to a distant dream temple is unnecessary. You can create your own personal dream temple and hatch a healing dream within your mind. Contacting your inner physician is an exciting adventure.

Ancient Healing Gods Appear in Modern Form

Meier implies that in modern psychiatric practice, healing dreams seem few and far between. This is probably due to the difficulty in creating atmospheres conducive to such happenings. Patients must be inspired with a faith in a savior god, a role to which the modern therapist cannot do full justice. I tend to disagree with this statement because I have personally conducted dream incubation seminars where the focus is on creating an atmosphere of faith in the healing power of the soul. This is done through dreams and establishing rituals of preparation that have a high rate of success for all kinds of personal problems.

These accounts from the ancient Greek dream temples may sound like UFO sightings. I, however, don't think that all these healing dramas are fabricated soap-opera stuff. I see them as posing a question: where have all these gods gone? They have gone back to where they originated—right in our own psyches. The gods of healing do reveal themselves, and sometimes the ancient ones appear in new guises. Doors to the healing kingdom of dreams are open. People just need to knock.

In the example that follows, a modern dreamer raps on the entryway, and she is promptly greeted by Asklepios, who is apparently alive and well in the modern psyche. The dreamer wanted help with a chronic physical problem. After writing all the answers to personal questions (see the next chapter), she lay down on the floor and listened to the dream induction. That night she had the following dream:

An Ancient Healing God Appears

I walk toward the restrooms in the hotel lobby where the dream seminar is taking place. Out of my peripheral vision, I see a very tall, imposing person dressed in a beautiful colorful robe of gold, red, and blue material. His exceptionally long hair and beard are white. I walk past him and suddenly realize it's Asklepios, the Greek god of healing. I become so stimulated and excited that I wake myself up and then regret not having approached him for help.

This contemporary dreamer was totally surprised and excited to see that the ancient healer was alive and well. Time, it seems, doesn't change the content, only the form.

Dreams respond to our needs and make the inner demand that consciousness evolve. Myriad energizing symbols reside in the psyche, and dreams utilize these resources for renewal of body and mind. Although Asklepios was the god of healing thousands of years ago, he remains a universal symbol, modernized in successive generations. Until this dream, this young lady was unaware that a symbol that could help her affirm her own healing existed in her dreaming psyche and could be called upon.

The Inner Physician Is Regularly On Call

The inner physician is always on call! Trudging miles to a clinic or calling for appointments are unnecessary. The crucial issues are making the effort to visit the inner doctor and heeding the wealth of information that is prescribed. What makes the interior medical doctor such an expert is the comprehensive knowledge and acquaintance with the physical causes and manifestations of our illnesses, our emotional makeup, and our thinking patterns, any of which may be the root cause of personal medical problems. Access to built-in diagnostic equipment can produce accurate diagnoses. There is a tremendous fusion of physical, mental, emotional, and spiritual knowledge. The interior physician who has a divine connectedness, profound skills, and wisdom can forge this intimate and comprehensive knowledge of the causes of imbalances into cures.

A cartoon on the Internet depicted a robed and bearded man descending a mountain path. When he reached the bottom, he saw that an expectant crowd had gathered. A hush fell over the throng as the bearded man stood before them. A man in the gathering suddenly cried out, "Our headaches are finally over! Here is Moses with the tablets!" Everyone cheered.[5] Over the years, great numbers of patients have heard doctors say, "Take two tablets and call me in the morning." In fact, when we feel physically sick, our most common response is to run to the medicine cabinet to cure whatever is ailing us. I'm not suggesting taking appropriate medicines or consulting doctors is unwise or unnecessary. They're very necessary. However, it is extremely important that you also visit your healer within so the inner expert can help guide the effectiveness of any treatment. Moses's tablets were not created to be quick fixes for outer symptoms. Instead, they were meant to serve as the essential guides needed to cure inner causes of spiritual imbalances that were expressing themselves in the outer symptoms of greed, anger, egocentrism, and other such negative emotions. So, too, does the doctor within help to cure the inner causes of physical imbalances that are manifesting themselves as physical sickness.

Additionally, our personal physician can help to identify the source or sources of our illness and can guide us toward appropriate remedies and professional help. Our inner health expert has known us and will continue to do so intimately until death. We can, therefore, look forward to continual health monitoring because that healer never leaves our bedside. Throughout history, every human being has had a twenty-four-hour hot line to that expert medical help long before the appearance of telephones or even carrier pigeons! That's because each healer's office and medical equipment is directly inside every patient. Today the magic of the new millennium is that we are waking up to this inner healthnet. We can all learn to connect to and direct the natural healing energy, and it's essential that we do. Worldly riches cannot buy us good health, and without good health, we are poor indeed.

Getting In Touch with the Inner Healer

How do we find our inner doctor, and how do we express our belief in that inner doctor's wisdom and healing capacity? There are multiple ways: through hypnosis, meditation, guided imagery, and our dreams! By focusing our dream incubation and induction phases on getting to the source of sickness manifestations, we are inherently declaring the belief that important and enlightening information directly related to healing will come. Further, we are laser-beaming a purpose into our forthcoming dreams that will knock directly on the door of the doctor who cures.

Actually, it was Dr. Albert Schweitzer in *Out of My Life and Thought* who first used the phrase "the doctor within." Having mingled with and observed many different cultures all over the world, he came to what he considered a "universal conclusion" about sickness and healing. He determined that the primary factors actually making the difference between a patient remaining sick or becoming healed lay directly within the patient. Those factors are *intention* and *faith*! The clearer the intention to become well and the stronger the faith in ultimate health, the greater the chances of becoming healthy.

According to Dr. Schweitzer, whether it's a doctor in a modern, high-tech Western hospital or a witch doctor in the African jungle, each performs a ritual appropriate to his or her culture. A physician actively administers a specific treatment designed to eliminate a defined disease, and the witch doctor doles out a special herbal potion and chants an appropriate incantation to exorcise a specific evil spirit. The physician and the witch doctor are each performing the same service. In both cases, in order for the patient to be healed, that person must energize the "medical ritual" with faith in the practitioner and in the ritual. In doing so, the ill person activates the doctor within. Once the doctor within is energized, the sufferer receives an appropriate dose of mind medicines, and consequently, healing happens! Schweitzer observed this happening time and time again. The clearer the intention and the stronger the faith, the faster the healing![6]

Energizing the doctor within and his mind medicines with all the waking intention and faith that can be mustered is the first important step toward getting well. For a complete healing, decoding the messages contained in the symptoms can be vital. After that, making the necessary lifestyle changes becomes the decisive factor. Real healing does not mean just healing symptoms. To Jung, it meant that patients needed to understand the meaning of their lives and their suffering and to be what they were with no pretenses.

Look at it this way. Sitting on a tack will cause pain. A person could stay seated and take some painkillers, but that would be like pulling the battery out of a smoke alarm while staying in a burning house! The source of the pain must be removed. Get off the tack! Flee the burning building, and put the fire out! Lifestyle changes are often what are necessary to stop the body from manufacturing symptoms.

The Inner Physician in Dreams Has Great Expertise

While tacks and fires are obvious signals, most causes of physical distress are not. It's not a simple task to discover and understand the vital messages contained within symptoms. To dig up the deep-seated message, the next visit must occur in the far-reaching recesses of the subconscious mind. Here lies in wait the genuine inner healer who knows how to provide an ill patient with remedies. People dream every night, but now preparation with a definite focus takes center stage.

The subconscious mind is always aware of the cellular condition of the entire body. When illness or injury strikes, it can provide vital diagnostic information about potential dangers as well as important messages that can guide and complement any medical treatments that may be needed. All this information will appear in the guise of vivid and often dramatic images. These graphic symbols occur at the onset and throughout the duration of the condition. Frequently, they will even appear before the condition has been detected, and they will also help monitor the treatment a patient is receiving. They can even inspire curative measures.

From personal experience, I can attest to the power of the dreaming mind to diagnose the problem, comment on treatment, view the illness as a learning experience, and predict the outcome. When the physical body is hit with illness, the victim has an immediate appointment with the greatest medical expert he or she will ever meet—a masterful diagnostician and treatment specialist who is always on call and has access to the total physical, mental, emotional, psychological, and spiritual database contained in a single body.

Dreams Helped Heal and Guide Me through My Cancer

Before describing how to prepare for a healing adventure in the next chapter, I would like to share a few personal dreams relating to my cancer and also those of seminar participants whose illnesses were dramatically impacted by their dreams. These examples demonstrate the early warning system and potent healing force that resides in the psyche and manifests just on the other side of sleep. If you believe in your dreams, they will never fail to provide insight and healing.

In 1994, I developed severe urological symptoms that were diagnosed initially as benign bladder cancer. The doctor who removed my tumor tried to assure me that it was not malignant. He said he had performed hundreds of similar operations and invariably could tell if the tumor was pathological. But just to be safe, he would send the tumor for a biopsy. During the night of the operation, I had the following dream.

I am in a small cabin situated on an elevated setting in a dark forest.

The darkness is illuminated by a full moon. Below the cabin, about fifty yards away, is a very small circular pond approximately twenty-five feet wide. Surrounding this body of water are huge crocodiles as wide as the pond. They are packed together, no more than a foot apart. Their mouths are wide open, as if biding their time until a good meal could be pounced on and devoured. I thought they were waiting for me, and I knew if I stepped out of the cabin, I would become a quick snack for the crocs. I also knew the cabin was safe but that eventually, I would have to leave and get on with the business of living. I awoke and sensed instantly the dream was about my cancer and immediate action was necessary.

The crocodiles were a warning about a hidden danger. In the wild, they are tremendous eating machines and can shred and devour a thousand-pound buffalo in a matter of minutes. One fact that stayed in my mind was that they were stationary and poised for something to come into attack range. The body of water symbolized my bladder. I knew I was safe from being ripped apart and eaten alive as long as I remained in the cabin, but I was aware that reality was waiting for me on the outside. I couldn't stay inside forever. My fear was intense. I felt I had to act fast, and so did the doctor.

A cancer diagnosis has a great deal of psychic fallout. Although this dream somewhat prepared me for the laboratory results, being diagnosed with malignant cancer rocked me to the core like an 8.0 magnitude earthquake. The human body resembles the earth in that both are subjected to storms and stresses that can alter their physical forms. Our lifestyles can reconfigure our bodies and subject them to a variety of traumas and diseases that produce intense psychological reactions. Little did I know how much soul unfolding was waiting to take place within me. Disease can be the main route that breaks down barriers to the inner world and all its wisdom. Not only did I want my health restored, I also wanted to know what was going on in my soul. And of course, the quickest route for me to that inner knowledge was my dreams.

My physician, Dr. Lau, had a strong sense of compassion and a touching sensitivity to my needs and fears. He even held my hand while I was wheeled into surgery and said, "Don't worry, Art, I won't let anything bad happen to you." Very reassuring. He even smiled knowingly when I came in for the biopsy report and shared my crocodile dream.

I knew I would get well after I woke up the morning after the diagnosis and was not dead yet. I thought cancer was a death sentence, but I had survived the first day! Way down deep inside me, I realized that this was another trial by ordeal and that eventually, it would shift me to another level of awareness. I don't think I went through the denial process, since recovery rates for my type of cancer were high. And because I knew that divine forces operated within all people, my hope was elevated. No matter what treatment an ill person tries, optimism can motivate the body to secrete healing biochemicals that have a beneficial effect.

I began treatment, opting for a combination of chemotherapy and a variety of holistic health practices. I ate shark cartilage, spent close to $100 a month on grapes (which supposedly contain powerful antioxidants), almonds, and hot castor oil packs to detoxify the liver. I prayed and meditated daily and even hugged trees, asking their trunks to transmit healing energy into my body. I also created a guided imagery that featured lions and crusaders on white horses protecting my castle and pond from any attacking crocodiles. The lions assaulted the crocodiles, ripped them to shreds, and made beautiful Italian shoes out of the skins. Even when the crocodiles laid their eggs, the lions would dig them up and devour them. I still do this imagery today during my daily prayers.

When the ill go on a healing quest, their odyssey is as much an inner journey as an outer one to heal symptoms. That is why I incubated my dreams daily, seeking health guidance and answers to inner personal questions. Although my conscious mind couldn't seem to penetrate into the deeper layers of meaning that this illness had for me, my dreams did. Several dreams informed me that the cleansing and healing process had begun. One dream showed me hosing down an area that was already clean, which told me I was overdoing it. This probably related to the castor oil packs on the lower abdomen for liver detoxification. Obviously, I was going to extremes; so I stopped.

The Learning Behind the Cancer

After about a month of treatments, I wanted to know what I needed to learn from this experience. After all, cancer can be a major wake-up call. I kept asking myself: what was this illness trying to teach me? Had my mind led me into treacherous waters? Why couldn't a broken toe have served the same purpose? In answer to my questions, my inner doctor sent me two dreams that struck at the heart of my belief system.

In the first, I was being interviewed on a radio talk show. The host asked me a question about a common dream that millions of people have. I thought: how wonderful! But as I started to respond with the answer, I said to myself, "This media stuff is all bullshit! Why am I doing this?" Suddenly, I didn't feel like doing it anymore. In actuality, I had a radio talk show called "Dream Talk" and had frequent fantasies about becoming a national celebrity who could take calls and give an immediate, accurate interpretation of a dream. I wanted to be a star dream interpreter for the rich and famous. And now I realized it was self-serving. My ego was hungry for expansion and needed to be fed. In fact, my ego was a slave because it needed continued enhancement from outer sources.

My second dream provided me with still more important information. I have included this dream in chapter 6 (Unveiling the Mystery) because I received tremendous insight when a dream-seminar class used a dramatic group dream interpretation process that went far beyond what insight I got from just working the dream myself. This technique that is easily learned and does not need professional guidance is the most powerful and intelligent approach to dream interpretation I have ever experienced.

A Dream Heralds My Wellness

The last and final dream related to my illness signaled recovery. It occurred about four months after the diagnosis and demonstrates that from beginning to end, the full ramifications of illness can be revealed in dreams.

I am in an enormous empty room whose ceilings, walls, and floors are made of old, unfinished wood. The ceilings are a good twenty feet high, and there is a very large entrance door that, as I watch, abruptly flies open. In gallops an enormous horse. He is immense and impressive—a colossal animal close to ten feet at the shoulder with a beautiful, shiny brown coat. My guess is he is a mixture of thoroughbred and workhorse. A tremendous sense of power and health radiates from his being. His hooves clatter loudly on the floor. Terrified, I back away from him. He sees me and trots over. I am frozen in place. He rears up on his hind legs, and with his head almost to the ceiling, he gently rests the hooves of his two front legs on my shoulders, locking me in my standing position. Terrified, I look up into his face and slowly he moves his head downward to my face. Very gently, and almost ethereally, he kisses me on the lips. He turns his head sideways so one soft brown eye is visible. Out of it pours such an intense love that I begin to cry, overwhelmed that such a profound feeling could be directed toward me. I begin crying and awake doing the same. The feelings I bring with me are immense love and sadness. I know my cancer is gone.

This dream left a vivid imprint in my dream storehouse and soul. I cherish this dream and reflect on it often. Archetypal dreams have prodigious power and can never be forgotten, because their impact is indelible, and they contain meanings that go far beyond the ordinary. Perhaps these extraordinary dreams can never be fully grasped; part of their enduring power resides in the very fact of their mystery.

To me, this dream is highly spiritual. Why couldn't a voice have just said to me, "You are healed"? That would not have been enough. I needed the wonder of the symbols and the emotional experience that helped deepen the encounter. My goal was to get rid of the cancer. My soul's goal was more extensive—a new attitude and a shift in values to honor service to others. My first reaction to that powerful horse was fear—I hadn't an inkling of why he approached me and held me fast with his hooves on each shoulder. Perhaps he wanted to make sure I didn't flee so he could get his message across. He was a mighty-looking animal with such a light and tender touch! What further struck me was how healthy and vibrant he looked and how, out of this great beast's eye, came what I can best describe as a limitless and unconditional love. He created within me an invitation to accept all this passionate caring.

The horse can be a symbol of many things: sex, animal nature, the physical body, instinctual power, freedom, etc. But this was a very special, almost mythical horse. I immediately thought of Pegasus, the winged horse who was the messenger of the gods. His prodigious soft brown eye held understanding, compassion, and the deepest adoration I have ever experienced in any gaze, from an animal or a human.

"Big" Dreams Dredge Up the Swamp

This dream was astonishingly accurate. It related to the one major area in my life that has perplexed me to no end: love. And now my dreams were confronting me. I realized that at times, I had been afraid to offer my love freely and unconditionally to my beautiful wife of thirty-seven years and my two sons. I had been critical and judgmental. When friends didn't live up to my expectations, I usually stopped putting energy into the relationships, ending them. I also grasped that I was afraid to give my love freely because of possible rejection.

Even the great Jung in his autobiography, *Memories, Dreams, Reflections*, struggled with the enigma of love. "In my medical experience as well as in my own life, I have again and again been faced with the mystery of love, and have never been able to explain what it is."[7] My illness and this dream helped me fathom that inviting love into my life both inwardly and outwardly is one of the keys to health. Ramakrishna said the singular purpose and ultimate destination of human life is to cultivate love. In the New Testament, a life without love is a barren land: "I may have strength to move mountains; but if I have no love, I am nothing" (1 Cor. 13:1–2). I had heard these words before, but now they were more than an aphorism. They were the key elements in self-healing and in solving the riddle of human life. I finally understood that the true path of life was lit by love, and the real issue was to put that understanding into everyday action.

We realize today that the body-mind-spirit connection makes us more responsible than ever before for preventing illness and participating in the healing adventure. One of our greatest allies in our healing odyssey is the unconscious mind and its dream power. Dreams can:

- Diagnose
- Prognosticate the outcome
- Direct treatment
- Cure
- Reveal underlying lessons in the illness
- Give dietary direction
- Help maintain bodily health

Anyone who has had a helpful dream about their bodily condition knows without doubt that the inner universe is very much concerned with the state of their health. Sometimes the path to well-being takes a humorous turn as it did in the following dream that occurred to a woman in one of my workshops.

A Toxic Bagel and Lox

I am standing by a lake. A bagel with lox and cream cheese comes flying over the trees that line the lakeshore and lands in the middle of the lake. As it sinks to the bottom, the lake becomes stagnant. All the vegetation and the fish die! A voice says, "In order to clear up this lake, you must fill it with oatmeal." I take off my shoes and wade into the water. As I feel the oatmeal squishing between my toes, the lake's fish and vegetation return to life.

Here was an example of a dream humorously "commenting" on the food that was harmful to this young woman's digestive system ("polluting the water"). Her poor diet needed replacement with a more wholesome regimen.

Smoking Depletes the Body

Years ago, when I was smoking more than two packs of cigarettes a day and not feeling well, I dreamt three nights in a row that I was drinking a quart of orange juice. On the third night, I awoke from the dream, immediately went to the kitchen, and made a quart of fresh orange juice. I drank the whole thing! The next day, I felt much better. A few months later, I read in a health journal that excessive smoking depletes the body of essential vitamin C. My subconscious mind knew my body needed that and directed me toward an outstanding source of vitamin C! I not only began drinking orange juice regularly but soon quit smoking.

Smoking cigarettes is one of the most difficult addictions to break. I know this and so did Audrey, a young mother with two small children who begged her to stop her habit. She often responded with, "Be patient. It will take a long time for me to break this dependence." After many months of her children exhorting her, she had the following dream.

I dream of a large, black, middle-aged woman who sits with her arms folded, just looking at me sternly. She says nothing and just sits there with an aura of power and determination projecting a "can do" attitude. I wake up with her image and have never smoked since. That was over twenty-five years ago.

If Audrey could package her dream, she could improve international health.

Lupus Disease

When I first started giving dream seminars, I decided to focus one particular seminar on dreams and healing. Just before people left to go home and sleep, one woman who had chosen to ask her dreams for help with her Lupus disease—an immune system malfunction that can damage joints, skin, blood vessels, and organs—fell asleep and had the following quick dream.

I am in a doctor's office with a physician dressed very traditionally—white pants, white coat, and a stethoscope around his neck.

He looks at me intently and says, "The reason you have Lupus disease is because of your tremendous anger and rage at your brother. The way to cure it is—"

She never got to the end because I was bringing the group out of the dream induction (guided imagery) just as she was preparing to hear her cure suggestion.

What timing! I would imagine the doctor would have suggested ways to deal with her rage, but we'll never know. What was so interesting about the workshop was that everyone's dream about their physical condition had an emotional basis. In other words, attendees wanted guidance for physical problems and instead got dream information about the emotional roots of their illnesses.

Stabbed in the Back

This next dream demonstrates how destructive thoughts create a malignant emotional environment that is fertile ground for an affliction. George worked in the movie industry as a skilled sound technician. Competition was intense because of elevated salaries and limited job opportunities.

I am at work, and a black demon batlike creature attacks me from behind, striking me in the back in the thoracic region. I wake up and have a pain in that area.

George was a friend whom I loved dearly; I hadn't been in contact with him for about six months. His wife called me and said he had advanced lung cancer and would I please come and see him in the hospital. I raced to the hospital and found him in bad shape. Dolefully, he declared that he had given himself cancer. How? I asked. He said that nine months ago he had been "stabbed" in the back at work. Someone had lied and taken credit for work he had done. Unable to let go of the resentment, he built up hatred toward this fellow worker. As George's dream suggests, hatred eats away at us. The demon bat was the harbinger of the disease that took his life.

A Dream Helps Heal Emotional Trauma from Sexual Abuse

Jennifer, a college student, had done extensive work in therapy trying to overcome a history of childhood sexual abuse. She was at the point of finally believing in herself when she had the following dream:

> I find myself deep in a very green forest. Darkness envelops the scene except for a radiant light that seems to come from the heavens. A very old man, perhaps one hundred and fifty years of age, with long gray hair and a beard approaches me. He is totally nude. Standing in front of him, I also realize I am completely nude and have a small white owl cupped gently in my hands. The old man is directly in front of me, approximately a yard away. He urges me to let the owl go, let it fly away. I resist, but he keeps repeating the request in a soft, calm voice. After several repetitions of this appeal, I finally surrender and let the owl loose. For the first time in my life, I feel a freedom accompanied by a peace I had never known and a feeling of gratitude for which I can't find words. I experience this both while dreaming and upon awakening.

It took Jennifer a few days to fully process the experience. The owl was a symbol of the wisdom and clear

111

insight within her. She realized her dream was telling her she could trust herself and let go of the fear and shame the abuse had created. This was because the new understanding gained from the experience would be retained. Along with her work in therapy, her dream was the final key to opening the prison gates. Soon after, she completed her studies and became a therapist and an artist.

Healing by Wolves

This next experience seems to represent a powerful curative force in the dream realm that can be as effective as traditional medicine. Alice, one of my graduate students, began dreaming of wolves. Educational pressures plus adjusting to married life in a new state compounded her stress. Initially, the dreams were nightmarish. Several months into the semester, she was involved in a serious automobile accident resulting in critical neck, back, and arm injuries. Six months of physical therapy did not provide improvement. She was starting to feel frightened and hopeless when the first wolf dream appeared.

> Three wolves (two gray, one black) are warming my neck with their fur and massaging my body injuries with their paws. They move and relate to me in a way that communicates an important message: I need to take control of my injuries and nurture my body. When I awoke, the pain had lessened considerably. I continue to dream about them when I am not taking care of myself consistently. In fact, whenever I'm under stress in waking life, the wolves appear and provide a great source of comfort.

Although wolves appear in many dream books as symbols of deception, craftiness, anger, or domination, in this woman's dreams, they appeared as symbols of healing, comfort, and compassion. In Roman mythology, Romulus and Remus, twin sons of the god Mars, were abandoned and left to die. They survived only because they were discovered by a she-wolf who fed them her milk. Native American lore has many stories of wolves and wolf parts healing the sick and injured and teaching tribes how to survive by hunting and valuing family bonds.

My House Is Crumbling with Me Inside

The following dream warning was taken seriously and disaster was averted because the dreamer followed her instinct regarding the message. It's a clear example of how someone on the verge of a serious illness can have a compelling catastrophic dream replete with graphic and symbolic images even before the illness has been detected.

A client of mine, Claire, dreamt of a devastating earthquake a few weeks prior to a breast cancer diagnosis. Strong earthquakes are far from uncommon to California residents, but Claire resided in a Midwest area where they were almost unknown. Unable to shake the memory, she was haunted by it daily because she sensed it had some substantial meaning in her own life.

I am sleeping in my bed when suddenly my house begins to tremble and shake back and forth as if it was in the grip of some powerful beast. Initially, I am not afraid, but as the vibration and shuddering intensify, my fear turns to dread. Suddenly, portions of my house come crashing down all around me. Even though most of my dwelling ends up in ruins, I somehow end up safe. Oh, I have a few bruises, but I'm ultimately okay amid all that destruction.

In waking life, she felt fine and was taking excellent care of herself. She had recently completed a thorough physical exam, including a mammogram, and had received a clean bill of health. Her personal life was very satisfying, and she cherished her new job. What possible threat could be looming on her horizon?

Memory of the earthquake dream would not leave her. Finally, just to prove her feelings of impending disaster were inaccurate, she scheduled a second complete physical with another physician. Her instinct was sound. The first mammogram hadn't picked up the cancerous breast tumor, but her body had and shouted the message through the cataclysmic dream. After hearing the new diagnosis, she had a strange sense of calm about it all. She remembered that in the dream, she had ultimately survived the disaster and come out relatively unscathed. She saw the house as representing her body and symbolizing the fact that a part of her physique, like the house, would have to "break off" to keep her safe. And she was accurate. The dream led to her acceptance of the surgery that would not only remove the tumor, but also part of her breast as well. She was convinced the operation would make her well, and fortunately the cancer had not spread. She thanks her dream for being healthy today.

Dreams Can Help Maintain Your Health

Here are a few more examples that I hope will stimulate interest in seeking out the healing instinct in dreams, whether these dreams arise spontaneously or are sought through incubation. The words are those of the dreamers.

Dreamer 1:

A woman appears in my dream and urgently stresses my need to see an ophthalmologist as soon as possible. I will go blind if I do not! At the time of the dream, I had been diagnosed with an unusual eye disease and had been treated. Thinking it was cured, I had not seen the doctor for several months. It wasn't, and this dream saved my sight.

Dreamer 2:

I developed symptoms of fatigue, weakness, and occasional out-of-breath episodes during walking. These traits were very unusual and puzzling for me until I dreamt the following: *I am walking on a beach and uncover an old iron spike, which is barely visible in the sand. As I hold it in my hand, I feel a great power surge through my body. I start running and am able to accelerate to over two hundred miles an hour. I can't believe it. The force and the power in my body are tremendous. In reality, I can't even jog because of arthritic knees, but in the dream, nothing hurt. I am running like the wind!* Shortly after this dream I went to the doctor for a blood analysis. Findings indicated I was borderline anemic, so the doctor prescribed iron and B-12 supplements. My symptoms have disappeared.

Dreamer 3:

Eight years ago, I had ovarian cancer. *In my dream, I am sitting on the beach outside a friend's home in Woods Hole, Massachu-*

setts. The tide is coming in. I look to my right and see a wooded area with a path. Coming down the path is a very tall malelike being whose head is a ball of light. He is dressed in a long, deep red robe with bell-shaped sleeves. It has a gold braid trim and un-identifiable symbols in deep purple, green, and blue sewn on. He sits beside me, puts his arm around my shoulders, and tells me everything will be all right, and I lean on him. He gets up and re-turns to the path, pauses, turns back toward me, waves goodbye, and then disappears into the woods. The next thing I know I am in the ocean, and gentle waves are washing over me. I sense that the water is washing the cancer away. The dream was very help-ful in easing my tremendous anxiety over having a life-threatening disease. I felt strongly that the dream was conveying what the out-come would be, and I often went back to it in my mind when the anxiety was overwhelming. It was the greatest source of comfort to me at the time, because it told me that my path was not one of early death. It's been close to nine years!

These dreams speak for themselves. They may sound mysterious and unconventional, but they are authentic experiences that have produced real results. They can do the same for you. It helps to be a believer, but even skeptics have had these unique experiences.

When Lincoln was president he seldom attended church because people didn't practice what they preached. But being a firm believer in the divine, he frequently claimed to get down on his knees and pray to God to help him end the Civil War. When questioned why a nonchurchgoer would do this, he politely replied that there was no place left for him to go.[8] The same holds true for pressing physical and emotional issues. Conscious minds have limitations and boundaries, so trust that the dreaming mind can often provide what is lacking. Sometimes dream worlds are the only places left to go.

The Key to Inner Remedies

All of these dream experiences are indicative of inherited natural inner remedies that are provided through the sixth sense. Compared to external healing agents, they furnish a distinct truth about the subtler emotional and spiritual issues that can contribute to and even cause illness. Outer restorative health practices operate in the physical world and include all kinds of machinery and medicines that can be applied to heal the body. Joined together appropriately, they can present a total healing package.

Without the active participation of the conscious *and* subconscious minds, achieving wellness can be an extremely difficult task. We must consciously want to be well and seek whatever we need to achieve wellness. Equally important, we need to muster our subconscious forces and resources toward that end. Contacting the inner physician in dreams is a very powerful way to do just that! Dreams can provide a surprising diagnostic index and healing modality of our physical, emotional, and spiritual state of being and even direct us toward wholeness.

The examples demonstrate how dreams spontaneously manifest effective health guidance and practices. They can also do it upon request, as the next chapter will demonstrate. You can get solid advice on diet, alternative treatment recommendations, preventive measures, manipulation, and surgery. If you dream of eating a pile of green peas, go out and buy a few pounds. Or if you dream of jogging, you may want to consider that activity. What would you do if you dreamt of bathing in an Epsom salt bath? Would you try it? A client of mine did with positive results. Often dreams are literal. What criteria would you follow to determine if the suggestions you receive are in your best interests? Ask yourself if it's well-grounded advice. Check it out by doing a little research. Dreams, which have your best interest at heart, would not propose any actions that threaten your overall health. If you are a recovering alcoholic and you dream of drinking, don't do it. That kind of a dream may not be literal but a warning that the tendency is still active. Use common sense. There are important and less important dreams, just like conscious thoughts. Chapter 7 will further explore this concept.

When doing dream incubation for health, don't be surprised if you fail to find a kindly bespectacled doctor greeting you at the door. The inner physician can take many forms and might appear as an image that relates to wellness, wholeness, or wisdom. No matter what the form, the symbol, or the action, your belief in your "physician within" will energize the power and potency of what that "doctor"

dispenses to you. The symbols of healing are varied and individu- .
ally tailored. Here are just a few examples: a beam of light, magic
water, an old Chinese herbalist, color, an animal, lightning, flowers, a
beautiful temple, a pill or injection, tasty food, a rainbow, a medicine
man, a traditional-looking doctor, a magic potion, a circle.

The next chapter provides you with the skills to program your
dreams on any issue with which you need help. This is an exciting
adventure because the unconscious/superconscious mind has access
to information sources that dwarf the Internet. Learning to use the
dream incubation process can uncover this previously concealed
information, like treasures that have been hidden at the bottom of
the sea finally rising to the surface. If you want to know how to get
rid of warts, ask. If you want help with a chronic illness, just ask. The
inner physician is always available.

Chapter 5

DREAM INCUBATION:

HATCHING YOUR GOLDEN EGG

Those who have compared our life to a dream were right...
We sleeping wake, and waking sleep.

Michel de Montaigne

Inviting the Guest of Honor

When a hen sits on an egg, it's not just an ancient barnyard ritual. The act has a specific purpose, and in its own way, is sacred. The hen is performing an incubation "rite" that both protects the fragile egg and nurtures its precious contents. The embryo inside is able to develop into an entity that will eventually break out of its shell and show itself to the world.

Incubated dreams are like that. They require protective and nurturing "rites" so they, too, can break out of the subconscious mind into consciousness. The specific incubation and induction rites elaborated in this chapter can help a dreamer receive the embryo of rich wisdom growing within the subconscious mind. What is remarkable about the unconscious mind is that it contains everything the conscious mind lacks so it can produce what is missing and needed.

The last chapter demonstrated that dreams are pregnant with potential. They are authentic special-delivery messages that can not only heal, but also bring forward the missing pieces that help complete the puzzle of our lives. Individuals are the oak trees in the acorns and the flowers lying latent in the seeds. As human connections to the inner world deepen, the unfolding of these treasures increases. This mysterious broadcast station transmits enlightening information that can transform body, mind, and behavior. The great Einstein attributed his general theory of relativity to a dream he had as an adolescent. He dreamt he was on a sled going faster and faster down a hillside. When he approached the speed of light, the stars above distorted, and the heavens bent. He admonished his colleagues, "Learn to dream."[1] Whoever coined the phrase "Sleep on it" deserves grateful thanks.

In the Greek dream temples, "hatching a golden egg" took time and preparation. I have streamlined the process. The method I have developed will require only a brief interval before bedtime on any evening of choice. But before I describe this approach, I would like to share a brief history of how it originated.

The Origin of a Modern Dream Incubation

At my dream seminars, people ask how I got interested in dreams. I covered this somewhat in chapter 1, but I'd like to add other reasons now. I knew nothing about the dreaming mind, as I stated earlier, until I started psychoanalysis with a Jungian analyst during my mid-twenties. It was just one of those moments—a spontaneous combustion event—when my dream of the magic stone with the cross after the first session ignited my curiosity. For the first time in my life, I felt in touch with something sacred. Thus began my life-long interest and enthusiasm about dreams, which eventually led to teaching both professional psychotherapists and laypeople about the tremendous value of dreams.

As I was working toward my master's degree in marriage and family therapy, I took a hypnosis class. Two unique things happened to me: an out-of-body experience and a past-lifetime regression. These events altered my thoughts about the human soul and the continuity of life. My previous concepts about these two areas were based on what I had read in psychology books. But having these experiences allowed me to bridge the gap between knowledge and comprehension.

I also was meditating twice a day for about forty-five minutes per session, and during one of these occasions, I heard a powerful male voice command me to "open the dream center." I came up out of the chair like a jet pilot ejecting and flipped the light on so I could examine the room to see if anyone else was there. I was alone. To this day, I cannot say for sure whether the voice came from within or without. A few months later, I opened a dream center and began giving lectures and leading small dream groups.

It was at this time that I read C. A. Meier's *Healing Dream and Ritual*, which centered on the ancient Greek healing temple at Epidaurus. After finishing the book, I started thinking of how to create a modern version of this ancient ritual by condensing this practice into an updated version that didn't take two or three months but could be a complete experience over a single weekend. I began piecing together a series of activities that would lead to participants selecting an issue that was resistant to solution and prepare them to have a meaningful dream on that subject the first evening of the seminar. Then using various dream interpretation approaches the second day, members could begin resolving the problem. Progress was slow until I had one of those "there are no accidents" experience. Three writings literally fell into my lap that helped me organize, simplify, and intensify the experience. The universe had provided me with exactly what I needed. Jung would have said this event demonstrated synchronicity, a coincidence of events that seem to be meaningfully related.[2]

The first book I found was *Living Your Dreams* by Gayle Delaney. Her phrase-focusing technique helped me clarify how I could prepare people in the first stage of going to sleep with the intention of solving a problem.[3] Henry Reed's *Dream Incubation Ritual* provided elaboration on the incubation ceremony.[4] The last book, Montague Ullman's *Working with Dreams* was the most helpful and dynamic book I have ever read on group dream interpretation. In the next chapter, I will offer the basic outline, process, and results of Ullman's group dream interpretation procedure.[5]

The Guidelines and Method

Dreaming is a natural function. You do it approximately two hours every evening. Many people who have an extremely persistent problem will occasionally have a dream that gives sound counsel and a fresh approach to resolving the issue. Dream incubation greatly increases the probability that you will have a creative problem-solving dream about any complicated issue of your choice. When I was giving weekend dream seminars and using this approach, the success rate was 95 percent on the first night. Some people took an extra day or two before the requested dream appeared.

Asking dreams for guidance may be one of the most meaningful endeavors an individual can undertake. The inner mind from which help is sought is a limitless Internet: it contains vast arrays of personal data about you and objective data about the universe. Sometimes these dreams are literal; at other times they are symbolic and will need interpretation. My clients and dream-seminar participants have used this method to incubate dreams regarding careers, health, money, creativity, and spirituality—just about any subject where help is needed.

In this chapter, I will focus primarily on two phases of dream questing—the incubation phase and the induction phase. Both of these stages are vital to successful dream missions. These rituals do not involve any kind of voodoo magic or unnecessary mumbo-jumbo. They are very practical and proven tools to help dreamers find necessary guidance by trusting the subconscious mind to work out a creative solution.

Expectation—The Placebo Effect

One of the primary ingredients of any ritual is *expectation*. It is one of the most powerful tools you can use in any area of your life, particularly if that expectation is expressed in a way that helps focus your mind and energy toward the creation of favorable results. Be careful not to confuse expectation with wishful thinking. They are very different concepts. Wishful thinking is just that: *wishful* thinking. Expectation is much more! It is the act of sharply or clearly defining a desirable future occurrence and taking the necessary steps to make it happen. You engage in special expectation rituals all your life, especially if it involves something that's important and life altering.

Take, for example, wedding ceremonies. Why can't two people just say, "Okay, we're married"? Or, since state or religious laws require a presiding third party, why doesn't a couple wearing everyday clothes just get a license and pop over to a magistrate or minister who recites a few simple words and then declares the couple married? Most of us require something much more meaningful. Why? Because we're taking an important life-altering step! The wedding ritual gives the act weight, and most significantly, it induces a degree of expectation from both parties. Birthdays, New Year's Eve celebrations, and even the act of choosing lottery numbers are usually subject to some sort of ritual. It's a ritual of expectation and is viewed as a rite that will somehow help to ensure success in a new undertaking, whether it's a marriage, the beginning of a new year, or the possibility of winning the jackpot!

The placebo effect mentioned in the earlier chapters demonstrates how control-group patients who receive harmless substitutes instead of real medication improve because *they think* they're receiving the actual medicine. Therefore, they expect to get better! Prayer and meditation have finally been accepted in the medical and scientific communities as having a positive impact on health. Prayer and meditation are both rituals of connection to a Higher Power beyond the conscious realm, a power that is expected to help comfort, heal, and present solutions to problems. Scientific experiments seem to bear out the truth of those expectations. Whether the positive results of prayer and meditation are due to the real existence of an external Higher Power, some higher form of ourselves that is also part of a Higher Power, or just the power of our inner selves (or some combination of all the above) cannot be measured by science. However, science has only just begun to measure the astonishingly positive results of the rituals of prayer and meditation. Just twenty short years ago, it would have been considered medical heresy to conduct scientific studies on something as intangible as prayer or meditation.

While the following notions are not as yet mainstream, these studies indicate a strong shift among doctors toward accepting the view that there may be more to health than medical tests and more to healing a patient than prescribing pills and using scalpels. Let me paraphrase a few examples of the studies that were discussed in the June 24, 1996, issue of *Time Magazine.*

In 1995, Dartmouth-Hitchcock Medical Center conducted a study, and researchers were astonished to discover that one of the most effective predictors of survival among 232 heart-surgery patients was the degree to which the patients said they prayed and meditated. Those who did not pray or meditate experienced more than three times the death rate than those who did! In a study of thirty female

patients recovering from hip fractures, those who prayed or meditated regularly and regarded a Higher Power as a source of strength
were able to walk much further upon discharge and had less depression than those who did not. Other studies have shown that men and
women who pray and meditate regularly have half the risk of dying
from coronary-artery disease as those who did neither.

A classic study provides yet another incredible example of how
belief and expectation have the power to heal. Pregnant women suffering from morning sickness were given syrup of Ipecac, which induces
vomiting. However, they were told that the medicine was a powerful
new cure for nausea. Soon after they were told this, women totally
ceased vomiting and no longer suffered from morning sickness. While
prayer or meditation was not involved, *belief*, or rather, *unabated expectation* was really the cure. In fact, it was so strong, it even overrode a
medication that should have had just the opposite effect![6]

Imagine how strong the mind must be to accomplish such feats.
In one example, the mind consciously appealed to a source beyond
itself for help with the absolute belief that the "source" existed and
would help cure the condition. In the other instance, the body
responded to the mind's belief that it was receiving medication and
the absolute expectation that that "medication" was curative. In both
instances, rather than general expectations, there were specific ones.
The idea of being given a particular medication (even though it was a
placebo) had definite expected results. Each prayer or meditation was
specifically focused on the resolution of a precise problem. In both
examples, the power of those conscious expectations brought about
astounding results!

That same, powerful mind is available to us every single day and
night, and it can help us achieve "miraculous" things in our lives.
While people are sometimes adept at exuding beliefs and expectations
in their wakeful state, they have no idea how to appeal to the great
sleeping genius that resides within us all. We just have to learn how
to tap into it to use its great knowledge, wisdom, and power to help
us solve specific issues and achieve aimed-for goals. The information
we receive comes from the inner mind and its vast connections to a
Higher Consciousness. But how do we access that sleeping genius
and receive the necessary guidance? Expectation is the golden key!

It offers the inner genius acknowledgment and shows that no doubt exists regarding what it can provide. It is therefore essential that we have faith in this Higher Power, a firm belief that it can furnish us with precisely what we want.

The Pygmalion Effect

Let's look at a few more studies that deal with rites of expectation. These studies illustrate how positive expectations will yield positive results, while negative or unexpressed expectations generate just the opposite. Incidentally, self-fulfilling prophecy is called the "Pygmalion effect." The name was borrowed from the George Bernard Shaw play *Pygmalion*, in which Henry Higgins transforms a Cockney flower girl into a lady who convinces others she is an aristocrat. The story illustrates the premise that people behave in ways that reflect others' expectations. Your subconscious mind is no exception! It reflects the expectations of your conscious mind.

Robert Rosenthal, an experimental psychologist, and his students put this Pygmalion effect to the test in a laboratory experiment. Half the college students were told they were given "maze-bright" lab rats. Actually these rats were no different than the ones given to the other half of the students who were told they had been given stupid rats. The results were astonishing. The so-called "maze-bright" rats outperformed the others! Since all the rats were really the same, their sterling performance happened because their experimenters *thought* they were brighter and *expected* them to be more intelligent. Sounds crazy, but it's true![7]

Let's consider one more example of the Pygmalion effect: expectation as a self-fulfilling prophecy in action! Robert Rosenthal and Lenore Jacobson concluded that if laboratory rats could act smarter because their experimenters thought they were, the same phenomenon might occur in a classroom full of human subjects. They embarked upon one of their most controversial studies. The researchers gave students in a particular lower-income neighborhood a pseudo-test that would supposedly identify the "intellectual bloomers." The teachers, unaware it had been a bogus test, were given the names of 20 percent of the students and led to *believe* they were "bloomers" with greater potential, even though there was no real correlation between their label and their actual abilities. Eight months later, those students showed significantly higher IQ gains than their fellow students who were not labeled "bloomers." How could this happen? Rosenthal inferred that the teachers encouraged greater responsiveness from the students from whom they expected more. They called upon the students more frequently, asked them more difficult questions, and gave them more time to answer, because they expected the students to be able to respond well![8]

Now, if more expectation directed toward other people (or even animals) can elicit a greater amount of successful responses, imagine the wealth of inventive messages an individual can bring forth just by believing and expecting answers from the dreaming mind. Becoming the hen by creating specific nurturing conditions will allow the dreaming mind to hatch and break through to the conscious mind.

The Dream Incubation Process—The Steps to Hatching Your Golden Egg

There are four primary steps in bringing forth a problem-solving dream.

1. Select the issue you need help with.
2. Write answers to specific questions relating to your problem.
3. Perform a presleep preparation of relaxation and guided imagery.
4. Record your dream in a dream journal as soon as you awaken.

First Step: Selecting a Subject to Dream About

Going to sleep with a definite intention will stimulate that part of the psyche that is already engaged in sorting out the critical issues of your present situation. Choose any problem or question that needs attention and is ready to be explored. The dilemma should be significant so that sorting it out would contribute favorably to life-satisfaction. I suggest staying away from unimportant issues. These don't have the emotional investment that meaningful problems do, and the dream response could be weakened. I emphasize getting clear about the issue and about where the impasse is. Questions that are open-ended usually have a more creative response. Here are a few examples of what people have chosen in my seminars:

- What is my true destiny?
- What happens when we physically die?
- In what ways do I contribute to the problems in my marriage?
- What is my special gift?
- What can I do to cure my headaches?
- What's next in my spiritual growth?
- How can I create greater self-confidence?

Other authors who have written about dream incubation suggest not asking questions that can be answered with a yes or no. I disagree. One participant, a real-estate broker, asked her dreams, "Should I continue in my current job?" She dreamt she was driving down the freeway and saw a huge billboard that said in bold letters, "Don't Stop Now!" This dream occurred a few months before the California real estate market began its boom. Remember the unconscious mind has intuitive access to time frames that see far into the future. The conscious mind only has statistical data to make an educated guess.

Here are some engaging and intriguing questions related to specific life interests that could bring some thought-provoking results.

- What was my past lifetime?
- Why am I so interested in Eskimo culture?
- What is the basis for my fear of touching a knife?
- What does love at first sight really mean?

Second Step: The Questions to Answer

Selecting the subject you need help with identifies the life area that's most in need of dream guidance. The next step is writing the answers to a series of questions relating to the issue you have chosen. There are many reasons for this.

The subconscious mind will have more material to ponder and reacts more favorably when it knows that you are at a standstill after stretching your conscious mind to its limits. Human beings are meant to live their lives consciously and to make decisions accordingly. I think the unconscious mind operates most effectively when it knows conscious thinking has gone as far as it can reach. At that point, it takes action and delivers what was requested in a novel way.

Writing the answers to the questions will help focus both the conscious and unconscious mind on the issue for which dream guidance is sought. In fact, at least during your first attempts at dream incubation, the questions and answers could be reviewed each night before entering sleep to improve the chances for the requested information. It may take a few tries, but the inner mind wants the self to be happy and successful and will do all it can to make that happen. But it needs help! The inner and outer worlds are so vast that the subconscious mind needs a "roadmap" from the conscious mind in order to know which area of that enormous world is causing concern. Only then can it determine which path is best so the desired goal can be reached. When looking inward for guidance, the right conscious input must be given in order for a dreamer to receive the most effective subconscious output. When this kind of preparation is coupled with *absolute belief and expectation*, the answers will come, and the results will not disappoint.

Take time with the questions, and answer each one as fully as possible. If some don't apply, skip them. Try to write out your answers in one evening, which should take approximately thirty to sixty minutes. Then think about the questions during the next few days and see what additions or alterations you may want to make, and write them down. Don't just answer a few of them and then lay them aside for a while. It's important to do them all at once, because they're all connected and have a specific flow. However, if time is limited, don't let that deter you. If you must answer them in more than one session, then by all means, do so. *Remember, there are no right or wrong answers!* There are only your honest thoughts and feelings. You may find that reviewing your written answers at a later time might just springboard the conscious mind into new ideas.

Eventually substituting questions of your own, either within the following groupings or tailoring new ones that would be more suitable for the subject of your choice, is perfectly acceptable. But, at least for now, don't miss answering the questions I've already provided here, since they could be used as the cues that will help shape a successful dream quest. They should help you interpret the basic feelings about daily life issues and also be a foundation for future incubations.

General incubation questions for most issues:

1. What problem, issue, or concern would you like your dreams to help you with? Select an issue that is giving you the most frustration—one for which you just can't seem to achieve the breakthrough that you want. Describe the issue in one or two short paragraphs. Include how it appears in your life context now and how it negatively affects you and your relationships and how long this unresolved problem has been with you.

2. What do you think has caused you to have this problem? (Include what you see as your responsibility and the responsibility of others.)

3. How have you tried to resolve this issue? Why do you think you have not been more successful? Why is this problem so resistant to being resolved?

4. What has this problem taught you about yourself?

5. In order to function in a relatively free manner, you must be somewhat free of resentment and fear. List any and all resentments you have in connection with this unresolved issue. It doesn't matter how petty they seem, just write them down. Do the same thing with fear. Again, even if they seem silly, write them down. Buried barriers need to be looked at before full healing can take place!

6. What opportunities do you think you have let go by or missed out on because of this persistent problem?

7. How do you feel about asking your subconscious/superconscious mind for a dream that could help bring healing to this area of conflict?

8. Consciously, imagine a dream in all its detail that could instantly bring healing to your problem. Write it down. Begin to develop an attitude of positive expectancy. Our minds begin to build what we expect to happen. Expect much, and you can attain much!

9. If this dream of resolution took place and affected your waking life, how would you and your life be different?

10. Do you think you get any benefits from keeping this problem unresolved? Sometimes, people remain unhappy because they have learned they can get attention from being this way. Think deeply on this question. On the surface there may not be any apparent benefits, but if you dig deeper inside, you may be surprised at what you discover.

11. What changes would you be willing to make in your everyday behavior to have this issue resolved? The idea of sacrifice is as old as the human race. You gain when you give. In the ancient Greek dream temples, sacrificing something of value was an important part of the healing process. What would you give to be rid of the problem? Would you give up a plea-surable habit such as eating candy or smoking? Would you give time—such as three hours of community service?

12. As you wind down from answering these questions, express what you are feeling. Are you energized? Absorbed? Confi-dent?[9]

The following question sequences are focused on two areas: healing information and spiritual growth. These examples could also give you some ideas of adapting the questions for specific subjects. I have spent more time on the healing questions because health can be paramount.

Incubation questions for healing:

You are in the process of preparing your dreaming mind to respond to your request for healing information. Just as the ancient Greeks undertook their healing-temple pilgrimages so, too, are you about to embark on your journey into your innermost being where your main healing power is waiting to come to life. Answering these questions is one of the necessary steps you must take in preparing your inner mind to send you dreams that can reveal the nature of your illness and even point in a direction that could lead to healing. Give serious thought and consideration to them. Do as much con-scious thinking as you possibly can on this subject. Illnesses are not just physical; they involve the total person. Your suppressed thoughts and emotions can seek expression in your body.

Physical symptoms are often an attempt to heal the psyche of unhealthy living, eating, and thinking. So give them your best shot. As in ancient Greece, incubating a dream for healing takes, time, patience, and strong effort. But it's well worth it. Journeys to the dream temples were not undertaken superficially. Seekers often had to take an arduous trek and travel great distances to meet the ancient healer. It may sound like an outward journey, but the real journey begins within. The answers to the improvement of your health may be found inside you, and this incubation process can lead you to them. The outcome could be as dramatic as what occurred in the Asklepian healing sanctuaries. You never know!

1. State the nature of your illness. Briefly describe your symptoms and how you experience them.

2. When and how did the illness occur? Was it a sudden onset or a slow developing process? What was happening in your life at the time of the onset? Can you relate the illness to an emotional situation? If so, describe it.

3. What healing methods have you tried? To what degree have they been successful? Why do you think they haven't been more successful? This question relates to your attitude toward the healing process. Are the healing methods you've tried more traditional or alternative? Do not blame yourself if the healing methods have not been as successful as you would like. Think of your illness as a greater challenge to learn more. Your dreams can be the source of information that could reveal the key to your healing.

4. How would you be different if you didn't have this condition?

5. Why do you think this condition happened to you? Do not blame yourself for your illness. Taking responsibility for your health does not mean getting blamed for the past, but it does suggest getting personally committed in the present. Illness is not a punishment. It can be a stimulant for examining which of your choices is off the mark.

6. What has this illness taught you about yourself that you didn't know before its onset? Think of your illness as an inner teacher who says it's time for certain lessons to begin.

7. Have other people been missing out on your special talents

and abilities because of your health issue? If so, how would they benefit if you were healed? Give yourself credit here! You have special talents and abilities; accept them, and know that people around you gain much from them.

8. How could you be benefiting from this illness? In other words, do you need this illness for any psychological reason? This question is not trying to place blame or guilt on you. It's asking you to examine your illness to see if you are using it to satisfy any emotional needs. For example, when people become ill, they often get the kind of love and attention they crave. Or they may find it easier to say no to an oppressive job or the annoying demands of other people.

9. What changes would you be willing to make in order to get well? Would you be willing to give up something? I am again bringing in the idea of sacrifice here. In the ancient dream temples, sacrifice was crucial. Would you be willing to give up any addiction (chocolate, smoking, TV, etc.)? Would you be willing to donate a few hours a week to some charitable cause?

10. What feelings are you experiencing as you complete these questions? Are you optimistic? Eager?

Incubation questions for spiritual growth:

1. Write a one-sentence description of what being a spiritual person means to you.

2. Elaborate on your response to question 1 in more detail, say, a short paragraph five or six sentences long.

3. In what ways do you fulfill this description? In what ways do you not?

4. How have you tried to become a more spiritual person?

5. In what ways have your dreams helped on your spiritual path?

6. If you could be the kind of spiritual person you would like to be, what would you be like?

7. With regard to your spiritual development, what areas (relationships, patience, church attendance, values, etc.) do you think need to be improved?

8. What holds you back from making changes in this part of your life?
9. If you did change in this area, what would you gain? What would you lose? Be aware that in any transformation, there is always an accompanying birth and death.
10. What would you be willing to give or give up in order to have this change become a reality?
11. All spiritual people talk of God (or a creative force or unifying principle). What is God like for you?
12. What feelings are you experiencing as you go through these questions? Are you inspired? Invigorated? Motivated?

Answering all the questions to the best of your ability, joined with a solid belief in the incubation process and an expectation that a creative response will come in a dream promises a fulfilling reply from the dreaming mind.

Third Step: Entering Your Dream Temple

After writing the responses to a selected set of questions, look at the drawings of the Greek dream temples on the next page: they feature Asklepios standing at the entrance waiting to greet you. Take your dream request and shorten it to as brief a statement as possible, and write it three times, once on the bottom step, once on the middle step, and once on the top step. Look at the first example with the written request repeated on each step. A blank one is available so you can use it for your own incubation.

The next step that took place at the dream seminars was a dream induction—deep relaxation and guided imagery with background music. As mentioned earlier, 95 percent of the participants came back with a dream the next morning, and the other 5 percent had their dreams shortly thereafter. If you would like the CD of the dream induction, see the order form on pages 246–7.[10] Meanwhile, just follow the instructions in the next three paragraphs.

Before doing the relaxation and final step in your preparation, reread your answers to the questions. If something new occurs to you, add it to what you already wrote. Be aware of how you are feeling, and then allow yourself to feel the emotion of achieving your goal.

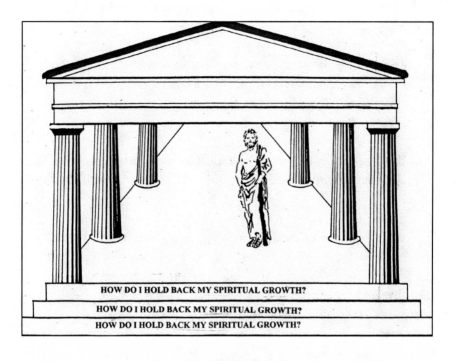

HOW DO I HOLD BACK MY SPIRITUAL GROWTH?

HOW DO I HOLD BACK MY SPIRITUAL GROWTH?

HOW DO I HOLD BACK MY SPIRITUAL GROWTH?

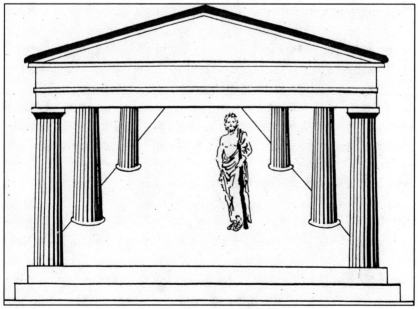

For larger image, go to www.dreamtechniques.com

Take yourself through a relaxation, and then say the following statement aloud three times:

> Tonight, this wise all-knowing portion of my mind will send me a dream that will help me finally resolve the most pressing issue in my life and free me to experience more of my potential.

You can vary it by naming the specific issue, or you can stick with a general statement. Modify it in whatever way feels comfortable for you.

Fourth Step: Enter the Dream Temple and Record Your Dream

Look at the picture of the dream temple, and imagine you are standing outside the entrance of a grand sanctuary with massive columns made of stone or marble. It is nighttime, and the air has soft warmth. Stars shine in the night sky and dimly illuminate the plants surrounding the temple entrance. You are dressed for sleep and know you are going to repose in this temple of dreams. As you walk up the steps to enter, you notice that imprinted in the stone is your request. Say it aloud. Do that three times, once for each step. Greeting you at the entrance is Asklepios, the Greek god of healing. Acknowledge his presence with a nod or gesture of greeting. Allow the greeter to take any form your inner mind produces. It can be a young man, an old man, a young woman, an old woman, an unusual animal, a child, a beam of light, a color, a modern doctor, a mythical figure—whatever strikes you. Enter the temple, and find a comfortable place to sleep—a bed, a cot, a soft and fluffy rug. Imagine yourself closing your eyes and seeing a light go on inside your mind. Then just go to sleep.

Record any and all dreams as soon as you recall them. Use the present active tense as if the dream is a description of what is occurring in the now. Don't concern yourself with the meaning; just get the dream down in as much detail as possible. Be aware of your feelings in the dream and include those in your recording. If you do not have a dream on this first attempt, record what comes to mind upon awakening; incubated dreams will occur on subsequent nights.

Further Suggestions for Success

I have heard of people who wear a special pair of pajamas when they do a dream incubation. You could say a distinct prayer over them before use. Other suggestions are using a specific pillow or sleeping in an area of your home that is just for incubating a dream. Create an environment that will be inspirational for dreaming. Do not drink alcohol the day of the incubation. Make certain that you have a notebook, a pen, and a flashlight for recording your dream or dreams. The possibilities for creating an environment to stimulate dream production and recall are boundless, because you can be as creative as you want.

How to Evaluate an Incubated Dream for Guidance

Mark Thurston, from the Association of Research and Enlightenment, offers excellent guidelines for evaluating a dream for guidance. No matter what kind of dream you have, it's important to evaluate the advice and counsel you obtain. It's careless to singularly follow guidance just because it came from a dream. I personally have never found the advice given or implied in any of my dreams to be harmful, and I believe that sound judgment coupled with the message and feelings evoked by the dream are often solid criteria for decision-making. However, Mark Thurston offers excellent guidelines for evaluating a dream for guidance. According to Thurston, guidance dreams will usually fit one of four categories:[11]

1. The incubated dream will state your issue or question in a different way with a novel point of view. This new perspective will often help you see the answer clearly.
2. The dream may foretell the outcome of a course of action if you continue on that path.
3. The dream gives you an unmistakably clear answer to your concern.
4. The dream doesn't address the issue at all but instead looks at another issue that may be more urgent than the one considered.

If you imagine that your dream is guiding you on a course of action, evaluate it on the basis of the following list:

1. Does the advice have the sound of truth to it?
2. Does it harmonize with the best I know?
3. Does it reach beyond my usual understanding, taking me to new ways of seeing?
4. Does the guidance seem practical and credible?
5. How is the information presented to me in the dream?
6. Has the guidance left me feeling optimistic and upbeat?
7. If I apply this guidance, do I see benefits coming to the people I am connected to and myself?
8. Does this guidance leave me with a clear, peaceful feeling?
9. Would a close friend agree with my interpretation?

These suggestions are all sound advice. Good luck on your inner and outer adventure.

Here are a few examples of incubated dreams and the results that came out of the group dream interpretation process in my seminars. Of course, my descriptions are brief, but they give a good idea of how powerful these incubated dreams can be, coupled with the interpretation process. These incubated dreams helped heal emotional conflicts and initiate spiritual enlightenment. Overall, this process produces trust that the answers lie within.

Dream 1

Question: How can I heal my emotional conflict regarding perfectionism?

This dreamer was a perfectionist who had a strong belief that others would value her only if she was perfect. She was deathly afraid of disclosing anything that would make her look imperfect. Depression was the mental-health issue.

Dream: I am making friends with my shadow. The figure is an actual shadowy character that has no defining features but is the shape of a human being.

Results: Her depression partially lifted upon awakening. When working in her dream-interpretation group, someone defined the shadowy figure as representing all her "dark" aspects, shortcomings and weaknesses that she was trying to hide from the public. The group emphasized that in order to find peace and happiness in life, accepting all aspects of herself was a necessity. Acceptance is also the first step to creating something new. Her assignment was to reveal her shadow parts that had been kept as guarded secrets to her group. She confessed her disdain for her looks, jealousies, manipulations, inferiority feelings, fake charm, etc. The experience was liberating.

Dream 2

Question: Should I leave my husband or work on the marriage?

The dreamer was seeing a therapist for her marital issues. She did not share any of her discontent with her spouse nor did she tell him about her visits to a psychologist. Consciously, he knew nothing about her frustration and dissatisfaction with the relationship of twelve years. She felt at a loss after so many years of not being able to communicate with her spouse.

> Dream: I come home, and when my husband opens the door to greet me, he immediately tells me he knows that I am leaving him, and he has cooked a special meal as a farewell. The table is beautifully set with candles glowing, and at my place setting is my favorite plant, a small red rose bush in full bloom. I awaken stunned.

Results: A short time after the dream, her husband started a complete turnaround. He became attentive, communicative, open to new experiences, sensitive to her needs, and took on more of the household responsibilities. She had never said a word to him about her marital unhappiness nor that she had contemplated ending the relationship. Nevertheless, the message penetrated his psyche. His love for her came through in her dream, and her message came through to him in the silence.

Dream 3

Question: How can I deal with my need to control others?

The dreamer had a need to take over activities and solve everyone's problems. She viewed others' predicaments as her own, believing people couldn't handle their own situations. She started early in life by taking care of everyone, even strangers. After sixty years of this pattern, she felt drained and needed to have more time for herself.

Dream: I am in a long line of hundreds of people walking slowly up a spiral walkway. It looks like the Guggenheim Museum in New York City. Only two people are familiar. One is an old friend, a devout Catholic, the pillar of her church, who is also a rescuer who stretches herself thin saving people. The other is a family member who is also Catholic and a devout church attendee who gives time to her own interests. As we pass what looks like a baptismal font, people seem to lift their arms and put something in the font itself. When I pass by, I see nothing in it and don't know what to do. Pressure from the line keeps me moving. I feel frustrated and disappointed at not understanding the situation. Everyone else seems calm, satisfied, and silent. Standing to the side is a male figure clothed in an earth-colored robe with a hood. I ask, "What am I to do?" A soft male voice replies in a whisper, "You just need to give a penny."

Results: Some deep learning resulted from the dream and the group process. She realized she didn't have to control relationships and give so much of herself. The robed man taught her to give just a penny and let others do their part and solve their own problems. To the dreamer, giving a penny implied just giving enough so that everyone takes responsibility.

Dream 4

Question: How can I overcome my performance anxiety?

This dreamer was a retired professional who had studied and mastered Bach piano concertos. He could not perform in front of friends or strangers because of tremendous performance anxiety. When he tried, his fingers became rigid.

Dream: I exit the rear door of my house into the backyard. My small dog has died and lies motionless on the grass. Deeply saddened, I bend down and gently pick him up to bring him inside. As I walk toward the house with his limp body, light originating from within my hands penetrates his corpse, and I can feel the warmth of life returning.

Results: The dream seminar group gave him the task of playing a Bach sonata for them at the piano in the foyer of the hotel where the seminar was held. With all that encouragement, he performed admirably. The effect of the dream coupled with the group support helped him break the cycle. What he discovered from the group interpretation and the actual performance was that if he tried to achieve perfection for ego gratification, his hands always froze. But if he concentrated on the message or feeling that the composer intended, without involving his ego, all went well.

Dream 5

Question: How can I have a greater personal connection to God?

The dreamer was a nun in a Franciscan Order and satisfied with her daily ministering to others. She longed for a more personal involvement with God and with the living breath of life.

Dream: I am on a beach of gold, sparkling sand surrounded by golden waters. On one side of the beach, people are fighting; on the other side people are laughing and playing. I am primarily an onlooker—watching people swim in the ocean, play in the sand, or just lie on the beach. Two giant tigers are quietly aware and silently overseeing the people in the crowd, who are oblivious to their presence. I play for a bit in the sand, scooping out a hole with my hands, and I swim in the ocean, feeling relaxed and at peace.

Results: She wondered if her answer lay in the message that she needed to relax and enjoy more of the beauty and fun in life. The dreamer connected to the idea that God is part of us, therefore getting closer to oneself gets one closer to God. She realized she could do nothing about the fighting in the world except be where she was, doing what she could to make her world a better place.

Now we move on to the heart of what dreams are trying to communicate.

Chapter 6

UNVEILING THE MYSTERY: GETTING THE MESSAGE

They say dreams are the windows of the soul—take a peek,
and you can see the inner workings, the nuts and bolts.

Henry Bromel

Unraveling the Mystery of Dreams

Dreams can be mysterious, but mysteries can be solved. Consider this bizarre and puzzling dream.

My boyfriend and I are standing in the kitchen dressed in bathrobes. We have just come down to get a bite to eat after making love in the upstairs bedroom. I feel something growing in my back, and I ask Jerry to take a look. He pulls up my bathrobe and says, "Oh my gosh, Joan, you have a penis growing out of your back! He proceeds to jump on the penis and have intercourse with it. I awaken shocked!

This was a real dream presented exactly as it was stated to me. Some dreams are heavy with meaning and linger on until they are interpreted. The unconscious sees and knows more and thus rallies its inner genius to reveal truthful facts in original and ingenious ways. Since dreams have their fingers on the pulse of a person's psyche, body, and relationships, whatever is hidden or neglected will rise to the surface. Dreams make a major effort to enlighten individuals.

Now a Freudian analyst could have a field day with this dream. All that rich sexual symbolism is just waiting to be interpreted. This is the stuff that dreams—some of them, at least—are made of! I am reasonably certain a Freudian analyst would say the core meaning is

141

strongly sexual in nature. The symbols have predisposed meanings, and the final message probably concerns issues arising out of childhood Oedipal conflicts.

I looked at my client and said, "I think he's screwing you behind your back." She responded with a big smile and said, "I guess that at some level I was sensing that." Later, she discovered that he was not only cheating on her sexually but also financially. Dreams can be funny, shrewd, and inventive. This dream was a pun, a humorous play on words. Screw has many different connotations, but defrauding her behind her back made the most sense to her. No dream book could have interpreted this message and its unique delivery.

Dream work is not a science; it's an art form. A dream of a pig could mean something a lot different to the owner of a meat-packing plant than to, say, a teacher. Freud tried to make dream interpretation into a science. He failed. Science consists of a body of laws that are rational, objective, and testable through a logical methodology. One thousand experiments will show the same result. Drop two identical golf balls simultaneously off the top of the Empire State Building, and in all instances each ball will take the same amount of time to hit the sidewalk. However, if a thousand artists paint the Grand Canyon from the north rim, what each artist creates will be unique. Truth in science is revealed by consistent results. Artists, on the other hand, reveal truth subjectively by coming up with varying results. So the same dream can have several different interpretations. Therefore, the pursuit of objectivity is an empty illusion. Results of dream work must be determined by their contributions to an individual's life. If they give the dreamer understanding, motivate him or her to action, reveal hidden information, or open new horizons, they can all have value. If dream work enriches lives by providing road maps for inner territories that are impervious to the conscious mind, who cares if it's unscientific?

Human beings have an intense hunger for meaning and truth. That's why people love to tell stories and produce original dream symbols. The unconscious mind knows we are molded of divine material, so in a particular sense that makes humans omniscient. Revelation of this fact is often made through dreams and their symbols. Dreams are so distinctive because we are all so one-of-a-kind that it is difficult to compose general guidelines for all dreams. Each person has to explore these inner revelations as an individual on a fact-finding expedition seeking to bring to light inner treasures. I will share several different interpretational methods and also recommend what I consider to be some of the best books on dream interpretation in the bibliography.

Dreams as Questions

It is very important to start off simply when learning how to work with dreams. This first method I describe is an extremely effective and basic way to get at the core meaning of a dream quickly.

One unique way to get at the heart of a dream is to think of a dream as a question and then state it in question form. Many dreams do not give you answers but pose questions that need a response. This approach generally applies to dreams—especially brief ones—where the action and issue are relatively clear. It certainly will not apply to every dream. This technique can get right to the heart of a dream and help a person examine attitudes, values, thoughts, feelings, and actions. A question can often stimulate replies and affect an individual in a more significant way than straightforward answers. The key is focusing on the situation and action rather than on what each symbol means.[1]

Examples of Questions

Most of the dreams that follow were shared at my dream workshops, and the audience asked the questions. Dreamers had the option of responding or not. Often the dreamer would just acknowledge if the question was on target.

1. Dream: I am a prisoner in a state penitentiary.

Restate the dream in question form: In what ways do you feel enclosed? How do you keep yourself imprisoned? What would it take to liberate yourself from confinement?

2. Dream: I am a passenger in a car that is somewhat out of control. I do not know who the driver is.

In question form: Where in your life do you need to be more in control? How do you allow others to steer you around?

3. Dream: I am in college on my way to take a final exam, but I'm late, don't know where the room is, and am totally unprepared.

In question form: Where in life do you need to be better prepared? How do you prevent yourself from being ready? Where in life are you being tested and feel like you could fail?

4. Dream: It's nighttime, and I am trapped in a house that is about to be demolished by a bomb that's been planted in it. The house has been evacuated, but somehow I've been left behind. I must escape before the bomb detonates, so I run from room to room, but all the doors to the outside have been locked.

In question form: Where in life do you feel trapped in an explosive situation? How have you put yourself in such a precarious predicament?

5. Dream: I am in front of a movie theatre, and many people are walking around. I notice some shiny, glimmering coins lying in the gutter. I bend down and pick some up, filling my pockets to overflowing. There are many more coins, but I am surprised that no one else seems to notice them. People just appear to walk by the coins without detecting them.

In question form: Where do you see value that others don't? What inner treasure have you recently discovered?

6. Dream: My husband's youngest bother and I are at a boat launch trying to get an outboard motor boat under way. The brakes on the car slip, and everything—trailer, boat, and car—slides into the water. A speedboat comes racing by, punctures a hole in the roof of the car, and I watch as my car spirals downward to the bottom of the lake.

In question form: What family situation are you involved in where you need to apply the brakes? How does "speed" cause problems for you?

7. Dream: I see the end of the world coming, because I am driving a pick-up truck along a riverbed that is rapidly drying up. People alongside the road are stockpiling sticks. Suddenly, I am with somebody in a place that is very green with vegetation. There are large trees that have fallen and been topped. No bark is on the trees, and they look like huge dry bones.

In question form: What area of your life could be drying up and has stopped growing? How would the end of your current worldview benefit you?

Remember, it is the conscious mind and waking life that often wobbles, is muddled, and needs a guiding force. Sometimes it's difficult to carefully pay attention to ways the unconscious mind tries to remedy the ego's distorted and unhealthy perspective. The above dreams in general represent the outcome of unclear thinking when awake. In one way or another, they seem to say to the dreamers: "Look, this is what you are producing. Your fears, negative thoughts, emotional blindness, and insecurities are creating these situations." When you're on the right track, however, favorable dreams will encourage you.

The Theme—The Simple Story Line

The first time I read about a method for determining the theme of a dream was in Mark Thurston's *How to Interpret Dreams*. This book helps get a dream message down to its bare essentials in a process that could otherwise be complicated and vague. Although working with the symbols is neglected, the theme approach can provide clarity for taking action.

A dream is a form of reasoning. The subconscious mind reasons inductively (thinking that goes from a specific observation to a broader generalization), whereas the conscious mind does so deductively (thinking that goes from the more general to the more specific). Dreams present the images, events, and series of actions, and the dreamer attempts to discover an underlying and unifying theme that ties all this together. What needs to be sought is a *simple story line* that restates the essential plot. Such a story line provides a basic scheme of what is happening in the dream by treating the dream as a whole. In this way, the dreamer can simply and directly tie the dream back to waking life. Rushing to interpret the symbols can break the dream into components without seeing how all these parts fit together and impact each other. Once a simple story line is found and its correspondence to waking life identified, interpretation becomes much easier.

To discover the simple story line, here are a few easy suggestions:
1. Focus on action words (e.g., verbs).
2. Use generalizing words like *someone, somewhere,* and *something.*
3. Keep it as short as possible—similar to the TV guide. One sentence is enough.
4. Say it several times using different words.

Keep it simple. This approach is designed to help discover that portion of waking life that coincides with the theme of the dream experience.

Here is an example Thurston gives in his book:

Dream: I am in a hurry to get someplace, and so I speed up my automobile. I notice my car license is being written down. Soon after, I am stopped by a policeman, which greatly delays me.

Simple story line:
1. Trying to rush results in a big delay.
2. Rushing things in life often backfires and takes even more time.

Dreams get much clearer when a theme is brought to light. Creating a theme sets the tone for an interpretation. Although it is not the whole explanation, it helps find the big picture and points in the right direction. Stripping the dream of its symbolic details and focusing on the action allows a dreamer to match the theme to the life area that best suits it.[2]

Look at the following list of dreams, and try to write at least one theme for each dream. The responses given in the dream seminars are at the end. Just follow the outline above.

1. I am in a small rowboat at sea. I put my hand in the water, and a killer whale grabs it. Terrified, I try to yank it out of his mouth, but the harder I try, the harder he grips. Soon my whole arm is in his mouth, and I think the end is near. I accept my fate and stop struggling. The whale, sensing that I have given up the struggle, releases my arm and swims away.

2. I am sitting at a table, perhaps fifteen feet long, with Frank Sinatra. He is at one end, and I'm at the other. It is a romantic dinner—candles, wine, etc. Suddenly I feel something pressing against my vaginal area. I reach under the table and realize it's Frank's penis. I think, "My gosh, it's fifteen feet long!"

3. I see a beautiful Indian sand painting framed on the sidewalk. People come and just look and admire it. I can't resist and touch it in the center. When I do, the whole thing implodes upon itself.

4. I am standing on the front porch of a mountain cabin. I hear an explosion and look down the hill just in time to see a man fall from a gunshot wound. Farther away, I see another man holding a smoking rifle. To my amazement, I see the wounded man get up and start to run away. But the man with the rifle shoots him again. This happens several times, but the victim always gets back up and runs.

5. I'm in an average-size house, and I open a door into a room off a hallway. The room has an enormous pile of human feces shaped in a pyramid structure. There is a large spoon inserted into the pile at my eye level. I know I must eat the whole pile. As I put the first spoonful close to my mouth, the odor is overwhelming, so I drop it and run out of the room.

6. I'm at work and I notice I am still pregnant. It has been over two years, and the baby still has not come out.

7. This is a recurrent dream. I am walking along a path, and I encounter a poisonous snake. We lock eyes, and I know if I make one false move, the snake will bite me, and I will die. It is always the same. I get locked into the same positions.

8. I am riding a pony in the countryside. Dusk is approaching, and I notice billowy clouds looming in the sky. I am wearing a Victorian-style suit, and riding alongside me is an unknown friend. As we approach a very steep hill, we dismount and crawl on our bellies up to the summit. When we reach the crest, the hill drops away to a vast emptiness that is both enormously wide and exceptionally deep. I feel this tremendous sensation of awe in my stomach, and I exclaim, "Wow." My friend turns to look at me and says, "Yeah, that's the dharma."

9. I am standing in front of a small wooden table that has about one square foot of compacted earth resting on top. Planted in this mound of earth is a pine tree about one foot tall. The grass under the tree is drooping from lack of water, and the same is true of the tree. I gently pull the tree out of the earth with my right hand, and I notice how dry and scraggly the roots are. As I begin digging a deeper hole to transplant the tree, I realize that I am shirtless, and the digging, coupled with a warm sun, causes me to perspire. Suddenly, the top of the tree starts growing. It spreads up my right arm, across my shoulders and down my left arm. It clamps on really tight, and I realize that the tree is trying to get moisture from my body.

10. I am walking down a tree-lined street. From a distance, all the tall trees seem barren, but when I approach them, I notice that the first tree I come in contact with has hundreds and hundreds of little pieces of paper suspended from strings. There are no leaves here, just all these little pieces of paper suspended from strings. I reach out and grasp one to see it closer and realize, to my amazement, that it has my name written on it—George. So does the next one and the next. Every tree is filled with these little pieces of paper with my name written on each and every one.

Possible Themes for the Above Dreams:

1. What one resists persists.
   - Someone is safer when he stops struggling.
   - Surrendering to a situation can create freedom.

2. Something or someone wants to connect to me in a big way.
   - Something trying to reach me is concealed from view.

3. Some things are better left untouched.
   - Keep your hands where they belong.
   - Some things are just to be admired and not meddled with.

4. Someone has the capacity to keep going in spite of being wounded.
   - Someone has the resiliency to bounce back from adversity.

5. Someone has to consume something that is very repulsive.
   - Someone is overwhelmed by a disagreeable task and flees the situation.

6. Someone is holding back personal growth.
   - Someone may not be able to grow in a currently held job.
   - Someone may need a change to give birth.

7. Being rigid can endanger someone.
   • Letting go of control could lead someone to safety.

8. When someone gets "off his horse," the world opens up.
   • Humility can lead to deeper understanding of the world.
   • Someone who observes the dharma deepens life meaning.

9. Someone's growth needs attending to.
   • Perspiration is as important as inspiration.

10. Someone's name is so common it grows on trees.
    • Everywhere someone looks he sees himself.

Symbols

Symbolism in dream work is very complex and would need countless pages and extensive experience to do the subject justice. With this in mind, I will offer a brief selection of the best ideas to foster understanding of symbols in dreams. I've also included several readings in the bibliography. The group technique explained at the end of this chapter is possibly the most profound and dynamic way to help people understand their dreams. But then again, you may come up with your own method of arriving at the inner meaning of your dreams that's even more effective. Go with whatever works.

I have often heard the complaint that dreams are difficult to understand because of all those symbols that are so hard to figure out. Many people think dreams are nonsense, because the symbols can be so confounding that grasping the inner meaning of a dream is daunting. The problem does not lie in the dream, but in the conscious mind's resistance to accepting and attending to its own shortcomings. Dreams seem to want us to close up the shop of daytime thinking and enter the mysterious landscape of metaphor and inductive logic. Sometimes dreams do say it simply, but most often we have to think artfully about these esoteric messages. While our minds are not trained to break down barriers to the extraordinary knowledge that flows from dreams, the unconscious, with nature's help, insists that we keep trying.

Dreams speak in symbols because nature intended it that way. In *Peace, Love and Healing*, Dr. Bernie Siegel has an imaginary conversation with the Creator about simplifying the delivery process in dreams. Dr. Siegel asks why we just can't go to sleep at night and have a flash card appear telling us what symbols mean and how to live our lives. The Creator replied that he had tried the cards but because there are so many languages, he would have had to make flash cards for each one, which would have added another day to creation. He couldn't afford the time, so instead, he created universal symbols that everyone could understand with a little effort. Dr. Siegel recommends we pay close attention to these symbols, because they come from the soul. As a surgeon, Siegel often found dreams of immense value in helping him diagnose illnesses and offering suggestions about impending surgeries.[3]

Nature is economical; it doesn't waste energy. Since dreams are natural phenomena, they, too, are economical. One brief dream with a few key symbols can sum up a whole lifestyle issue. For example, a businesswoman who was a supervisor had a recurring dream of a leopard waiting in a tree for prey to come within killing distance. She complained about her relationships with colleagues at work who never invited her to parties outside the office. When I talked to her about the behavior of a leopard, she was shocked when she realized that the leopard waits in stealth until the opportune moment and then swiftly swoops down upon its victim. Someone in the office had even told her that she dealt with people in exactly the same way— "pouncing" on her colleagues when they least expected it. She got clear on the message, but the real work would come in applying the message in the conscious world.

We could attend a drawn-out speech and become periodically inattentive and at the end have forgotten everything that was said in a few minutes. But a picture paints an enduring image that can last a lifetime. Nature wants to deliver powerful messages that capture our attention without hoodwinking us. Freud stated that dreams are symbolic in order to conceal the real message so people wouldn't be shocked into an awakening; dreams, after all, are guardians, not disturbers of sleep.[4] Jung, however, emphasized the natural quality of dreams. According to him, there was no reason to assume dreams were a cunning strategy to lead us off course or protect our sleep.[5] When outer events and words aren't working, a dream comes to "wake us up." Our inner self will use whatever device is necessary to rescue us from ourselves. That's why dreams can make our hearts pound, our spirits soar, our knees quiver. They want to change us and redirect us to new heights.

Symbols represent so much more than the object itself. Although elements in dreams may be identifiable as part of ordinary daily life, their meaning is much deeper and more profound than the apparent external connotation. Jung saw symbols as complex facts and ideas that were not really understood by the conscious mind and were therefore representations of the mind's potential.[6] Symbols are the growing edge of an expanding awareness alive with possibilities. There is not just "one meaning." The most important factor in understanding a dream symbol is to explore personal associations the dreamer has to the symbol.

Dream books on symbols are not the answer. The basic ingredients of dreams are not like recipes found in cookbooks or explanations listed in symbol dictionaries. Approaches like this lead to static conclusions with little or no connection to individual dreamers. These types of helpmates may be used as a starting point but should not be taken as the final statement. For example, if you dreamt of a Bible, a dream symbol book might say this symbolizes spiritual study, or the like. But what if your association with a Bible was being hit over the head with it by the pastor for not paying attention during Sunday school? Many symbols have more than one meaning and often depend on the dreamer's life situation. For one person, fire in a fireplace could mean warmth, romance, or family values. But for a fireman, a fire could represent disaster.

Jung, who is the foremost authority on the nature of dreams and dreaming, made an unbiased declaration when he stated that he had no theory about dreams.[7] Each dream had to be examined on its own without considering fixed theoretical positions. If you pay genuine and sincere attention to a dream, it will reveal its intention about where the unconscious is guiding you.

The Brakes Don't Work

In the following example, the unconscious uses a symbolic scene to try and warn of impending danger.

> I am driving my car down a steep mountain road during day-time with my girlfriend seated beside me. Accelerating beyond the safety point as I approach a sharp curve in the road, I apply the brakes to slow down. The pedal goes to the floor, and nothing happens; the brakes do not work. I lose control, fail to round the curve, crash through a flimsy barrier, and soar out into space. A huge chasm is below. The car flips over, both doors fly open, and my girlfriend and I are flung out into the air. I know we will hit the canyon bottom thousands of feet below and the car will crash on top of us. I awaken, terrified.

The dream was an intense warning for the dreamer that whenever he was out of control, his behavior could lead to disaster. The automobile could depict the body, its condition, and also a person's lifestyle. Brakes could be symbolic of discipline, restraint, or will power. Failing brakes indicate lack of control over thoughts and actions. The dreamer was in the entertainment business and was completely out of control with a cocaine and alcohol addiction. His unconscious mind told it like it was. When the dreamer and I discussed the message, however, he pooh-poohed it, and I never saw him again.

This dream has a dramatic structure that's similar to a stage play. A cast of characters and time and place are introduced. The story unfolds, and the plot is revealed. A conflict ensues, comes to a head, and something positive or negative happens. In many cases, though, dreams are too fragmentary to be so well defined.

Here is a dream that doesn't quite have the same structure. It is the recurrent dream of an alcoholic:

> I fall out the window of a tall building, hit the ground, bounce up, flap my arms, and fly away.

This is an excellent example of how a common action, flying,

153

does not have a universal meaning but is particular to the dreamer. He is an alcoholic who frequently loses his psychological balance but can't stand to be grounded to reality and so escapes by drinking. Being grounded means being responsible, and every time that issue comes up in his life, whether it has to do with paying bills or servicing his car, he has this dream that indicates a desire to flee from reality.

A young man in the movie industry who was an excellent cartoonist and writer was struggling with home and work issues, as revealed in the following, richly symbolic dream:

I am home, and I think my wife and children are there (two male teenagers); they are, however, shadowy blurs. I have recently had some medical procedure performed in which the top of my head was very cleanly cut off like the lid of a pot. Apparently, my brain has been surgically removed for repair, cleansing, or some kind of adjustment, and my still-open skull is empty and smooth inside, like a bowl made of cream-colored bone. My wife hands my brain back to me, and I hold it in both of my hands. It's like a great big encapsulated mass of quivering jelly. Gravity keeps shifting the bulk toward my left hand, almost like one of those childhood slinky toys. I raise my left hand higher than the right so that the jellied mass shifts back toward the center of the whole brain, creating a symmetrical mound of matter. Time to put it back in my head and get back to the world and about my business. I set the brain inside the skull, then put the domed skull-top back into place and walk outside. I'm embarrassed that people will see the obvious thin scar (somehow already healed) that encircles the entire top of my head. Being bald, I have no way of concealing it. People will know that I have had radical surgery. To make matters worse, my brain keeps shifting to the left inside my head, making my head actually begin to tilt in that direction. I see the reflection in the mirror, and I am pleasantly surprised to discover that I have blond hair growing and wispy bangs in front that almost completely conceal my scar. Not bad at all!

The setting is the home with all family members vaguely present and an awareness of a medical procedure that was performed to repair his brain. It needs cleaning and an adjustment. So we can assume this dream relates to the way his mind functions in this situation. A popular theory is that the right brain and the left brain are responsible for different modes of thought. Whichever side of a brain dominates will determine the primary way a person thinks. Each of these parts of the brain sees the world in an immensely different way and often doesn't understand its counterpart. Simply put, people who are left-brain dominant tend to specialize in the language functions and are generally more analytical, logical, and objective in their thinking. Those with right-brain dominance tend to experience the world through feeling, imagination, and intuition and tend to think in symbols and images. They see the whole picture rather than its parts, as the left brains do.

The dreamer has had his brain (thought process) worked on, and his wife hands it back to him. In the dream, as in the waking world, she had a more balanced, holistic way of thinking and constantly struggled to help him gain a more comprehensive picture of his life. But the tendency for his brain is still to tilt to the left. Eventually the jellied mass rearranges itself in a more central position creating a symmetrical pattern, and he is ready to reenter the world and get back to business.

It was interesting that his work as a writer and cartoonist demanded high right-brain involvement. And he was quite successful at it. The left brain took over in the home, which was quite beautiful and situated near the ocean. What drove him berserk was his need for cleanliness and orderliness in this new house. When his teenage sons came in, unwittingly depositing sand on the kitchen floor, or when their rooms were messy, his emotions erupted. One small smudge on the floor meant the family was doomed to live in a pigsty. He was very critical of them and unwilling to make the effort to gain some control over this narrow perception. This, in turn, left him open to frequent depressive episodes. So living in a prime location and having a solid career wasn't enough for him to enjoy his family. Focusing on just this one aspect of his home and being unable to connect to a holistic approach caused him a great deal of aggravation. Evidently, more right-brain emphasis was needed.

Although the skew of the brain was still to the left, the conclusion of the dream indicated that the dreamer was developing some new insights of high value. New blond hair (his hair was brown) could be a symbol of the outer manifestation of some new thoughts and attitudes that would counter his rigid perceptions at home. The scar could symbolize the residual effect of his one-sided thinking. But when he was successful in getting his mind more balanced, his general outlook improved, especially where his family and work situation were concerned.

Compensation

Jung's grasp of the dreaming mind surpassed all that came before him, and his doctoring of the human soul was sought by people from every area of the globe. He left theory aside as much as possible when analyzing a dream, stating he didn't know where his ideas came from or whether his style of working with dreams deserved the name of "method." He was not concerned if his speculations about dreams were scientifically validated. His sole criterion was whether what he offered a patient worked or not.

Jung was convinced that one of the major functions of dreams was to restore balance to psyches with one-sided attitudes. This is no different from what the ailing body does when it mobilizes its resources to recover. Homeostasis is the tendency of living things to actively maintain fairly stable conditions necessary for proper and constant functioning. Break a bone, cut your finger, or raise your body temperature, and a host of human healing potentials are ignited. Broken bones stop growing, cells adjacent to a wound multiply then cease growing when healing has occurred. And when the body starts overheating, perspiration is triggered to cool it down. The same thing occurs in the human psyche's attempt to heal itself..

As seen in the cartoonist's dream of his own mind, the psychic makeup of human beings tries to maintain equilibrium, especially when it becomes unbalanced. Just as happens physically with the body, when we go too far in one direction with our thoughts and feelings, a dream often attempts to bring us back toward the middle to restore balance. Jung discovered this principle when he was reproached in a dream for having too low an opinion of one of his patients who had loose morals. In his dream, he saw an elegant woman standing on a castle tower. He had to look so high to see her, his neck hurt. When he recognized the woman as one of his patients, he awakened with a painful neck. He quickly realized that she was put so high in his dream, because in waking life, he had a very low opinion of her. His unconscious was attempting to compensate for his one-sided attitude. She was not a bad woman; rather he had to grasp that he was a judgmental analyst.[8]

The unconscious mind will weave dreams in impressive contrast to ideas held in the conscious mind. When the conscious attitude leans too far in one direction, dreams will counter this by producing images that contrast glaringly with that attitude so the mind can restore balance.[9]

Examples:

1. A timid man who was employed in a position far beneath his capabilities dreamt that he was a boxing champion fighting with great bravery and defeating all challengers. His dream was trying to help him change his attitude about himself so he could find his courage, take more risks, and uncover his greater abilities.

2. A man who took his wife for granted and often ignored her emotional needs dreamt she was being admired and sought after by countless lovers. His attitude changed upon awakening.

3. A woman who moved much too quickly in life and was constantly on the go dreamt that her car overheated, and she was stuck. Her psyche was trying to warn her to slow down.

4. A teenage girl dreamt her mother died and she was grief stricken. This young girl was so dependent on her mother that her psyche was trying to get her to exercise more independence.

5. A woman who admired her boss dreamt he was using cocaine and acting like a fool at a social function. Her boss did not take drugs, nor did she have any conscious or unconscious desire to see her boss embarrassed. The dream was trying to reduce her boss to human proportions so she could respect her own abilities more.

Volumes have been written about the many facets of Jungian dream work. It is not in the scope of this book to add to these descriptions. However, I do offer recommended readings in the bibliography that share insights into Jung's concepts.

Group Dream Interpretation

What I would like to present now is an abbreviated and adapted approach to working with dreams that was developed by Montague Ullman and Nan Zimmerman in *Working with Dreams*. This technique went beyond Jungian and Freudian dream work by taking the expertise away from the professionals and placing it in the hands of laypeople. The process is the most dynamic and helpful approach to dreams I have ever experienced. I adapted this method to suit my needs in the hundreds of dream seminars I gave for many years. Before I describe the method I eventually adopted, I will explain what Ullman and Zimmerman developed. It's my belief that their work will stand for a long time and gain in popularity as people become more aware of the deep learning that comes from dreams.

The Process

According to Ullman, a group size of eight is ideal, and five to ten is workable. In my seminars I found these numbers too limiting, especially when the enrollment was large. Because the process was so effective and engaging, even small groups of three or four were remarkably efficient according to the evaluations of the participants. Much depended on the perception and intuition of the small-group members. The process itself is impressive, because the way it is structured is so nonthreatening that the dreamer can hear the most intimate thoughts and feelings about his or her dream without feeling defensive.

Dreams tell it like it is, but often the telling is shrouded in a mystery that needs unraveling. Because most people do not know how to decode the mystery, help is necessary to overcome it. Before a group gets started, their intimate disclosures must be respected. The group must not divulge the identity of the dreamer to others outside the group. Secondly, the dreamer is always in charge of the process, which includes sharing a dream or stopping the procedure whenever he or she chooses without any explanation. Control must remain in the hands of the dreamer because of the intimate knowledge revealed in dreams. Sharing a dream in a group experience is very special and personal. Concealed in all those symbols can be highly emotional issues that bring out just about every feeling in the human emotional spectrum. What can surface is truth that has been suppressed or repressed and blind spots that have been uncovered. When camouflage is peeled away, the truth can be painful.

There are four stages in this process. I will add my adaptation after listing Ullman's steps.

Stage 1

Someone volunteers to share a dream. At first, the most recent dream or a short dream is preferable. It's somewhat simpler working with dreams that are not too complex, because they take less time to work through. Group members listen intently and take notes if they choose. When the dreamer is finished, the group can ask questions on the content only to help clarify what happened in the dream. If there are any characters in the dream that are part of the dreamer's waking life, they can be briefly described. There is no attempt at interpretation at this point.

Stage 2

a. Now group members take on the dream as if it belonged to each person. At this level, people share the feelings the dream evoked in them. For example, someone might say, "In the beginning of my dream, I feel angry and helpless, but in the end I feel in control and hopeful." Group members *never* use the pronoun *you*, always *I*. I'm emphasizing the *I* position because use of *you* can seem accusatory and put the dreamer on the defensive. There are no wrong responses. The point of this exercise is to make people sensitive to the fact that dreams originate in feelings and express feelings. All of these statements are projections from the group members and may or may not be valid for the dreamer.

b. The group interprets the symbols and images as if they were their own. They should be looked at in metaphorical ways:

What might these images say about personal conflicts, life situations, relationships, feelings, etc? People share whatever occurs to them without concerning themselves about relevancy for the dreamer. Again, there are no right or wrong answers. Members always share by prefacing their statements with, "To me, this image in my dream would mean..." What stage two is trying to do is create a reservoir of possible meanings for the dreamer.

Throughout stages 2A and 2B, the dreamer does not respond to anything that is said but simply listens and takes notes on responses that are meaningful.

Stage 3

The dream is returned to the dreamer, who is invited to respond in any way he or she chooses. To what degree have the responses been helpful? What are the dreamer's personal thoughts and feelings about the dream? What might the main message of the dream be? Responses are shaped in any manner the dreamer chooses.

If further work is required, the group and the dreamer can have a conversation that helps relate the dream to a current life situation. Generally, about twenty to thirty minutes are spent working on an individual's dream. It can be longer or shorter depending on the time constraints and the needs of each group.[10]

I modified this process to accommodate a weekend seminar. The last activity on the first evening was dream incubation. People would select a major life problem or concern that had been unresolved and then answer the personal questions relating to that issue (see chapter 5). Final preparation for dreaming that night was the dream induction, which was done while people were stretched out on a carpeted floor. From there, participants left the seminar quietly and went right to bed after reviewing what they had written, adding more if they chose.

Upon returning the next morning, usually 95–100 percent of the participants came back with a dream relating to their major life issue. After discussing the concerns people had about recalling dreams, I distributed large sheets of white cardboard and provided everyone with a set of colored marking pens. Each participant was instructed to draw the dream that had occurred the previous evening and color it the best they could. To demonstrate many different styles, I showed numerous slides of artwork done in previous seminars, which ranged from simple to complex. The only guidance I gave was to try not to draw stick figures, because it's hard to determine character from those images. What I discovered about the dream-drawing exercise was that things people cannot grasp entirely in their thoughts can be expressed pictorially. There seemed to be more awareness and insight because of the drawings, and reaction to the images had a stronger emotional tone than verbal descriptions. Participants loved doing the illustrations, which seemed to give both the dreamer and the group a sense of freedom to express feelings.

When groups were formed (they ranged from three to eight members depending on the size and length of the seminar) and someone wanted to share a dream, the picture would become an important part of the presentation. A description of the dream-incubated problem, the dream itself, and the accompanying images would give the group much more information about what the dreamer was struggling with. I found it to be exceptionally helpful, and it cut down the time it took to get to the main message.

Bringing Dreams to Earth

The other change I made was in the final phase, where I added one more step. When the dreamer finally agreed upon the main message, the group suggested a practical assignment relating to the message that needed completion within a certain amount time. Tasks would be specific to the dream. After deciding which tasks would be appropriate, the dreamer selected one or two and agreed to accomplish them within a specified period of time. I know many people who understand their dreams perfectly, but their lives never change. *The key to dream work is applying what is learned in the waking world; insight is not enough.*[11] The task and its fulfillment are the testing ground, and proof is in the doing. After the group interprets the dream, a deepening of understanding occurs that anchors the learning, raises consciousness, and invigorates the dreamer.

Here are a few examples of tasks that evolved out of the group dream work at one of my seminars:

- A young man dreams he is caught in the gears of a huge machine. His thinking and approach were too mechanical and logical. He agreed to read a book of poetry and report to the group.

- A woman dreams of making love to her boss whom she despises in the waking world. She agrees to be more loving, thoughtful, and kind and to use these values to win him over. By complimenting him on minor things such as his clothing, a mannerism, his promptness, etc., she achieved some remarkable results.
- The husband in a long-lasting marriage dreams his wife dies. His dream is trying to separate him from a strong dependency on her. He agrees to spend a day alone and learns a great deal about his inner need for independence.
- A young woman has a solid idea for a new business, and her dream encourages her on this path. Her doubt was persistent, so the group assignment urged her to write a short brochure on the name of her business, the services it offers, and the benefits people would gain from it. She did this and eventually opened up her own business.
- A woman who was sexually abused by her father dreamt she had a friendly discussion with him. She had been alienated

and disconnected from him for many years, so the group assigned her a letter-writing task, which she completed and mailed. She finally received a deeply apologetic response that laid the groundwork for future reconnection.

I have seen many lives advance because of dreams and because the dreamer was encouraged to take a risk based on these messages from the soul. Dreams throw open the gates to growth and healing.

The Collective Imagination of the Group Process

Ullman's method stresses the collective imagination of the group. The technique frees people to use their imagination, intuition, and feeling, three assets Jung claimed were essential for successful dream work.[12] Participants brought diverse views to the interpretation process, which provided alternative choices that opened up a host of new message possibilities for the dreamer. There's a certain playfulness about the technique that's quite a stimulating experience. Group interpretation enables the participants to lose themselves in the process, allowing them to get to deeper emotional levels where the inner message often lies. Taking on someone else's dream as their own was so nonthreatening to people that those who shared dreams could, without fail, hear the most personal revelations about themselves without feeling judged. According to evaluations, the whole process was so meaningful that people in the seminar formed their own groups to continue their dream explorations after the seminar was over.

Here is an example of how the dream incubation and group dream process work in unison, unfolding step by step. During a particular one-day seminar, several people fell asleep and had their dreams during the dream induction. I always asked for a volunteer so I could demonstrate the group process before I assigned people to smaller groups. This was often a golden opportunity for a participant to get tremendous feedback and gain insight into his or her personal issue. This seminar had about seventy-five people, so the feedback and deep understandings were prodigious. One young lady volunteered right away because she had fallen asleep and had her dream immediately.

The Dream Request: Why am I a social worker when what I really wanted to be was a rhythm and blues singer?

The Dream: I am approximately eight or nine years old sitting at a desk in the basement of my best friend's house. Cynthia was my dearest childhood friend in elementary school. There is a file cabinet next to me, and stacks of papers are piled on the desk waiting for me to file them in their proper place. This really is work for an adult. I am sad.

Question Period: Many questions were asked to clarify the setting and the character of Cynthia, her best childhood friend. Cynthia was certainly a free spirit who did exactly as she wanted with no regrets and always seemed to feel good about what she did. She was true to herself—a natural child. The dreamer was a compliant child who did what she was told and often didn't feel okay about it. Because of the family situation, she had to take care of brothers and sisters at an early age and revealed that she felt she missed out on her childhood. Laden with adult responsibilities, she carried this attitude into adulthood and neglected her real inner desire and talent, which was music, especially singing rhythm and blues. She revealed that she had practiced for years, even taking voice lessons, and she often sang to herself when she was alone. She was terrified of performing for others and had subtly concealed this talent and desire from her closest friends.

Feelings Stage: The group took on the dream as their own and shared feelings from the *I* position. Here are some of the responses:
- I feel resentful, because I'm too young for this kind of work.
- I feel stuck in the basement, and I want to go out and play.
- I feel overwhelmed by all this responsibility.
- I feel envious of Cynthia, because she has such freedom to do as she pleases.
- I feel angry at my parents for not recognizing my needs.
- I feel such admiration for my friend because of her self-styled independence.
- I feel I've neglected my musical talent to please adults.

- I feel excited and energized knowing what I know now. I don't have to be the way I have been. Maybe I can begin doing what I want.
- I feel alone because I have nobody to share my secret with.
- I feel sad that I'm doing what I don't like, and I'm alone.

Of course there were many more responses, but these more or less sum up the feelings that the dream evoked.

Symbol Interpretation Stage: The group now took on the symbols and action (or lack thereof) in the dream and projected their own meanings onto them as freely and honestly as they could. In other words, individuals assumed they created these images and interpreted them as symbolic of their own struggles and issues. It was not a question of being right or wrong. Creating a possible reservoir of meanings for the dreamer was the key goal. Very often, the actual dreamer would say, "You know, I would never have thought of so many of these responses myself." Input from the group brought clarity to the dreamer struggling to understand the message. All statements are shared from the *I* position.

- To me, the basement represents the lower self—that part of me that has been programmed with values and attitudes that don't belong to me.
- The basement is a place where I can't get enough breathing room or air, and I can't see the outside world.
- Stacks of paper that need filing represent my missed childhood. Things need to be put in their place, and what I would really like to do is make paper airplanes and fly them around the basement.
- Cynthia is my teacher. My attraction to her fills me with desire to change.
- File cabinets are cut and dried for me. The work I am doing is boring and uncreative.
- A huge stack of papers means there is no end to this for me. I'm stuck where I don't want to be.
- To me, Cynthia is such a free spirit. She wouldn't be doing what I am doing if she didn't want to.
- Cynthia's house is a place of freedom, independence, and

joy. Here I am in the basement, confined to the lowest level, and I don't even contemplate how I'm going to get out. It reminds me of the saying, "In the land of plenty, I'm picking peanuts."

These are just a fraction of the reactions. When people start responding in a group situation, a momentum builds, and members start feeding off each other's ideas. As the process continues, the group gets to deeper and deeper levels of interpretation and understanding.

The Dreamer Takes Over

This dreamer could relate to almost everything that was said. Initially, she never realized the full meaning of the dream until the group began taking the dream on as their own. Her feedback about the process was insightful. She never once felt threatened, because every response came from the first-person perspective, and she was able to hear all this information about herself with an open mind. She was not being accused of anything. If a response was totally off the mark, she was able to just let it go.

She gave more details about her background as people questioned her about her past. To a large degree, childhood responsibilities prevented her from socializing with friends. Carrying this programming to help others into adulthood, she became a social worker so she could continue to rescue and care for others. Suppressing her real love, singing, she practiced alone and never shared this secret with others.

The Task: When it was time to suggest a task for her to perform in relation to what her dream had uncovered, there were many suggestions.

- Invite a few friends over to her house and share with them her secret passion.
- Invite these friends back for a brief rhythm and blues concert, and sing for them.
- There are several clubs with open mikes, so sign up and perform one song. Ask friends to accompany her.

One task suggestion in particular shook the rafters: *I want to hear you sing now in this workshop right in front of all these people.* The whole seminar got behind the request, encouraging her to take a risk and put it all on the line. It took several minutes, but finally she grabbed the mike out of my hand and proceeded to belt out a song. She sang a cappella for a good two minutes, and when she finished the audience gave her a rousing applause. They did it not so much because of her courage but because she had real talent. She had slain her dragon and exited the cave as a heroine. When she finished, she was not the same person. Her face lit up like a neon sign. Transforming fear into courage helped free her creative juices. She said she began to imagine what the power of this experience might mean to her life from this point forward. Until then, her fear had closed down her full potential. To me, it's always a remarkable experience to watch how a brief dream coupled with a group interpretation and a fulfilled group assignment can crack open the cosmic egg.

Learning from My Cancer

The final dream example is one of my own and concerns my cancer experience (first discussed in chapter 4). The reason I chose this dream was that it was a relatively small group and no one volunteered to share a dream in front of the class. People first needed to witness the safety of the environment and how extensive and helpful the group input could be to a dreamer who was willing to take the risk in sharing highly personal material. Selection of this dream demonstrated the complete process of incubating and recalling the dream and then having it interpreted through the group method. My incubation question was very specific. I wanted to know what I had to learn from this illness.

I wrote my incubation question three times on the temple picture steps.

"What is the wisdom my illness is trying to teach me?"

The Dream: I am walking along Hollywood Boulevard on my way to meet with a television producer about a show on dreams. I'm either supposed to be the star of the show or a guest. As I step off a sidewalk onto a street, I realize I am wearing a polyester leisure suit—a maroon jacket and plaid pants. I enter a studio and walk by the producer's large office. When he sees me, he quickly draws the curtains. I can still see a few figures inside involved in a discussion that I cannot make out. The producer looks in my direction and then quickly turns away. In that instant I knew his invitation was all bullshit; I had been hyped up and now realized it was the empty and phony "call me for lunch" moment.

The Question Period: The group wanted to know what was going on in my life before my cancer diagnosis. As mentioned in chapter 4, besides doing my dream seminars and running a successful private practice, I wanted to be the darling dream interpreter of the movie stars. My strongest desire was to eventually have my own television show on dreams. The closest I got was a radio show called "Dream Talk," which lasted six months. People called in, shared their dreams, and I worked on the interpretation. It ended because I wasn't very good at the banter needed to fill the empty spaces between calls. What I needed was a live audience. I sought publicity; I had several feature articles written about my work in major newspapers and had appeared on national television shows in New York, Los Angeles, and Boston. Several opportunities came along, but none of them ever panned out. Apparently my self-esteem was all about self-aggrandizement.

My disease was really talking to me through this dream. How I detested those polyester suits—wrinkle free, but with no style, no substance. I was pursuing a goal for personal glorification, and my inner healer was trying to tell me that my motivation was a synthetic, artificial fiber. The Hollywood producer's invitation was as serious as the phony "Call me at the office, and we'll do lunch" offer one frequently hears in the entertainment industry. An ego time-bomb was ticking, but my conscious mind couldn't hear it.

With this input, the group began processing my dream.

Feelings Stage: The group took on the dream as their own and shared feelings from the *I* perspective. Here are some of the responses.

- I feel so out of style and cheap.
- I feel inappropriate. In fact I feel like a phony.
- I feel a lack of substance in my outer image.
- I feel slighted and disappointed, because I am barking up the wrong tree.

- I feel I've wasted an effort, because I have been deceived.
- I feel misguided by my own desires.
- I feel so cheated, because I chased a pot of gold at the end of the rainbow that didn't exist.
- I feel fraudulent. My dreams went up in smoke.
- I feel so hopeful in the beginning of my dream, but as I proceed to my meeting and get rejected, I feel like a fool.
- I feel optimistic that maybe now I can find my higher values and goals.
- I feel shut out of my dreams.

These are just some of the feelings expressed by the group, and many of them touched me emotionally.

Symbol Interpretation Stage: The group now interpreted the images by projecting their own meanings into the symbols, creating a pool of ideas for me, the dreamer to choose from. Here is an abbreviated list of the interpretations that emerged:

- To me a leisure suit is a synthetic fiber, so there is something not genuine about it.
- Hollywood Boulevard is a site of many broken dreams. Every waiter and waitress is an actor waiting for that big break to stardom.
- A Hollywood movie or TV producer is a real hustler. They can be dishonest, manipulative, and wily. I think I may have been deceiving myself all along with my dreams of being a media star.
- Closing the curtain in my face was like my play had ended. The drama came to a close, and once again my dream came to an end.
- I think I finally need to accept the fact that this path leads to a dead end.
- To me, the closing of the curtain meant a portion of my life had come to an end.
- I personally dislike leisure suits, because they seem so dull and even comical. They are like a make-believe outfit, a pretension, a fake.

The group nailed down the very clear message coming through this dream. I was using my ego to inflate my self-image. Shortly after this dream and my cancer recovery, I substantially reduced my private practice and stopped giving dream seminars, because I realized I was doing it more for me than for the participants. I discontinued the radio show and a short time later went into full retirement for a few years. Eventually, I returned to giving dream seminars with a new perspective, which is described in the epilogue. Sometimes one has to leave something and return to it with a new set of attitudes and values. In my case, I no longer needed to feed my ego and could truly give of myself to help others. When the ego loses its grip, there's a broader sense of freedom and a beginning of wisdom,

So behind my cancer was a most dramatic message: "Stop using the ego to puff up self-image, because it leads nowhere." I was starting to grasp the true nature of myself, and it was about time. The group wanted to give me tasks to help me continue along this newly chartered course. Here are some of their suggestions. Many of them were very humbling but were said in a compassionate way and I sensed the group was able to identify with my struggle.

The Tasks:
- Don't try to be the center of attention.
- Don't fish for compliments.
- Try not to talk too much.
- Don't frequent places that boost your ego, e.g., go to restaurants where the "rich and famous" eat.
- Avoid name-dropping.
- Practice moderation and humility.
- Listen more than you speak, and when you have nothing to say, be quiet.
- Don't practice one-upmanship.

These are all solid suggestions, and I have incorporated many into my life. I've become more conscious of how the ego tends to grab center stage.

We have so many conscious stories that we share, but what really defines us is the motivation behind what we offer in conversation. I'm sure many of you have met people who are always trying to be one step ahead of you. You tell them you have a headache, and they respond with, "Well, I've had brain surgery." You caught a one-hundred-pound tuna, and they caught a five-hundred-pound marlin. You went sailing in a forty-foot yacht to explore the islands off the coast of Georgia, and they searched the Greek Islands in a one-hundred-and-twenty-foot yacht. They take the wind right out of your sails without asking you a question about your experience. One-upmanship is the quintessential ego game. But the stories that come from the unconscious, the stories from inside tell a different tale and expose the motivation.

The Connecting Thread

The group process was immeasurably helpful in stimulating my mind to go deeper and look for the links in my ego-issues chain. There is a continuity in our inner lives that is consistent and persistent. I immediately related this dream to my first big dream, which I described in chapter 1—the need to sacrifice the fork and spoon or feeding of my ego to gain the magical and meaningful stone. My dreaming mind was trying to break down this smaller self so I could become cognizant of a fuller self. In the face of a potentially terminal illness, one often reflects on the past for causes and connections. From this dream, I recognized that my ego-centeredness helped create my past depressions and disappointments. Whatever I was trying to achieve was fueled by my need to impress people with my knowledge and what I could do with it. When I failed, I was racked with feelings of inadequacy and stupidity. I had made it all about me when essentially it needed to be about doing my best to be of service to others.

There comes a point in our psychic lives when we must go beyond the boundaries of what constrains us. A broader self wants to be born at a certain stage in our daily lives, and blocking it could put us in peril. Our psyche is a living, breathing force with its own itinerary and timetable. Like despotic kings, big egos get kicked off their thrones and must learn to be servants of the divine force within them. When I look back, I can see more subtle raps on the door that I didn't want to hear. It's easy to overlook what is important—to not take time to separate the gems from the junk. At times, the path is dimly lit, and the landscape seems unfamiliar. But when the message finally and firmly shows up in the body as a life-threatening illness, hearing aids are turned up to full volume. We may know certain things intellectually, but dreams make us feel it in the gut and shrink us down to just about the right size. Dreams say what they think. They peel the ego disguise right off of us, and what do we discover? Our real self!

To me what is most interesting from this inner experience is that the millions of dollars we rake in, the power we brandish, and the celebrity status we reach measure outer life. In dreams, the script is rewritten because what is success in the outer realm could mean poverty in the inner one. We steer a course in the external world hoping it leads to great success, but the inner sage says we're off course and resets the compass. When the energy that builds the ego is withdrawn, the borders of the larger personality expand. We become much more aware of "higher self" qualities. The soul needs to be nurtured, and if the roles we assign ourselves can't provide this nourishment, the inner source will nudge us toward a regimen that will. We can't go against our true current without paying a big price.

Ways to Encourage Sharing in a Group

Ullman offers some thoughtful ways to encourage sharing in a group:[13]

1. Emphasize that the dreamer is in control of the process from beginning to end. The dreamer decides how much self-disclosure is revealed and if and when to stop the process at any stage if the heat of close examination gets too uncomfortable. When I noticed a strong emotional reaction from the dreamer, I always brought up the option of stopping coupled with a compliment for going this far. Sometimes I would interrupt the process and change the subject so the dreamer could get some breathing room.

2. When a certain intimate issue surfaced, I would always ask the group if they could relate to that and perhaps share a few personal details. It's reassuring to the dreamer to know that other people have a similar problem and learned to deal with it.

3. The group needs to be made aware of and respect the vulnerability of the dreamer.

4. Whenever applicable, I would encourage people to share painful personal experiences associated with their dreams but emphasize that the benefits far outweighed the distress.

This whole process is certainly not what you would call a scientific approach. You never know what is going to come up during dream incubation, and the same uncertainty exists with the group interpretation. Another group could respond in a totally different way. People have to trust that dreams and their interpretation are beneficial—sometimes uncomfortable, but never harmful. For Jung, understanding dream symbols was a matter of great importance that could enhance mental health. It was a natural and complete process, an organic activity devoid of complicated or superimposed theory.

Benefits of Group Dream Interpretation

There are several benefits that arise out of the interpretation process:

1. Anyone concerned about mental health needs to take more personal responsibility for the maintenance of his or her own psychological well-being. The incubation process and the group-interpretation technique present an exceptionally user-friendly medium to accomplish this.
2. No experts are needed for this work, which equalizes participant authority.
3. Confidentiality gives the group a stronger bond and encourages more intimacy.
4. There are so many different responses and contributions offered in a group setting that a wider range of potential insights exceeds what a single person could offer.
5. Having the dreamer in control of the process lessens the possibility of a defensive posture.
6. Lack of commitment to any theoretical position makes group members feel qualified.
7. Each shared dream in the group often contains meaning and guidance for many group members.

When dreamers are confronted with personal truths and are free to accept or reject them, there is a natural response to welcome the truth. A natural quality within every individual recognizes the curative force in truth. Putting all theories aside allows for a great deal of freedom of expression in the group process. The group interpretation is more like play therapy. Most people have played "house" as children where roles are divided. All the kids play their parts and relate to each other, but there is often one rational child who kills the fun by saying things like, "Just because you're wearing the stethoscope doesn't mean you're the *real* doctor." End of game! The statement is right, but it is also wrong. Play can be fun. You don't want to get too rational. Play releases stress, elevates the spirit, expands self-knowledge, connects people to others in a positive way, and stimulates creative thinking. It also can cultivate empathy and respect for the thoughts and feelings of others in a diverse group.

I have done these seminars countless times, and I am always amazed at the initial handicap of people who know too much about dreams. In Los Angeles, I had many mixed seminars of professionals (psychologists, social workers) and lay people (musicians, cartoonists, housewives, lawyers, doctors, nurses, writers, actors, actresses, etc.). The ones who were dream-theory deprived were often the most sensitive and imaginative. They didn't have to think in Freudian or Jungian terms and trusted their intuition, especially those in the creative fields. A belief and confidence in that inner voice enabled them to get somewhere without a roadmap, whereas others educated in dream theory sank like stones whenever a complex dream came up. My revelation in these early seminars was that the key ingredient in helping others understand their dreams was intuition. That is why Ullman's group dream-interpretation process, without fail, produced remarkable results. When groups began trusting the process, they mimicked Sir Isaac Newton who sat under that apple tree mulling over gravity until he eventually came up with the universal law of gravitation. He trusted his hunch.

Intuition

Intuition is instant inner knowing. You don't know how you know or why you know, you just know that you know. Professional athletes know of this. A famous hockey player once said you don't go where the puck is but where it will be. Great athletes *feel* the direction in which they need to go. The best fishermen seem to know where the fish are. Intuition is as natural as breathing. Many people who participated in group dream interpretation had never worked with dreams. By trusting their intuition they were able to offer penetrating insights into complex dreams.

Animals have instincts, and we have intuition, which comes before logic. How often have you thought of someone a moment before the phone rings, and you know who it is? Information just comes to you—trust it.

Writers, composers, scientists, and politicians have all been the beneficiaries of intuition in creative dreaming. The list is impressive: William Yates won the Nobel Prize for literature in 1923. One of his most famous plays, *Catherine ni Houlihan*, came to him in a 1902 dream. No other play by Yates more clearly expressed the cry to break free of English rule. William Blake, one of the greatest creative and mystical artists Britain produced, claims to have been taught his illuminated printing technique by his deceased brother in a dream. Harriet Tubman used her dreams to find safe routes for escaped slaves seeking freedom. She even dreamt that Lincoln freed the slaves a few years before the Emancipation Proclamation. Srinivasa Ramanjuan (1887–1920) was a great mathematical genius of India. Many of his formulas led to new directions in research in continued fractions and infinite series. He claimed that a Hindu goddess would appear in his dreams and offer mathematical formulae, which he could verify upon awakening.

Giuseppi Tartini, an eighteenth-century composer dreamt of the devil playing an astonishing music piece on his violin. It became the basis for his famous violin sonata, "The Devil's Trill."

Dr. Marcia Emery's *Intuition Workbook* is an excellent guide to unlocking and trusting intuition. She says we are of two minds that differ dramatically. The logical mind is analytical, rational, and highly verbal. This aspect of our minds instructs through the use of words and sentences. Our intuitive mind transcends rational analysis and awakens us nonverbally. This part of our mind is highly creative and instructs us visually through images, symbols, and metaphors.

Dr. Emery interviewed many business people to see how they

experienced intuition. According to her interviews, intuition could be defined as:

- Knowing without conscious awareness.
- Arriving at decisions without any sequential logical steps.
- Random thoughts and hunches that smoothly move to conviction.
- Knowing what to do in any situation without having to think about it.
- A "gut feeling" that allows one to make decisions that contradict the facts.
- A subconscious knowing without cognitive analysis.[14]

I asked members of dream groups how they experience their intuition. Some have experienced it through the body—a knot in the stomach, a pressure in the head, warmth in the heart. Others have experienced it through feelings—mistrust around a new person or situation, empathy for what another is going through without being told. Intuition can be premonitions that come in the form of an ominous feeling about a future event. It can also give you the sensation of being connected to the universe, that life is bigger than you, and that you're an integral part of the whole. Intuition doesn't figure things out. It presents you with things already figured out.

The next chapter will examine the full range of the dreaming mind. Some of the experiences that people have shared about their dreams can leave you breathless at the limitless extent of the dreaming mind's capability. Not just famous individuals have this potential; average people with a little guidance can dramatically expand the capabilities of their minds.

Chapter 7

DREAMS HAVE NO BOUNDARIES:
ALL DOORS OPEN TO THE DREAMING MIND

The soul in sleep gives proof of its divine nature.

Cicero

A fundamental spiritual secret is progressively being revealed at both the material and metaphysical levels. At one time, the universe was seen as a great machine, but today many see it as a great mind that has no boundaries, is infinite, and contains all time and all space. We can see this growing inner awareness manifest in the material world as "globalization." Our universe is shrinking thanks to the Internet, cell phones that can reach around the world, and high-speed aircraft that take us rapidly any place on the globe. The world is becoming one. Walls are coming down. This has always been true for our inner world but is now manifesting in the external world.

Consciousness May Have No Limits

In 1929, Edwin Hubble, an astronomer at Cal Tech, made the brilliant and revolutionary discovery that the universe is not static but expanding. Jung stated that perhaps consciousness has no limits and may be capable of indefinite extension. When we look at history and science, we see that every boundary that existed has ultimately vanished. The Berlin Wall came down, just as the impediment to unleashing the power of the atom disappeared. We are starting to realize we have unlimited creative power that will inexorably revolutionize our consciousness. All of us see things we never thought would be possible—and it's only the beginning. We are diving beneath the little waves on the surface to an immense kingdom within us. Edgar Cayce's model of the mind and consciousness is a good place to get an idea of the larger picture. His work provides a foundation for unraveling dreams.

Edgar Cayce's Model of the Mind

Henry Reed's *Edgar Cayce on Mysteries of the Mind*[1] and Mark Thurston's *How to Interpret Your Dream*[2] give unique and thorough explanations of Cayce's model of the mind and its relationship to dreams. The following descriptions and diagrams are a partial summary of their interpretations of Cayce's readings on the nature of the mind and dreams.

Cayce, known as "The Sleeping Prophet," had remarkable abilities. By entering a self-induced trance, he was able to tap into a superconscious mind of infinite knowing. He could sleep on a textbook as a child and remember its complete contents without ever reading the book. As he matured, he could diagnose the illnesses of complete strangers down to the minutest details and then locate a medicine in a distant pharmacy that would help heal a patient. He claimed we all have this ability because all knowledge is within. Whatever has been known throughout history as well as the seeds of all that will be known is within our own mind.

The One Mind

Figure 1 gives a visual rendering of Cayce's idea that the mind is as infinite as the universe. The universe is a great mind, and we all share it by being connected to it. Representing the entire mind is the total star with each offshoot depicting an individual. That's roughly 6.5 billion connections. To individuals, it may feel like the mind is just what happens inside the skull. But according to Cayce's model, the mind is a reality in itself. It's a living actuality that is not

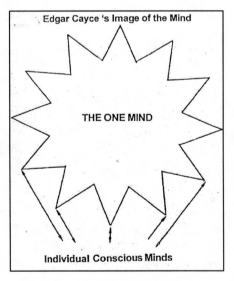

Figure 1

just positioned in the brain but is unattached to a physical body. Like the universe that continues to expand and evolve, this mind never dries up but seems to have unlimited creative resources.

This One Mind is like the air we breathe. Air does not just exist in our lungs; it is everywhere and has an independent existence. The mind is outside the limits of an individual's perception and exists independently of the human brain. We are much bigger than our physical dimensions. As discussed in chapter 3, dreams attempt to communicate that we are beings of cosmic significance and our lives have a sacred meaning in a creative universe. Our task is to search for that abundant and immeasurable intelligence.

The Conscious Mind

The conscious mind is a miniscule portion of the total mind. When compared to the unconscious mind, it is like an island whose main body is below the surface of a vast ocean (figure 2). Conscious mind is the level of mind that humans are most familiar with because logic is the ruling force coupled with the capabilities of concentrated focusing on specifics, ignoring distracting surroundings, and the ability of sense discrimination. Like a flashlight, the conscious mind can illuminate a limited locale and is a great and remarkable evolutionary step, but as you can see in figure 1, conscious minds seem disconnected and distant from other conscious minds. This separation between people and between the conscious mind and its foundation is the invention of the conscious mind. Although we have achieved great benefits from this portion of our mind, its main misfortune has been its separation from the One Mind. This in turn has led to hatreds, rivalries, and wars. To overcome this illusion, we must surmount these false notions of the

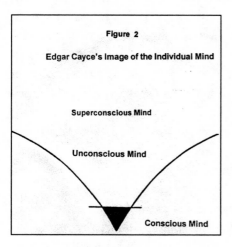

Figure 2

179

conscious mind. For the mind to express its full creative capacity, it needs to be introduced to the giant on whose shoulders it rests—the unconscious and superconscious, which together comprise the transpersonal mind.

The Subconscious Mind

Fortunately for us, a huge portion of the mind compensates for the conscious mind's tendency to generate feelings of separateness. Freud's concept of a dark interior laden with evil secrets and tendencies has been superseded by a new illumination. Jung and Cayce's ideas about the mind's deep recesses indicate a great ally with a mind-boggling storehouse of natural resources awaiting discovery. The subconscious mind has a diffuse but greater awareness of its total surroundings. In a sense, it has a built-in radar screen. Its hypersensitivity allows it to pick up data the conscious mind misses, even when we are oblivious to our environment. Not only are the events detected, they are also interpreted. So while the conscious mind remains unaware, the subconscious is able to analyze surroundings and determine their significance. We may be told we have five senses, but the subconscious adds the sixth sense, a psychic perception. Its sensitivity is unbounded. It records a reaction even when someone is just thinking about another person. Nothing escapes its memory, even those experiences buried in the distant past. It has a symbolic logic, and it can think creatively, solve complex problems, and employ telepathic powers. And it can do all of this outside conscious awareness.

Jung was the first to introduce the idea of a two-level unconscious. The first level is a personal unconscious or reservoir of personal memories and experiences. The second is the collective unconscious, which is an archaic mold of original images and patterns that are inherent in all humanity. Like Jung, Cayce depicts a subconscious mind that includes a personal unconscious and a number of levels beyond that are universal and reachable by all.

The Superconscious Mind

Beyond the subconscious mind is the *superconscious mind* (see figure 3, following page). When we connect with this level of mind, we experience the oneness of all life. Qualities of oneness and wholeness are granted to every human being at birth. The paradigm of the superconscious mind is our potential, and we must work toward realizing its capability. Most of the world's religious traditions have promoted various exercises to help people awaken from the mistaken notion that they are separated from the One Mind.

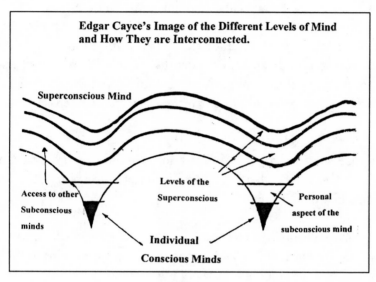

Figure 3

These ideas obviously confirm that each and every individual has deep roots that project into the universal mind. From these roots sprout ancient symbols that arise spontaneously in the psyche representing ideas never consciously thought. Education and experience have little or no influence in their production. They are instinctual to the mind itself and spontaneously create ancient symbols that help diagnose our personal problems. Nature has been kind to us by providing these communication lines to the source of this great wisdom whose truths govern all attributes of existence.

According to Cayce, telepathic abilities reside in the subconscious, whereas intuition and clairvoyance operate through the superconscious mind. These stretch the mind far beyond normal conscious functioning. Today we call it the transpersonal mind, and it goes far beyond ego consciousness, where each mind is distinct from the rest. As we experience the subconscious and superconscious, the mind expands. In the process, the ego is not destroyed but is transcended. We can even experience that at the subconscious level when awake. Many people who are in long-term close relationships have experienced thought sharing: one person thinks of something, and then the other starts talking about the same subject. Or a therapist hasn't seen a client in a few years, and for some unknown reason can't stop thinking about that client. The next day the client calls for an appointment. Even more dramatic telepathy, intuition, and clairvoyance come out in dreams. In the depths of the mind of every person, a divine mind exists, a mind that is unlimited and penetrates all life. This great transpersonal mind is most active in the sleep state.

A Mouse in a Ramshackle Building

Alice shared that her youngest son was hiking the West Coast Trail on Vancouver Island between his junior and senior year in high school. Her dream follows:

My son is hiking in the wilderness and discovers an old wooden ramshackle building and sleeps there for the evening. A little mouse scurries around throughout the evening.

When he arrived home and shared his experience, he related the exact same happening right down to the little mouse. Boundaries are transcended in dreams. This is not an uncommon experience between people who have a strong emotional bond. One could even say the mother had a built-in video recorder and television set that enabled her to view her son hundreds of miles away. The mind is unimaginably capacious, and experiences like this dream show us time and space dimensions wane in the realm of the psyche. Borders exist in the conscious mind, but the dreaming mind is beyond measurement. Dreaming minds can instantly travel to places the body cannot.

Abraham Lincoln Sees the Future in Dreams

President Abraham Lincoln recounted the following dream to his wife a few days before his assassination:

About ten days ago I retired very late because I had been waiting for important dispatches from the front. Having been in bed a short time, I soon began to dream. There seemed to be a death-like stillness about me. Then I heard the subdued sobs of many people weeping. I left my bed and wandered downstairs. I went from room to room but the mourners were invisible. No living person was sighted, but the same mournful sounds met me as I passed along. All the rooms had light, so all objects were familiar to me; but where were all the intensely grieving people?

Alarmed and puzzled, I wondered what this could all mean. Determined to find the cause, I continued on until I arrived at the East Room where I was met with a sickening surprise. Before me was a covered casket on which rested a corpse wrapped in funeral garments. Soldiers acting as guards surrounded the coffin. There was a throng of people and many were weeping pitifully.

"Who is dead in the White House?" I asked one of the soldiers. "Why the President" was his response; "he was killed by an assassin!"[3]

Lincoln assigned great authority to his dreams. On the morning of that tragic day, he shared with General Grant that he expected important news from General Sherman that would be of vital national significance. Grant wanted to know why he felt that way. Lincoln replied that since the war had started, he had a dream before every critical occurrence of national concern that he believed foretold events to come.

We don't know why dreams like this happen to some people and not to others. Of course, we all have the capability, but maybe these types of dreams happen more frequently to those with open minds; and when they do happen, they are taken seriously. As mysterious as it sounds, we can know what will happen before it happens, because the past, present, and future exist in the timeless seam of our psyche. These dream happenings are created before the event and come fully formed out of somewhere. We tend to know future events without knowing the details leading to them. Science may view foreknowledge as an old wives' tale, but when people experience these dreams, they fortunately disregard what science has to say and pay attention to their own instincts. But we have to be careful here, because this part of our mind forecasts the future in a few distinct ways.

The Future Is Not Etched in Stone

Sometimes (which was not the case for Lincoln) dreams offer speculation and warning rather than prophecy. As such, they are able to foresee the outcome of a series of events whose final conclusion is not etched in stone. When I was doing couples counseling, one husband had a recurring dream that his wife was running off with another man, and he was running after her beseeching her to stay with him. He actually woke her up after these dreams and asked her if she was having an affair, and she said no. In reality, *he* was the one having an affair, and finally after two months of these dreams, he told his wife he was in love with another woman and was moving out. He left and pursued the other relationship for nine more months until it ended. At that point, he wanted to return home. Meanwhile, his wife had started dating and had very strong feelings for a new man in her life. The husband was now pursuing his wife, pleading with her to give the marriage a chance and begging her to give up her new relationship. His dream had forecast the possible outcome of a sequence of events. This is similar to what happens in a national election. When only 5 percent of the votes are cast, complex computer programs can analyze statistical data and project the possible outcome with surprising accuracy. I have had many clients who had warning dreams about chosen paths and logical outcomes: if they continued to take drugs, their lives would be endangered; if they continued to steal from their companies, they could end up in jail; if they continued to ignore their children, they could end up strangers. The future is not fixed: your choices affect whether a dream's forecast will or will not manifest in the future. Watching over us like a concerned parent the unconscious mind shifts the wind to push us off on a new course. We get a sneak preview of what's ahead if the air stream stays steady and the rudder holds firm. It's the choice of the conscious mind to avoid disaster.

Clairvoyance of the Holocaust

Many dramatic and clairvoyant dreams were collected during the ugly reign of Hitler. In the *Third Reich of Dreams, The Nightmares of a Nation 1933–1939*, Charlotte Beradt collected an extraordinary body of dreams from people living under the Third Reich. No special interpretation skills were necessary to decipher their meanings, because their messages were unmistakably clear. What was apparent here was that beneath the world of logic and reason lay a buried world of horror that dreams illuminated. The collection, dreamt by Jews and non-Jews, demonstrates how a brutal totalitarian regime destroyed the foundation upon which life rested. Themes repeated in the dreams included loss of identity and continuity, depersonalization, helplessness, homelessness, constant threat, and paralyzing fear. These dreams could foresee the future consequences and forecast that violent dramas were to unfold. One of the most chilling of prophetic dreams was that of a twenty-two-year-old girl whose delicately formed almost Semitic nose dominated her face in such a manner that she concluded everyone would imagine her to be Jewish. Consequently her dreams were permeated with noses and identity papers:

> I went to the Bureau of Verification of Aryan Descent (which did not exist under this name) and presented documentation certifying my grandmother's ancestry, which I had acquired with considerable effort. The official looked just like a marble statue and was sitting behind a low stone wall. He reached over the wall, grabbed my paper, tore it to bits, and proceeded to throw the pieces into an oven that was built into the wall. And he remarked, "Think you're still pure Aryan now?"[4]

One can see from this dream the contempt for anyone who did not have the "right" heritage. We cannot help but notice how analogous this is to the mass murders and incineration of millions that were just around the corner.

A Dream Ushers In a Nobel Prize

How nerve transmission occurred was a mystery until Otto Loewi (1873–1961), a German-born physiologist, had a recurring dream that solved the problem. He thought there might be a chemical transmission rather than an electrical one, which was the general position of science, but he was unsure how to affirm his conviction. He pushed it out of his mind until seventeen years later when a dream prodded him to investigate it again.

> The night before Easter Sunday of that year, I awoke, turned on the light, and jotted down a few notes on a tiny slip of paper. Then I fell asleep again. It occurred to me at 6 o'clock in the morning that during the night I had written down something most important, but I was unable to decipher the scrawl. The next night, at 3 o'clock, the idea returned again in a dream. It was the design of an experiment to determine whether or not the hypothesis of chemical transmission that I had uttered 17 years ago was correct. I got up immediately, went to the laboratory, and performed a single experiment on a frog's heart according to the nocturnal design.[5]

It was a simple but elegant experiment utilizing the hearts of two frogs. The results demonstrated that chemical substances modify the heart function. Loewi was awarded the Nobel Prize in 1936, sixteen years after a dream that helped unlock one of the secrets of life. The unconscious and superconscious produce dreams and resolve issues that seem impenetrable. Our minds are online twenty-four hours a day, and with the conscious mind asleep, great depths can be reached because there are fewer distractions and easier access to limitless sources of creative information. August von Kekule revolutionized organic chemistry when his dream presented the molecular ring structure of aromatic carbon compounds. Dreams revealed to Nobel Prize–winner Niels Bohr that electrons in an atom follow specific paths.[6] Dmitri Mendeleyev, a Russian chemist credits the discovery of the periodic table of elements to his dreams.[7] Handel credited his dreams for the musical insights he needed to produce portions of his *Messiah*. And as mentioned in a previous chapter, Albert Einstein claimed that during adolescence, a dazzling dream in which he rode a sled at the speed of light causing the heavens to bend and stars to distort was the basis for his theory of relativity.[8]

You Will Find Your Answer in Kansas

This following experience is an extraordinary example of the range of our dreaming mind. The subconscious responds to our needs and requests. Its orbit has magnificent breadth and depth; no subject is exempt from its scrutiny.

One of my clients had been employed in a responsible executive position for a company that was sold. His severance arrangement enriched him with a large sum of money and opportunities to develop his own investment business; but his real passion was inventing. I introduced him to dream incubation, and he responded in a most dramatic fashion. He had been working on an invention that needed a small customized motor that would run reliably, consistently, and quietly. Unable to perfect it himself, he sought help from a number of West Coast companies, none of which could produce it to his specifications. So he went to his dreams and got a surprising response.

> I am in a coffee shop. As I eat my hamburger, a strange man sits down at my table, looks me in the eye, and says, "You will find what you need in Kansas." I know he is referring to my invention.

As he reflected on the dream, he realized that he didn't know anyone in Kansas but had a business acquaintance in Kansas City, Missouri. He called this man and asked him if he would look in the yellow pages to see if any small motor manufacturers were listed in the area. There were none in Missouri and just one listed in Princeton, Kansas. He called, and, of course, it was just the company he needed. He faxed his specifications, and the perfect prototype was built.

Our unconscious mind has access to a National Yellow Pages telephone book. Of course the rational explanation would be that he heard about this company but had forgotten this information, and his unconscious mind reminded him. Logical explanations cheapen the experience. He had never been to Kansas, but apparently Kansas had come to him.

Dreams Are on Both Sides of the Law

Tommy Glenn Carmichael was a master inventor who designed cheating tools that bilked casino slot machines out of millions of dollars. His career began in 1980 when a friend introduced him to the inner workings of a mechanical slot machine and a popular cheating tool. A five-cent machine was his first victim. After he applied his tool to it, he walked away with $35 in nickels bulging in his pocket. The American Dream was in his grasp until the introduction of high-tech slot machines. Old machines that relied on a combination of electricity and physics were replaced with computer games. The complicated new machines made his chosen task more difficult. Undeterred, Carmichael purchased one of the newest versions and labored for six months, attempting to exploit it for profit. A dream solved his problem:

> I walk into a casino and see myself playing a slot machine. My cheating device is working spectacularly. Upon close examination, it is a thin piece of metal shaped like a wedge that has a piece of piano wire tied to it that slides into the machine. I awaken excitedly and know how to build it.

He eventually built the device known as the "slider" out of spring steel and guitar wire. By inserting the slider through the payout chute, Carmichael could trip a micro switch, which emptied the container holding the payload. Carmichael's dream became a reality to the tune of $1000 per hour. His lifestyle changed dramatically and included expensive Jaguars, glamorous cruises, and two house purchases. However, his luck eventually ran out, and he served jail time coupled with three years of probation plus banishment from gambling casinos.

Who knows what circumstances led Carmichael into his crime career? He found a way to manifest the all-too-human tendency to want something for very little effort. He had questionable moral integrity. His unconscious mind reflected his conscious attitude, which was focused on the rewards of illegal activity. The face one turns to the unconscious is often the face it turns back. If the conscious mind's moral system is unprincipled, the unconscious mind lacks moral intention. If his dream contributed to his illegal and immoral goal, there is no reason to assume its intention was otherwise. This dream shows the inner truth and reality of the dreamer. It doesn't say what ought to be or what ought not to be. We have to draw our own conclusions.

A Dream Helped Win World War II

One of the main purposes of the dreaming mind is to help the conscious mind solve problems. When we sleep we have a creative computer that's online that can predict and combine elements into new and original configurations. What seems too dense to fathom consciously can often be penetrated and unraveled when we sleep and dream. The dreaming mind can leave conventional logic behind in search of original paths. We think when we sleep, but in a very different psychological and physiological state. I am not intimating that all dreams lead to poignant outcomes. But because of their unique capacity, they can enhance and improve on what the conscious mind has done in the waking state.

The case of David Parkinson clearly demonstrates the power of dreams to shape history and create pragmatic technology. In 1940, Parkinson was a twenty-nine-year-old engineer who was working on a potentiometer (an instrument for measuring electromotive forces) as an employee for Bell Telephone Laboratory in New York. The device was similar to a lie detector test in that a pen was used to register voltage on a sheet of paper. His work was not connected to a military project. Something, perhaps world events, stimulated him to dream the following:

I found my-self in an anti-aircraft gun crew. I don't know how I got there—I was just there. The men were Dutch or Belgian, by their uniforms, and their helmets were German, French, or English. A gun fired occasionally. The impressive thing was that every shot it

189

fired brought down an airplane. After three or four shots, one of the men beckoned me to come and take a closer look at the gun. When I drew near, he pointed to the exposed end of the left pivot. Mounted there was the control potentiometer of my level recorder. There was no mistaking it—it was the identical item.

He discussed the dream with his boss, who was working on an amplifier that could add and subtract electricity. Their combined effort produced an analog computer to accurately perform mathematical calculations to gauge movement and position of flying airplanes. Bell Lab executives contacted U.S. Army officials, who were fascinated with the idea of replacing complicated slow-acting mechanical predictors used to pinpoint aerial targets. First production models were named the M-9 and were introduced into combat in 1943. Not every shot brought down a German bomber, but its main accomplishment was lowering the number of shells fired per kill from thousands to one hundred—a remarkable ratio. August of 1944 saw the weapon destroy eighty-nine of ninety-one German V-1 rockets launched from Belgium. Developed from his dream, Parkinson's weapon strengthened Great Britain's air defenses against the German Luftwaffe and aided in the eventual defeat of Adolph Hitler.[9]

We Are Drawn to the Future

As mentioned earlier, dreams are at least one step ahead of us. It seems that all life-sustaining or life-giving operations progress in a forward direction. Seeds germinate, expand, grow roots, sprout leaves, and bear vegetables and fruits. All life seems to be pulled forward by some inner blueprint or spirit toward its impending completeness. The subconscious contains the faculty of future envisioning and sees things laid out endlessly. Parkinson's dream is a great mystery and deserves the challenge of an earnest explanation, not a casual dismissal as mere chance.

Many wise people from scientific fields trust their dreams to help them make breakthroughs when they are stuck. Floyd Ragsdale, an engineer at DuPont, dreamt how to repair a Kevlar machine that produced material for bulletproof vests used in the Gulf War. The breakdown was costing the company $700 a minute. Ragsdale not only located the problem, he dreamt the solution that saved many American lives and several million dollars for the company.[10]

From a dream in 1782, William Watts, a British plumber, invented the modern method for producing buckshot.[11] Elias Howe perfected the sewing machine by dreaming an accurate design for the needles. In the early 1990s, Alan Huang, head of optical computing at Bell Laboratories, had a dream that solved the complex problem of using optical laser circuits in place of conventional circuitry that led to the development of laser computers. Indeed, some physicists have claimed to seek a resolution dream whenever they are stuck on a problem.[12]

Many cultures believe dreams have powers beyond the conscious mind. Anjali Hazarika, of India's National Petroleum Management Programme, cultivates corporate creativity by conducting dream workshops for oil-company personnel, a course unthinkable for a U.S. firm. Participants in these courses seek solutions for both personal and objective problems.[13]

We Are Also Drawn to the Past

This following example is a remarkable event that demonstrates the ability of the dreaming mind's capacity to explore the deepest reaches of our universal Internet for every subject imaginable. There are no limits to what it can track down.

The dream involved the Edgar Cayce readings and occurred in 1977, more than thirty years after Cayce's death. A middle-aged New Zealand woman experienced symptoms of dizziness and fainting spells, pains in her side, and discomfort with her kidneys, bladder, and liver. Unable to diagnose the causes of her complaints, a physician treated her for low blood sugar and a disparity between red and white blood cells. The symptoms remained constant, and she felt wretched. A friend convinced her to pray for guidance. She did and in a short time had the following guidance dream:

> I see myself looking at one of Edgar Cayce's readings and can clearly see that the case history number is 1880.

She related the experience to her friend who wrote the Association for Research and Enlightenment for a copy of the reading on case

1880. Upon reviewing the material, she was astonished to discover that the case, which took place in 1939, dealt with someone who complained about the same symptoms she was having. Cayce's diagnosis outlined mercury poisoning as the cause. He also delineated a treatment program. The woman contacted her mother and asked if she had been exposed to mercury as a child. Her mother told her that as a child, she had bitten off the end of a thermometer and swallowed the contents. The dreamer asked her doctor to test her for mercury, and when he refused she went to another whose test proved positive. She then started following the Cayce regimen and was symptom free in a few months.[14] The woman was familiar with some of the Cayce readings, which totaled in excess of 14,000. The impressive aspect of her experience rests in the fact that she was directed to the specific case relating to her condition.

Great Political Dreams

Throughout history, many dreams have been recorded that influenced major events. In fact, some very famous leaders have regarded their dreams to be as real as their thoughts in waking life. These dreamers considered the dreams commands from a higher source to do something significant. Napoleon, on the night before the battle of Waterloo dreamt twice that a black cat ran from one army to another, and that his army was demolished. He ignored the dream and lost decisively. Dr. Mossadegh, the Prime Minister of Iran in 1951, had a dream encouraging him to nationalize the oil industry. In the summer of 1950, his doctor prescribed an extended period of rest because of his deteriorating health state. He dreamt one night of a person emanating a bright light who said to him: "This is not a time for rest, arise and break the chains of the people of Iran." Despite his exhaustion, he worked with the Iranian Oil Commission, which eventually adopted the principle of nationalization.[15] President Lyndon Johnson had several dreams in which he found himself paralyzed and helpless to alter his condition. In one dream he found himself swimming in circles unable to get to shore. These dreams reflected the bewildering situation that was the Vietnam War and made a major contribution to his decision not to seek another term.[16]

Gandhi Heals a Nation

In 1919, Great Britain controlled India and passed laws that did away with juries and even trials. This resulted in chaos and civil unrest throughout India. Burning, ransacking, and insurrection were daily occurrences. Gandhi pleaded for moderation at mass gatherings but was drowned out by inflamed crowds. Powerless to push forward his agenda of nonviolence, he withdrew to a friend's home to fast and pray for answers. Several days passed before he awoke from what he considered to be a prophetic dream.

Gandhi saw all the people of India suspending their usual business activities for a complete day. Opposing religious factions—Hindus, Sikhs, Muslims, Jains, Buddhists, and Parsi—had ignored their own sacred festivals to participate in this mass protest and pray together. It was a strike involving a complete shutdown of workplaces and shops, a form of civil disobedience (*hartal*) that Gandhi instituted as an anti-British movement.

Gandhi believed this was a directive from a higher source and beseeched the Indian Congress to notify all religious sects to practice *hartal* immediately. His own party scoffed at the idea, but Gandhi persevered and wrote letters to religious leaders throughout India, sharing his dream and summoning them to assemble under a non-sectarian standard. Most of them came and gathered together for impressive prayer rituals. Violence was reduced, and the opposing factions joined as one voice. Britain's colonial administration became powerless and was forced to repeal the despised laws and restore to Indians the rights of British citizens.[17]

Time Boundaries Have Permeable Walls in Dreams

When it comes to time, dreams seem not to be subjected to the chronological constraints of the waking world. Past, present, and future have illusive qualities in the dream state, and it is not uncommon for information to come right at us from the future. Even Einstein believed the distinction between past, present, and future was a persistent illusion. Perhaps it will be left to science to explain how this dream mechanism works, but until then, dreamers will have to evaluate these experiences in a personal way without the approval of science.

Certain dreams alert the conscious mind to danger, and sometimes we have the opportunity to take a different course of action or at least prepare ourselves for the jolt. Precognitive dreams may not agree with outer events in every detail. A mixture of the symbolic with the literal can be present. So the question, which is not easily answered, is: how can we determine the symbolic from the psychic? Before answering that, I'd like to share a prophetic dream that was literal but not detail specific. The story was a feature article in the *Syracuse Herald Journal.*

A four-year-old boy climbed out of bed in the early morning, woke his mother, and told her she had killed him in a dream. It was the first nightmare he had ever told her. Weeks later, on August 16, the mother accidentally backed her vehicle into her son. Two weeks later, he died in the intensive care unit of University Hospital in Syracuse.[18]

One of the major problems of precognitive dreams is that they are not carbon-copy reproductions of the actual event—elements get obscured. If the boy's description of the dream had included exact details, perhaps the mother would have been more vigilant day in and day out. When a dream seems to foretell a negative event, it may be wise to trust your instincts and take precautions.

Identifying ESP in Dreams

Was the mother a careless driver? Did his unconscious pick up the danger? It's hard to answer these questions with any certainty, but it is best to remain on the side of extreme caution. My original question was: how does one differentiate the psychic from the symbolic? How do we know the headlines of our inner newspapers are accurate before the fact? Mark Thurston claims many of our dreams have some degree of psychic information. ESP is an attribute of the soul itself, so we all have the potential to access it. In sleep and dreams, we edge closer to soul connection. Cayce emphasized the concept of oneness that allows us to harmonize with the superconscious mind and subsequently have access to original information and pending future events. It seems that all life is interconnected, because our universe is composed of essentially one energy.

Thurston suggests a threefold approach to help identify literal dream elements.

1. Accept the idea that dreams contain elements of ESP. People with open minds who believe in the reality of psychic ability do better on ESP tests than those who don't. When dreams that occurred in the past are examined with an open mind, it is not uncommon to find they frequently pointed to future events.

2. If you think and feel a dream is psychic, try to work out a practical way to apply the message. Observe the results carefully to help uncover your particular style of psychic dreaming. If an application is impossible, then look at the dream from another angle.

3. Literal dreams have common elements. Imagery is usually acute, not vague, and color memory is generally recollected. Symbolism appears normal, so people, places, and things are realistic as are their interactions. Events flow naturally with scenes having their own paced sequences. Any feelings of extreme significance in the dream, especially if it is a sense of urgency, could indicate a literal dream. If the dream is a favorable one that occurs before or after you have taken a new direction and you awaken happy, you probably have chosen the right path. If it's negative and you awaken with doubt, it may be a warning that a negative result is around the corner. By keeping a dream diary and faithfully recording all dreams, you can begin to pinpoint the personal signs and symbols that characterize your ESP.[19]

Here is a dream about ESP and gambling that is quite striking, because it accurately fits Mark Thurston's description. This experience is unique since it happened in a one-day seminar when we did the dream incubation in the morning. In a two-day seminar, we do the incubation late in the evening as the last activity before going to bed. Following are the exact words of the dreamer, who wrote me an e-mail soon after the seminar:

A Dream Hit the Jackpot

Hello! I wanted to thank you, first of all, for coming to St. Louis to speak about dreams. I attended the conference, learned a lot, and thoroughly enjoyed it. I don't know if you remember me or not, but when you did the dream induction and asked if anyone had actually fallen asleep and dreamt during that time, I was one of those people. My dream was that I went to Harrah's Casino with my mom and that she won a large jackpot. I walked around to the machine across from hers, and I also won a smaller jackpot myself. You suggested that some dreams are prophetic or literal, and so I figured what the heck! I'll call my mom and see if she's free after the conference. She was. We went to Harrah's and although the slot machines were in a different place than in my dream, we sat down side by side. She immediately hit a jackpot for $4150, and a few minutes later, I hit one for $600! Everyone at work said I should e-mail you to let you know. Wow! I was impressed! (I was also thankful that I had relayed our conversation to my colleagues during the lunch break so the next day when I came into the office with my news, they knew I wasn't making my dream up.) Just thought I would pass that along…

I wish I knew the secret of how this dreamer created a money-making dream. Sometimes the universe wants to give you a gift, and it's best to just accept it. She was not a gambler, nor was her mother. That experience has happened to a few of my clients in other forms of betting. A woman who had never been to the racetrack had a dream in which she was given the name of a horse that was going to win a race the next day. She called a friend to take her to the track, and the dream was accurate. There are many mysteries we have to live with.

Precognitive dreams describing future winners at the racetrack can be quite profitable, and many dreams of this sort have been recorded, but few have been as notable or as well validated as those of John Godley. On Friday, March 8, 1946, Godley, a student at Balliol College, Oxford, dreamt about reading the horse-race results in Saturday's newspaper, which had not been published yet. The names of two winners jumped out at him, and of course, the next day he bet on them and won. These periodic dreams went on for ten years. Fame came to him when newspapers from all over the world published his story. His remarkable case is supported by numerous testimonials. Many of his predictions were shared with his fellow students before the races had started. At least one was written down, witnessed, and sealed away. His largest winner was at the Grand National and went off at 18-1. He did not have a clue about why he was gifted this way, nor do others who share his capabilities.[20] Nature seems to bestow ESP gifts in specific areas on certain people. Why that happens is a mystery. What is important is that the average person can paranormally get a sneak preview of future events. A person may dream that a strange man dressed in a most outlandish suit coughs five times at an adjacent table in his favorite Italian restaurant. The next evening that man in that peculiar suit performs that exact insignificant event in his preferred eating-place. Information presented in this paranormal event has little importance beyond provoking the dreamer's interest in the possibility of foreseeing future events that could be of great value. Rational explanations for ESP events do not sufficiently explain how our subconscious mind can conceive of time as not only "now" but as somehow existing ahead of us.

Stock-market investing can be a challenging area for which to try to program dreams. An intriguing book written by Walt Stover, *Dreams—My Lamp unto the Darkness*, gives methods and cautionary guidelines for market investing. He also conducts a Precognitive Stock Market Dream Group, which fosters the use of intuitive material (dreams, meditations, visions, etc.) for the purpose of arriving at individual financial planning decisions. They can be located online at http://www.stockdreams.org.

Stover had been investing for years with disappointing results until he attended a lecture on dreams at the Association of Enlightenment in Virginia Beach at a 1983 conference. Even after several successful dreams, he still remained cautious until the 1990s when he started hitting pay dirt. Here are a few examples:

Stover read an investment magazine that recommended purchasing Johnstown America, a company that makes railroad cars. Several days after reading the article, he had the following dream:

I see a little railroad that starts up at the bottom of a steep hill. It keeps going up and up until it vanishes over the hill with the number twenty on it.

Taking this dream experience as a positive omen, he purchased the stock for $3.50 and sold it twenty months later for $22 per share. As the dream had indicated, the company literally vanished from trading when it was bought out and became a private company. For several years, it was delisted from trading.

His favorite dream in 2002 involved Corning Corporation and brought a six-figure gain:

> I see a circus performer ride into the ring on a unicycle. He rides around the ring several times with the ticker-tape signal GLM (Corning Corp.) emblazoned on the front of his shirt. On his back is a sign showing the current stock price at $2.50. As he rides around the ring, the unicycle seat keeps getting higher, and the price sign on his back increases to $5, then $7, then $10, $15, and eventually to $20.

He purchased the stock at $1.85, and the increases in the dream occurred as predicted. Four years later he sold out at $22 a share, which meant a handsome profit for him.[21]

The Whole Stock Market Opens Up

Edgar Cayce was a staunch believer in the power of dreams offering financial guidance. In fact, he thought a person could train himself in the art of pinpointing future financial conditions. He worked with a stockbroker who had advanced psychic capacities and encouraged him to further develop his ESP talent. Cayce assured the broker that great results would follow if he applied himself in the service of others, maintained his spirituality, and took care of family responsibilities. The stockbroker followed Cayce's suggestions and became a wealthy man. His forecasting abilities in dreams reached the level where the whole market opened up to him so he could ask any question about individual stocks or market trends and receive accurate answers. Dreams became his primary source of information about stocks.[22] Many wealthy people came to Cayce to get even richer, but his main criterion for guiding them in investment and monetary advice was their enthusiasm for serving others. Cayce's vision had no boundaries as proved by his consistent ability to see intricate particulars that influenced the financial world. He emphasized that the boundaries that limit the conscious mind seem to dissolve in the dreaming mind. The following dream is a prime example:

> An unfamiliar man is trying to sell me a radio. Someone then puts poison on the doorknob of my office door and urges me to come and touch it. I am very frightened, especially when he tries forcing me to touch the poisoned doorknob. I awaken in a cold sweat.

The sleeping Cayce said that a deal in radio stocks would be offered to the dreamer. The proposition appeared wonderful, but the poison on the doorknob was a severe warning about the negative conditions that would enter into the investment. Cayce's final statement was not to invest in radio stocks for the next sixteen to twenty days![23] Here we see how prospective dreams can be comprehensive. Not only did Cayce's interpretation indicate future events, but it also included warnings about potential danger.

A person has to be cautious and conservative in using dreams for investing. Just as many fail as gain. Some dreams are accurate, some partially correct, and others distorted. It is difficult to decipher what is true precognition and what is fabricated prediction. If an individual is interested in this mode of investment, it is wise to be levelheaded and learn how to read technical data on stocks. In business dealings, information may not register at the conscious level, especially when emotions are involved. However, amid all that static, the subconscious can pick up the most delicate of signals and transfer it to the conscious mind through dreams. Time, distance, and emotional barriers are nonexistent at this level, so information the dreaming mind sees as essential cannot be blocked out. For example, a client, George, was excited about entering a complicated and expensive business partnership with an associate that seemed destined for success. I taught him to incubate dreams to see if there was anything he may have overlooked, and he received two responses.

> Dream 1—I am walking down the street toward the business complex that my partner and I are about to purchase. As I approach the front entrance, I receive quite a jolt. A large sign on top of a

marquee has the name of the business emblazoned in bright neon letters. It is not the name we agreed upon but my partner's last name.

Dream 2—My partner is trying to steal money out of my pocket.

These are not what I call good omens and obviously ran counter to the optimism of his conscious mind. After he shared the dreams with his lawyer, they carefully reviewed the contract and found a clause that greatly favored his partner under certain conditions. The dream warnings helped him back out of the deal. What is concealed from the conscious mind can easily be perceived and revealed by the intuitive, dreaming mind. After all, over a million bits of information per second descend into our nervous system. That's a lot to process, but fortunately most of it is filtered out except that which is urgently needed by the conscious mind. Hidden details may be screened out of the conscious mind, but nothing escapes the perceptive ability of our sixth sense. Fortunately there is a mechanism that translates the subliminal mind's information into meaningful images.

Dreams Add Another Level of Truth in Relationships

As demonstrated in the last section, dreams can be an invaluable tool in financial dealings. They can be just as dramatic and revealing about relationships. People enter these unions and marriages with great hopes for a lasting intimate connection, yet there is no guarantee they will be successful. Matchmaking services try to guarantee that data collected from people will enable them to make a match that will be enduring. The mechanism that can be the most truthful is the most neglected one. The unconscious mind picks up everything of relevance and has our best interests at heart. A number of my clients had dreams about potential mates. Some were warnings, and some were encouragements. Where idealistic thinking, outer appearances, and emotional overload blinded clients, the unconscious could see the truth through the smoke screen. The following experience and dream ran counter to what the conscious mind valued.

Florence met two men who were close friends. She only wanted to date the tall, dark, and handsome one, but both asked her out.

Reluctantly, she made a date with the short and not-so-good-looking man. After the date, she dreamt the following:

> I see the short man with very broad, strong shoulders. I feel he could really support me. When I awake, my whole affect has changed. Ten days later, we started to talk about marriage, and that was thirty-five years ago. It's been a wonderful union. Without the dream, I never would have considered him.

One cannot see a clear image in agitated water. The dreaming mind can see to the bottom of the lake, no matter what turbulence is on the surface. The conscious mind can easily deceive itself, but the dreaming mind will recognize the false information consciously thought or communicated. Things may sound or look right but feel wrong. Dream images present the incongruity in picture form.

One of the most unheeded frightening symbolic warnings was shared at a dream seminar. Kathleen, a young woman engaged to be married, dreamt the following:

> I am shopping in a supermarket. Walking down an aisle, I see an unattended shopping cart with one item in it: a beautifully wrapped package with a colorful bow. I look around and do not see anyone it belongs to, so I grab the package, put it in my cart, and continue shopping. When I go to check out, a knife comes out of the package and literally stabs me in the heart, delivering a mortal wound.

The dreamer had no idea what this dream meant. When she shared it with her girlfriend, the friend mentioned the dreamer often referred to her fiancé as a "beautifully wrapped package." She ignored the dark clouds gathering on the horizon, dismissed the connection as ridiculous, and married. Two months later, her husband attacked her with a knife, and she barely survived. The message: when in love, don't ever underestimate the ability of the dreaming mind to speak the truth.

Another seminar attendee shared a dream that her life would end by being stabbed in the back when she was forty-two. Eight years after the dream, her husband left her for another woman. At the time, she was forty-two. Her unconscious mind saw it coming. The death was the marriage and the stabbing the betrayal. For a time, she did indeed feel as though her life had ended. Sometimes dream warnings are subtle and sometimes blunt and can project far into the future. Often it is difficult to read them, but it is wise to meditate on these dreams and ask for clarification if you are unclear about their meaning. The subconscious mind is highly suggestible and will frequently respond to genuine requests.

An Ideal Lover Turns Into a Voracious Rat

A middle-aged female client shared with me that she had found her soul mate and intended to divorce her husband of twenty-five years. Supposedly, soul mates are two people who are perfectly made for each other and destined to spend their lives together. They have a natural affinity and love for each other and often share a common life path and purpose. When I asked her to describe the relationship, she gushed out a litany of superlatives: "The sex is the greatest, we call each other ten times a day, can't wait to see, touch, and talk to each other, and above all, I am the apple of his eye." Of course, someone in this stage of lust feels the fire in every cell, making that person blind to reality. After about two months of ecstasy, she had a dream that put the proper perspective on what was happening.

A small rat crawled into my heart because it was cold and just wanted to snuggle for some warmth. Suddenly, the rat was hungry and started to nibble at my heart. Eventually, he ate up my whole heart, and when I awoke, I felt empty.

He didn't just perforate her heart: he ate the whole thing! In a few weeks, she saw the dream become a reality as Mr. Perfect turned into a parasite. Looking for perfection in a mate coupled with a problem-free relationship is a setup for disillusionment and disappointment. Many people who think they have found a soul mate and expect a relationship to be free of struggles and quarrels often get a dose of reality when their ship takes on water and starts sinking. From my experience of doing marriage counseling, the relationships that seem to work the best are those where mates encourage each other's spiritual development and completeness as individuals. Those unions that do not have this as a core value often get strained to the breaking point. Dreams often reveal when that moment has arrived.

My Executioner Is My Husband

Mary was in a long-term unhappy marriage—more than thirty-five years—and had many therapy sessions trying to let go of the relationship. Her husband had moved out three years before this dream, boasting he had three or four girlfriends. She was devastated, yet ambivalent about a divorce. This following dream was the deciding factor.

I am in a line of people moving toward a firing squad. Each individual moves onto a platform where they are shot to death. As I move closer to my turn, I begin complaining and state I will not cooperate. I refuse to step up onto the platform, and the slayer gets enraged at my resistance. I notice that the killer is my husband. He screams, "Get up here—I'll shoot you fast. It won't even hurt that much. I'll even smile when I kill you." I awaken terrified and horrified.

She didn't need much more than this dream to help her realize she was unsafe and needed to get away from him as soon as possible. She pushed to finalize the legal part of the divorce, which resulted in a fuller, richer life. In her case, a dream favorably tipped the decision-making scales.

If a troubling relationship occupies the greater portion of waking life, dreams will create an allegory that is a symbolic representation of the relationship's inner truth. The story will often illustrate its creative intent, which adds another layer of depth to understanding. The conscious mind may be the captain of one's vessel, but not listening to the inner navigator can cause the ship to flounder. Alberta needed her eyes opened to the role she had been playing in a long-term relationship. This happened when she had the following dream.

> I'm on a ship in very rough waters. My boyfriend loses his balance, falls overboard, and is drowning. I throw him a life preserver and haul him aboard.

Upon awakening, she suddenly realized her partner was saddled with many problems, and her role in their connection was to come to his aid and bail him out of his difficulties. She needed someone to lean on occasionally, so she ended the relationship.

Barbara was an unhappily married woman with three young children. Divorce was unacceptable because of her Catholic convictions. Her dream gave her the courage to override her religious beliefs.

> It is nighttime, and a huge gorilla is roaming around the outside of the house, wanting to do some damage. The beast begins pushing and shaking the structure as if it is a toy. My children and I are terrified.

When she awoke, she instantly knew the gorilla symbolized her husband—his limited intellect and unpredictable and irrational behavior. Catholicism had to take a backseat when it came to the safety of her children. She divorced him.

Career Guidance

Career guidance is not an uncommon experience in the dream world, especially if in conscious life, we are uncertain about our vocational direction. When it comes to careers, we tend to be practical and highly analytical and often neglect or are unaware of the intuitive power of dreams to direct us to more compatible and satisfying careers. Some of the major signs that indicate we are not in the right place for expressing our unique gifts and talents are: frequent stress-related illnesses, feeling unchallenged, or dreading going to work.

There is this omniscient central intelligence within us that has access to the minutest data about our talents, abilities, aptitudes, interests, and attitudes. If we put value on dreams, they can rescue us from an untenable situation or redirect us onto the correct path. And they can do it overnight! Often the crucial information needed for such redirection may not register at the conscious level. However, the subconscious can pick up the most delicate signals and transmit this counsel to consciousness through dreams. Similar to the healing dreams recorded at Epidaurus that helped incubants reclaim their health, this rejuvenating force wants to reawaken our true gifts.

In the 1980s, my wife and I were on a vacation traveling through Indian country and stopped at a Native American library in South Dakota. The librarian shared a most engaging story of a young Seminole Indian who had left the reservation, gotten a college degree, became a teacher, married, and had two children. He began drinking heavily and eventually lost his job, wife, and family. Despondent, he called his uncle at the reservation. In response to the man's tale of woe, the uncle said, "Come back to your Indian land, and we'll wait for a dream!" A dream! They trusted the soul to point the man in the right direction. What would happen if a Caucasian middle-class student called home and described his depression and troubles to his parents? They would most likely say, "We'll make an appointment with a psychologist who will prescribe a series of aptitude and achievement tests. We'll get to the bottom of this and find out what you should be doing." That's the conscious, rational approach. The last thing they would have considered was how a dream could be of value.

Like the Native American who trusted dreams to counsel him, here are a few more examples from dream seminar participants and from me that reaffirm choices, direct dreamers into careers, or offer sage advice. What these dreamers needed could only come from themselves, not outside sources. The rational boundaries of the conscious mind were breached by the impartial, spontaneous products of the unconscious mind, which were clear and simple truths.

A Dying Spirit Is Revived

Emily had this dream right before she left home in Texas to go to California and attend the Matthew Fox School—then called the Institute of Creation and Cultural Spirituality in Oakland at Holy Names College. Before leaving, she was depressed and felt hopeless after three years as a medical social worker in a hospital pulmonary unit. She hated the job; it was so hard to witness people struggling to breathe. She sold her home and quit her job. The dream occurred the night before she left for Oakland.

> I am holding a small blackbird in my hand. It is dying—struggling to breathe, lying on its side with an open beak, and looking at me forlornly with its left eye. I take a little water onto the fingertips of my free hand and let some drops fall into its mouth. The bird miraculously begins to revive. I wake up feeling that my spirit is reviving and being healed.

Her comment: "[The dream] told me I was doing the right thing to recharge my spirit. It filled me with enormous hope of revival and renewal and affirmed my pilgrimage to school for a master's in spirituality. It was not only the right thing to do; it was one of the most important experiences of my life. My soul would come to life again. I can still see the bird in the palm of my hand, beak open and struggling to breathe, its little black eye calling to me. As it swallowed the drops of water, life returned. Water is the source of all life, and my spiritual thirst had to be quenched. Currently, I am working in the field of spirituality."

Not only did she receive an affirmation of her decision to change direction, she had a real experience. Some dreams need little or no interpretation. The meaning of the dream is the personal experience that can generate feelings that last a lifetime and are prime motivators for taking action. The symbols add to the mystery, but the dreamer doesn't question their meaning in the dream, and when she awakens, she feels a rebirth of life and hope. At some level, the dreaming soul must know that these symbolic communications come from a source that transcends the rational mind.

I Was Told by the Spirit to Write

Jonathan, a dissatisfied mental-health professional had a dream that was very specific about a new career option.

> A male guide speaks to me while sending a pulsating energy through the soles of my feet. This energy electrifies my whole body. The spirit guide looks at me and says emphatically, "Write!"

His comment on his dream: "Thus began my writing career, initially with automatic writing and then a novel, *Cuckoo Forevermore*. It was published in 1996 and is similar to *One Flew Over the Cuckoo's Nest* but set in a children's psychiatric department in Sydney, Australia." Currently, he's redrafting the sequel and hoping it will be published in 2008. While the screenplay was never picked up, he moved to California at the end of 2007 with the expectation of pitching ideas and stories to the movie industry.

The guide's command to write reinforced signs throughout his life that he was meant to tell stories and be an author. His confidence and motivator buttons were pushed, so he started taking writing classes and never regretted his choice. Writing is part of his everyday life now, and he credits the dream with convincing him he will be a success as he develops his God-given talent.

This dream centered on what he considered the heart of success. Recognizing your own talents will help you define your life purpose and restructure your life as needed so that you can bring that talent to the world. Dreams can help in the recognition and pursuit of a fulfilling life path.

The Church Vehicle

Martha's dream came when she was in college struggling with uncertainty about her career path. As a result of this inner experience, she was able to decide on the direction of her life.

> I am asleep in the back of the church bus from my early childhood. When I awaken, I realize I am alone, and the bus is speeding without a driver. Jumping up, I race to the driver's seat, but I can-

207

not get the bus to stop or turn. It passes through the town's busiest intersections, yet I just can't figure out how to stop it. A very busy intersection with a red light is coming up, and just as I approach, the light turns green, and I get through safely. Eventually, I am out in the countryside surrounded by wheat fields. I know I need to either keep going down the road until I run out of gas or try and turn off into a wheat field. That's when I awaken.

From her dream, Martha realized that the church would be her "vehicle" through life. Currently, she is an ordained United Methodist clergy person who loves to drive the church bus! Her dream penetrated the thin wall of time and in that one brief moment allowed her a glimpse at her future potential.

Helping Others Climb Up Gets Me to the Top

Doris was a young woman whose direction in life was revealed by a dream adventure, which is particularly poignant because it demonstrates an often-overlooked truth about searching for a life path. Finding a relevant direction in life can be daunting. Many people get lost, because they get stuck on job selection. Doris's dream uncovered an underlying dynamic that made her mission easier. Look at the principle Doris practices in her dream.

I am climbing up a very jagged mountain, and it is taking a long time. I know I have to get to the top. About 95 percent of the way up, I hear a voice calling, "Help me, please help me!" I look back down the mountain, and I realize I have to help this struggling person. I do this and have just started back up the mountain when someone else calls for help. I go back again and assist him. This happens numerous times. When I finally awake, I understand that the only way I can reach the top is to be of service to other people. This is my calling, so I became a social worker.

There was no misunderstanding what this conveyed. Her dream was another one of those "real experiences" that touched the dreamer to the core and helped her decide what basic principle to live by. The dream had overtones of a religious calling. Her dreaming mind knew her special gifts and abilities and encouraged a career direction that would dovetail with who she was. Selection by the inner self usually assures a person of emotional satisfaction and fulfillment in career choice. *When a dream reveals a soul's primary inclination, it becomes engraved on the heart.* Because our dreaming mind deeply understands the very nature of our being and shares this wisdom in a dream, conscious search for that special career can be shortened dramatically.

A Great White Shark Wants Me for Dinner

Listening to the sixth sense as it manifests in dreams can help us avoid a lot of anguish in careers. When I was struggling to build a private practice, I was offered a high-paying position to help develop a new concept in support systems for single people in the Southern California area. The man who originated the project gave a slick graphic presentation about all the good it would do and all the money it would make for designated managers. Impressed by the electronic wizardry used to display financial gains, I told him I would think about it. That night I had the following dream:

> It's nighttime and pitch black, and I am swimming in an even darker and murkier ocean. In the distance, I see a huge great white shark bearing down on me, with the intent of making me his dinner. I awake in a cold sweat.

The next morning I immediately called and rejected the job offer. Someone I knew took the position and within six months, the whole operation folded with a lot of money missing. A great white shark is a voracious predator. The waters I had considered entering were fraught with intense danger. A person we think of as a "shark" is a rapacious, crafty individual who preys upon others through trickery. The conscious mind might sense something sinister when it is nearby, but the subconscious mind can detect it from a mile away!

Dreams are many steps ahead of us because of their access to facts and future consequences the conscious mind can't see. Jessica was a young woman who asked her dreams what the outcome would be if she accepted a new administrative job with much more responsibility. Her unconscious mind responded with a brief dream picture of a wasted, frail old lady. The dreamer couldn't comprehend what this image was trying to convey. After accepting the position and working in it for a short time, she realized that in spite of enjoying many aspects of the job, the work wore her out. She knew she had to quit. Even very short dreams with one symbolic image can have powerful meanings. A lot of information can be condensed into one symbol.

Illness can lead to a career choice. Recognizing a positive outcome from misfortune may take a long time in the waking world, but a dream can speed up the process. Betty was fourteen and a half when a serious accident left her hospitalized with thirteen vertebrae needing fusion. She was frightened and in great pain when a dream came to her rescue.

I am wild and out of control, just like a caged animal. Full of rage and pain, I begin tearing down the walls of my hospital room and angrily ripping the whole room apart. Worn out, I sit to rest on a cloud in the room. In a moment, I float out the room's window and have a most peaceful journey to my home so I can visit with my dog. It is all so gentle and calm. When I wake up I am surprised that I'm not feeling sad and mad about the accident. Instead, I feel less pain, and I know I can accept and deal with my situation. I had hated hospitals before this experience, and now I have this strong urge to become a nurse and help others overcome their afflictions. From that moment on, I became a kinder person with a bigger heart, and the desire to become a nurse increased. And that is what I am today.

Uncovering Concealed Talents

Outer activities may not have revealed our true creative capacities and skills, but invisible within us are talents and abilities. Our dreaming mind makes us aware of these creative potentials so we can utilize these gifts. Take the case of a thirteen-year-old boy I was working with who was unaware he had any musical talent until he had the following dream.

I am not only playing an electric guitar with the musical group I have put together, but I am the lead singer. It all feels so good and right.

He talked his mother into buying him an electric guitar, and within nine months, he had put together a musical group that was playing at local parties.

Another thirteen-year-old boy had this dream:

> I am sitting at my desk getting ready to study when I notice a blank piece of white paper lying there. I pick up a pencil, pull the lead out, and gold dust flows out of the opening and begins to pile up on the paper. It is real gold.

Gold is a precious commodity and often a symbol of personal riches (i.e., talents). I asked him if he had ever written creatively. His face lit up and he said that up until the sixth grade, he loved writing poetry and short stories. Then his mother told him that when he got into junior high school, he was going to give up that writing nonsense and become a scientist. I don't know what became of him, but if he is a scientist, I would imagine he's writing for scientific journals.

Sometimes a dream advises against an individual's choice of career. The previous two examples opened up possibilities that broadened the dreamers' self-images. Dreams have a unique way of spawning conditions where new talents and capacities are expressed. They can also discourage a seeker from biting off more than he or she can chew. We have a built-in book of wisdom that knows where we are gifted and where we fall short.

This next dreamer had been a nurse but decided to become an MD. After enrolling in a pre-med program that strained her to the limit, she had a mental breakdown and ended up in a psychiatric ward. During her stay, she had the following short, but enlightening dream experience that attempted to rescue her from further endangering her health through excess stress.

In my dream, a voice says to me, "Knowledge comes from college, but wisdom comes from the school of hard knocks." She chuckled when she awoke and realized the spirit has a great sense of humor. The dream helped her to see and accept the idea that the course was too demanding and an advanced nursing program would be more in line.

The unconscious seems to know what our endowments are, and when we put ourselves in tenuous situations, this inner sage will let us know if we are in over our heads. Conversely, when we have the talent and ability and are reluctant to put it on the line, the indwelling spirit may encourage us to take a risk.

The following dreamer was deeply concerned about discovering her true purpose and path in life. Unsure about moving ahead with insufficient knowledge, she dreamt:

> I find myself standing in a room full of junk. There is a female guide there who says, "You may take whatever you want to make you happy." I respond loudly with, "How am I supposed to find my life's purpose in all this junk?" She responds, "Oh, you're looking for the purpose of your life! You need to come here." I get excited and follow her into a large empty gallery. She goes to a far wall and removes a sheet of plywood to expose a massive machine that is at least four stories high. It is made of a shiny green metallic substance and has a dark chute—like an entrance opening. I know that to find my purpose, I have to climb in. I hesitate and wonder if I will get stuck and destroyed. When I look back at the guide, she is passively standing in a doorway waiting for me to enter. I am so unsure; then the guide sings a clear melody to me twice:
> A risk not taken
> Is a key unopened
> To a dream unspoken.

A quote by Robert Frost seems so appropriate for this dream: "Two roads diverged in a wood, and I took the one less traveled by, and that has made all the difference."[24]

Vision and desire are the first stage, but staring into the great unknown is not enough. You have to pass through it. Avoiding risk limits your chances for success and novel experiences. As Einstein said, "Nothing happens until something moves." If you're unsure about taking a new step, program a dream and see what the inner mind has to say. Life demands that we grow and change.

Dreams have the capacity to penetrate vast reservoirs of information and fill in the blanks that the conscious mind has missed. The unconscious mind is not just a concealed copy of the conscious mind. It can and does function from a distinct viewpoint. Above all, it unmasks the false and lays open the truth, which brings us to the final subject that is a common denominator of all people—physical death. But before delving deeply into what dreams say about death, I would like to share a dream experience that gives an added perspective to issues of living and dying. A woman was stricken with a ruptured liver, and her loved ones worried that she would not survive. After an eight-hour surgery, she had the following dream in recovery:

> I tell God I do not want to die and that what I was going through was so hard. This deep booming voice responds, "Dying is easy, it's just letting go! It's living that's hard!"

I pondered this when I awoke and felt a deep peace from it. It helped me choose to live! What a paradox! We would think it was the opposite.

The exhaustion from caring, loving, and living is very real; sometimes it feels overwhelming. Whether we are rich or poor, sooner or later the universal law of hardship strikes us all. Courage is called for when tragedy strikes, when intense pain envelopes us, or when bad luck frustrates us. When it's time to go, wouldn't it be gratifying to know we have truly struggled, succeeded, and loved and are being rewarded with a final peace for a job well done?

What Dreams Say Happens at Death

The fear of death is a core issue in most people's lives. No amount of money, power, or celebrity status can prevent this outcome. But there is mounting evidence that while we may die physically, our soul transitions to another plane of existence. The results of so many recorded near-death experiences (NDEs) may be indicating that the mind could exist independently of the physical brain. When a patient experiences an NDE, his or her electroencephalogram (EEG), which measures the electrical signals within the brain and records them on a graph, flatlines. In other words, no brain activity is registered, so the patient can't be hallucinating. But if, after flatlining, the patient regains consciousness, he or she often describes scenes in vivid detail that occurred when others struggled to revive him or her. The pattern is the same no matter what the individual's culture. Of course, the experiences vary. In Western culture, entering the afterlife often includes a passage through a tunnel and out into light. In other cultures, it could include taking a walk down the road to greet a familiar deceased person, or having to cross a body of water. If you are Christian, the guide you meet is likely to be a religious figure. If you are from India, it could be a Hindu. The devoutly orthodox are no more apt to have an NDE than the irreligious.[25] No matter who they are, when people who have NDEs are interviewed, their stories are strikingly similar and involve a review of life down to the smallest detail.

When I started my initial analysis with a Jungian therapist, he emphasized the importance of dreams as guiding principles. To stress this point, he shared the following story: a female client was diagnosed with terminal cancer. Unable to visit her on a particular day, he asked his associate if he would look in on her. When he arrived in her room, she was sleeping, so he pulled up a chair and waited until she awakened. Opening her eyes, she said, "Oh! Doctor, I just had such an unusual dream!" Her experience follows:

> I am standing in front of a full-length mirror, holding a candle in my left hand. Suddenly an arm reaches over my right shoulder and snuffs the candle out, but the image of the candle does not go out in the mirror. In fact, it gets brighter and brighter until it fills up the whole mirror.

She smiled at the therapist, sighed deeply, and died in front of him. There are a few common denominators that link all humanity, and one of them is that we will all die physically. Death is not evil or good—it's a fact of life and is in the background all the time. Staving off death has become a giant industry. The medical profession has become advanced enough that it helps people hang on to life even in the face of serious opposition. Maybe we just need to enjoy the scenery, because what dreams seem to indicate is that death is a transition. Energy doesn't die; it just appears to be transformed. Dreams point to existence and sustenance on another plane. What the caterpillar calls the end of his world is actually the beginning of the butterfly's universe.

A client of mine was dying of cancer and shared a remarkable dream that was directly the opposite of what he consciously believed. Before his dream, death to him was a candle being snuffed out— never to glow again.

I am
sitting on the roof of my
house in a lotus position. It is
nighttime, and countless radiant stars
beautifully illuminate the dark sky.
Suddenly a huge spoon comes out of the
sky and begins feeding me.

He died a few days later. In the dream his house could be a representation of his physical body. That he was sitting on the roof suggests he was in the process of leaving his body. The spoon that extended endlessly from the sky and had no source connected to it indicated that his superconscious was preparing him to be sustained by a higher source of nourishment. As a nonbeliever, he actually thought the spoon could be connected to God.

There are countless ways dream symbolism prepares people for the transition. A voice or a hand beckons one to cross a boundary. One dreams of cavorting with deceased relatives. A darkly dressed figure leads one into an unfamiliar land. A clock stops, indicating time has run out. If these dreams cause apprehension or a feeling that it's a premonition, followed by an impulse to put affairs in order and reconcile any leftover issues with friends and family, it may be the subconscious mind's way of reconciling the dreamer with the inevitable.

Dreams and Connections to the Deceased

Dreaming of people who are deceased can be understood on many different levels. These dreams can be an essential part of the grieving process, helping a dreamer deal with feelings of sadness and resentment over the loss. Often, the difficult confrontation with grief experienced at the conscious level can be mitigated in the dreaming world.

What seems to be most helpful is the visitation of the departed loved ones in dreams. These experiences produce two dynamic results: they help the dreamer to accept death and also to understand that life continues on another plane. I have often heard stories of those who have passed on reassuring loved ones in dreams that they are fine and love the dreamer dearly. This helps the dreamer make a quantum leap in the grieving process toward emotional healing. A dream shared in a seminar described a much-loved but completely demented grandmother living in a nursing home. Her granddaughter was unable to express what her grandmother had meant to her. In a dream, her grandmother was being pushed in a wheelchair up into the clouds. Her face was radiant with joy and love, and she turned and waved goodbye to her granddaughter. The dream occurred two years after the grandmother's death; afterward, the dreamer finally felt closure and the healing of her grief.

Samantha was married to an agnostic psychiatrist who died in an accident. She was experiencing a complicated grieving process until the following dream resolved much of the pain:

> My husband comes to me in a dream and reassures me that he is fine. He is aware how miserable I am without him, but he assures me that in time, we will be reunited forever, and everything will always be fine. And if everything will always be fine, then I can be

"fine" now! Fine was repeated often in the dream, and I found it very comforting. Coming from a psychoanalytic background, she interpreted this dream as a "wish fulfillment." And yet she had an overriding feeling of comfort as well as a really solid connection to her husband. This dream helped her grief work immensely.

Another dream in a similar vein but with a deeper message concerned the Jungian analyst I went to as a young man. He died suddenly at age fifty, and his wife was in her second year of mourning when she dreamt that her husband appeared to her at a party and told her to go out, date, dance, and enjoy life. Then he delivered a most startling message: "You must stop grieving for me, because your grief is holding me back from making progress with what I need to do." She began releasing him. Certainly one could look at this dream in many different ways. It could relate to her own personal growth and the need for the living to go on with their lives. But the unanswered question is, how can her grief hold back the progress of her deceased husband? The dreamer felt it related to both her personal development and the progress of her husband's soul.

There are no ironclad rules about what kinds of dreams mourners will have or how to interpret them. That is best left to the dreamer. Some mourners have dreams they are watched over and cared for by deceased ancestors. This universal belief has created rituals of prayers for guidance and ancestor worship. Probably the key factor in dream contact with the deceased is love, and when that message is delivered in dreams, it seems to impart greater confidence that life is a continuum and the connection has been authentically confirmed.

Following is an example of a dream that emphasizes it is important to the departed that their loved ones grasp what dying means.

I see a dark hole from which jumps a large black dog, a beloved pet that had died one year before. She is healthy, jumps into my arms, and seems thrilled to see me. Turning toward the hole, she beckons me to follow her. I step through it into a beautiful flower-filled field glowing with a bright light and stirring with a gentle breeze. Feeling peaceful and joyous to see her so well, I follow her as she runs ahead to a white arched garden gate that leads to a grassy knoll. I sit down in the warm sun, close my eyes, breathe deeply, and when I open them, my deceased grandparents are standing in front of me. They both look so healthy, young, and beautiful. I run to my grandfather, hug him a long time, and feel safe, warm, and protected. I shed tears of happiness. They both radiate light that doesn't seem to come from around them but from within. My grandmother cups her hands in front of her, and a small intensely bright rainbow appears in them. A thought comes into my head that says it's all about rainbows, and I should give this one to my mother. Feeling so happy to see them, I awaken sensing comfort, relief, and certainty that they had come to let me know they're alive and well on another plane of existence.

Some could dismiss this as just working through the grief or a wish-fulfillment dream. A rainbow is often symbolic of a covenant or promise of good things to come. Seeing a rainbow in a dream often stimulates a stronger emotional reaction than seeing one in nature because the dreamer senses something positive is on its way. For the dreamer, it was a real experience and offered connection to those she loved. For someone who has never had this kind of experience, it is very difficult to sense its true inner nature. Intellectual discussions about the continuation of life on another level can prove fruitless and frustrating. Common experiences such as being distraught after seeing loved ones in a coffin are dissolved when that same loved one comes in a dream and says, "I'm not in that box; I'm in Cincinnati or Boston or Las Vegas."

What about family members who have to decide whether to maintain a life-support system? A woman I know decided to let her comatose mother pass on, and the family was outraged. Her deceased mother came in a dream and reassured her she had done the right thing and that she was at peace and loved the dreamer very deeply. The dreamer has been content since the dream occurred and knows it was not her imagination but her mother's communication of love and support through the dream. Dreams seem to address the issue of death as a transitional phase during which the deceased continue their education about the mystery that envelopes living and dying. All these dreams counter many religious ideas about going to heaven and living the life of Riley. As one of my clients said, "What a gift these dreams are!"

This next dream is a reassurance that there need be no fear of death. The dreamer was not in mourning nor was her death imminent.

I am pregnant with my first child, and a female being comes to me in a dream and tells me she is going to guide me through death. We quickly move through levels that help me leave the earth plane. At first, I am terribly concerned for my family and their grief over my passing, but very rapidly my guide leads me toward a state in which I feel a deepening love and connection with all beings. It is as if I began my journey with a myopic focus, and as my awareness expands, I am totally encompassed by what feels like the most profound love I can imagine. I feel this love as much for strangers as I do for my family. In it is complete security and confidence in the well-being of myself and all others, separate, yet one. This dream changed me. I don't fear death. I feel certain it will be a wonderful transition.

As Plato said, "He whom love touches walks not in darkness."[26] There is no grander feeling than being touched by the spirit with universal love. It often can't be described in words. Only the one who has the feeling knows what that is like. Indeed, one of the main messages delivered by the deceased in dreams is to love, as suggested by this last dream recounted to me by another of my clients, whose mother was killed in a car accident in the late 1980s.

My mother comes to me in a dream and explains that anger, hate, and negativity are part of the earth world, and when you die, they leave you like old clothing, and all that is left is love. At the time of the dream I was not aware of spirituality and this type of love that my deceased mother emphasized. The dead are trying to make us more alive. I am now on a spiritual journey.

I don't think these dreams are talking about the idealistic and physical kinds of love that erupted during the 1960s. They seem to point to the unconditional love that unites, heals, connects, expands the heart, ennobles, and creates a feeling of oneness in whoever is fortunate enough to experience it. So many of the messages spoken by the deceased in dreams to various dreamers encourage going beyond the normal boundaries of love, which are often associated with romance, to the compassionate love that Jesus, Buddha, and Lao Tse emphasized. This message has pursued us for thousands of years. Now that technology is connecting all parts of the world, the deceased, along with the evolved living, are trying to strengthen this oneness with compassionate love, the most powerful binding force in the universe. Teilhard de Chardin, the great thinker and theologian wrote, "The day will come when after harnessing the ether, the winds, the tides, gravitation, we shall harness for God the energies of love. And on that day for the second time in the history of the world, man will have discovered fire."[27]

Chapter 8

RECALLING AND RECORDING
THE BOOK OF YOUR SOUL

They say dreams are the windows of the soul—take a peek
and you can see the inner workings, the nuts and bolts.

Henry Bromel

So many people have difficulty trying to remember their dreams. Crucial to this issue is *why* you should take the time or make the effort to recall dreams. In other words, what can dreams offer? By now you probably have a fairly good idea what dreams can accomplish. Some people search the planet for a guru to assist them in evolving spiritually. But everyone has a built-in mentor, a guidance system that functions all the time. Dreams can motivate and arouse intense emotions just as gurus can. Gurus are supposedly guides to higher spiritual planes, and so are dreams. There is no one who could know your needs and abilities and when to give you a metaphysical tune-up as well as your own inner spiritual master.

Reviewing What Dreams Can Do for You

Here is a quick review of what dreams can do for you and why you should remember them.

1. Dreams catch a glimpse of what's coming and can offer insight into the future.
2. Dreams recharge the batteries in our souls so we can advance spiritually.
3. Dreams help us see our defects so we can improve them.
4. Dreams offer cryptic messages that tell us what we need to change to live a better life.
5. Dreams deliver warnings about the consequences of behavior.

6. Dreams provide lessons for living a richer life.
7. Dreams diagnose illnesses, even impending ones.
8. Dreams provide health care and advice that is free.
9. Dreams open the door to those seeking truth and wisdom.
10. Dreams help overcome undesirable emotions.
11. Dreams communicate with the deceased.
12. Dreams supply inside information about relationships.
13. Dreams help create abundance.
14. Dreams make decision-making easier.
15. Dreams help us to become complete people.

Suggestions for Dream Recall

When you know you have had a special dream, how do you go about remembering it? I have my own way of recalling dreams when I awaken but can't remember the details. Sometimes I awaken without the thought of a dream, and at other times I know I have dreamt but can't recall any specifics.

This is what I suggest: When you awaken, naturally, lie still and focus your attention in the middle of the forehead, keeping your eyes closed. I usually say my mantra, *Ra-Rum-Kah*, silently and slowly with eyes remaining closed and focusing on my "third eye." This technique is about 75 percent effective for me. If nothing comes in a few minutes, shift to another position and try again. Do not distract yourself thinking about what you are going to do during the day. Focus!

Other writers have their own methods:

1. Suggestion plays an important role in dream recall. The subconscious is highly suggestive, so when you get in bed, state aloud that when you wake up you will recall dreams. If you have continued difficulty remembering dreams, see the order form for my CD, "Dreams, the Wisdom in Sleep." It's a relaxation and guided-imagery presentation that will greatly increase your dream recall and ability to program a dream on any subject.

2. Change your wake-up routine. Set an alarm clock on low volume a few minutes earlier or later than normal waking time.

3. Record your dream immediately after recall. Some great opportunities have been missed through a lack of diligence.

4. Keep a dream journal and a pen or pencil next to the bed, and if you are just too sleepy to record the complete dream, write down any symbols you can remember. Recalling these few images can trigger a complete recall. I have had success with using a small hand-held tape recorder so I don't have to get up to write a dream down.

5. Avoid alcohol, caffeine, and heavy meals before retiring for the evening. These can prevent a relaxed body and mind.

6. Develop rituals you think will help recall dreams. You might meditate, pray, listen to spiritual music, or go outside and admire the stars. There is no one thing that works for everybody, so experimentation is important. Whatever works for you is your key.

7. Develop a strong desire to recall dreams. This may sound obvious, and it is. A strong desire can create realities. Reflect on your purpose for recalling dreams. What do you hope to achieve?

8. Be patient, and do not attempt to force the issue. If you don't recall a dream upon awakening, get up and go about your business, but expect the memory to appear any time during the day. Somebody may say something or you may see a particular object, and suddenly recollection gets stimulated.

9. Don't dismiss any dream fragments. Recall of a short scene, an individual, a symbol, or even an uncertain feeling may hold the key to the dream. So record these bits and pieces, for in them may lie decisive clues.

10. Often dreams are recorded in reverse order, where the last scene in the dream is recalled first. It doesn't matter if you record it in nonchronological order. When the recall is complete, the scenes can then be placed in order of occurrence.

11. Appreciate and cherish your dreams, especially the big ones. These are great inner gifts from the spirit. They will stay with you for your lifetime, because they are meant for a lifetime. Years later you can return to these unusual dreams and still find inspirational, new meanings.

12. During the day, reflect on what you would like to dream about and the meaning of recent dreams. Establish your own criteria for planning dream incubations. When you think about dream recall, reiterate your intention of remembering them and consider appreciating what comes. *Treasure these gems that originate in the depths of your soul.*

13. Join a dream group or start one. There is enough material in this book to guide you.

14. Accept whatever comes your way. Sometimes dreams can publish our most painful secrets. A nasty dog biting people, a venomous snake threatening others, or a pathetic prostitute pleading for business may be symbolic pictures of an unflattering aspect of ourselves. Accept it. Your inner eye can see where you need awareness and correction. You are much more or much less than you realize.

15. Make sure you are getting enough sleep. You dream approximately two hours every night. The dream periods occur every ninety minutes and get longer throughout the evening. The last dream period in a seven-and-one-half- or eight-hour cycle means you could be dreaming the whole last hour of sleep. If you deprive yourself of sleep, you could be missing the bulk of your dreamtime.

16. Ingesting 50 mg of vitamin B-6 could help dream recall. Taking some vitamin C will help the body metabolize any extra B vitamins you consume. Check it out on the Internet and with a nutritionist.

17. Drinking a lot of water before going to bed can cause you to wake up during the night at least once. Generally these awakenings occur during REM sleep.

18. Go to sleep a little earlier than you usually do to make sure you catch the last dream cycle.

19. Before going to bed, read a few excerpts from a book on dreams or reread your dream journal to review a poignant dream.

Maintaining a Dream Journal

1. Create a dream journal that has a distinctive element about

it. Don't record your dreams on random loose papers. Using a quality product sends a message to the dreaming mind that you are earnest and serious about the project.

2. Journaling dreams will help you experience and discover who you truly are. Repetitive themes and symbols demonstrate progress or lack thereof. I have always enjoyed reading my dream journal to see how I have matured and progressed. Reflecting on your transformation is an uplifting experience. Some people claim that just recording their dreams has made dream recall stronger and easier to understand.

3. When recording a dream, don't concern yourself with what it means, as this could distract recall. Get as much detail down on paper as you can. Trying to interpret as you record could make you lose some important details. One of the most important but neglected aspects of dream recall and recording is focusing on the feelings generated in the dream. This element could be one of the keys in grasping the meaning.

4. There is no one style or singular way to journal dreams. What suits you is what feels right. Some people make quick simple drawings or sketches in black and white or color. Others create short poems or paste significant pictures in their journals. The important point is that you have a record you can refer back to and see how symbols and themes keep repeating and how premonitions arise in your subconscious.

5. If you are attempting a dream incubation, write about it in the journal before going to sleep. Dream responses to incubation requests can come days later.

6. Record the date and time of your dreams, and create an index or table of contents with page numbers for the important ones to which you want to refer. It's frustrating trying to locate a meaningful dream that has no reference points. It's also interesting to see if your dreams in the early morning differ from those that come to you in the middle of the night.

7. If you awaken in the middle of the night exhausted and resistant to recording, just write one or two words to help trigger the recall in the morning. Don't be overly concerned about punctuation and grammar. Recording the major symbols and

events before they dissolve is the main objective. Later in the day, you can elaborate when you rewrite the final story.

8. Put a title at the top of the dream. Create one that zeroes in on the essence of the dream. If you don't have an index, titles can help locate a specific dream and over time give you an accurate picture of recurring themes. "Airliner Crashes in Ocean," "Airliner Attacked by Terrorists," "Airliner Plummets to Earth," "Airliner Destroyed by Missile off California," might reveal that the same issue is alive and well in your life.

9. Don't ignore bizarre dreams. They are often presented that way because the unconscious wants to be certain you get the message. Most of us need a two by four between the eyes to awaken us. Dreams will give us exactly that.

10. Read selections from your dream journal to similar-minded people you really trust. They will often see connections and meanings that have eluded you.

A Few Notes of Caution

Learning to understand your dreams and apply their underlying meanings in the waking world is not an overnight project. It takes time and patience. When you think you have mastered the subject, up pops an unfamiliar and unexplored dimension of yourself that presents a new challenge. Stay patient, unruffled, and persistent. Just reflect for a moment on the majesty of dream gifting. *We are blessed with a navigational system that rivals the best in technological guidance systems.*

Remember: working with dreams is not just for entertainment and understanding. Many dreams beg the right questions to be asked because entwined in the symbols and actions are answers that can pinpoint the issues. Develop a plan of action based on a dream's main message and also a time frame to complete it. Generally, application changes us and puts us more in line with who we were meant to be. When acted upon, insights become real and concrete. You will start to feel a stronger sense of integrity and courage and have a truer sense of your own destiny, because you are rebuilding your house brick by brick.

If your dream encourages you to examine a behavioral pattern, an attitude, a relationship struggle, a financial concern, a health issue, or a career change, then phrase it in a way that sets it in motion: "I will diligently create and act out ways to change my negative attitude." "I will seek the counsel of a financial consultant to help me straighten out my finances." "I will upgrade my resume and begin exploring new job opportunities." "I will make an appointment next week to consult with a homeopathic doctor."

Following is a brief example from my dream journal.

11/1/06 Clint Eastwood Discovers a Fortune in Gold

Dream: I am in a room with Clint Eastwood and other men: we total twelve. Eastwood knows where $50 million is hidden—in an ocean cave in very deep water. I ask him, "Since we will all be helping you, what's your take and what's ours?" I then add, "I guess you will want 50 percent." He says, "More! I would like 60 percent." I ask him if he is sure he knows where it is. He says, "Absolutely! I've seen it in the cave under the water. It is deep, very deep."

Thoughts: Clint Eastwood to me is a very powerful force in the movie industry and society. As a director, he's innovative, creative, a natural leader, and reputed to be respectful to his actors. He gives them relatively free rein. As an actor, he is very talented and charismatic. Although he doesn't seem to say much in his films, there is a profound quality about his presence. He is also a very rich man. The $50 million mentioned in the dream is a lot of money. If it does represent material wealth, the project I am involved in will require me to pay a large percentage to get the help I'll need. The gold is also symbolic of great spiritual wealth or insight. And the number twelve is associated with cosmic order, the zodiac, the disciples, and twelve months of the year.

Task: I will return to meditation and contemplation this evening and will continue until I clearly understand what the $50 million in gold inwardly represents. I know that many dreams can take a long time before their inner meaning is grasped. That's a lot of money, energy, or wisdom that is waiting to be pulled to the surface, but it's deep, really deep.

EPILOGUE: THROW YOUR KITE INTO THE WIND

> I've dreamt in my life dreams that have stayed with me
> ever after, and changed my ideas: they've gone through and
> through me, like wine through water, and altered the color
> of my mind.
>
> *Emily Bronte*

I sincerely hope this book will inspire you to pay close attention to your dreams. There is one more experience I would like to share with you. This ends my story and hopefully begins yours.

Just as discontent with Roman Catholicism spawned the first Reformation, a desire to return to our spiritual roots motivates us today to revitalize out-of-touch religious practices. Church authority and dogmas no longer wield the power they once did. When atheists make the best-seller list of the *New York Times* and emphasize the irrationality of religious beliefs, we know the "times they are a changing." Where spirit was once exalted, the intellect now reigns and has accomplished astonishing technological innovations. But the intellect does not have access to the spiritual domain. People may have become much more intellectually, scientifically, and technologically sophisticated, but many are living in spiritual poverty. Religious activity and symbols have become enfeebled in most religious institutions, which creates a void within the innermost experiences of human beings. These activities and symbols have either been abandoned by the modern world's impact on the soul or they have met a natural death, and the new gods with their vital spirits have not yet reached consciousness. Although we may have numbed ourselves consciously, the spirit is not only alive and well, but is hidden in our innermost nature and can be experienced and felt in dreams.

C. G. Jung claimed that the majority of his patients were those who had lost their faith. The believers did not seek him out because, for them, church dogma and ritual served to fill the existential void. However, others, even when their goals were achieved in the material world, remained unhappy and unfulfilled, because they were satisfied with inadequate answers to the meaning of life. In these cases, Jung would often wait until the unconscious mind brought a dream that spontaneously delivered redeeming symbols that supplied what was lacking and necessary for patients to gain some insight into the meaning of their lives. Experiencing the wellspring or source of this animating energy can be a daunting experience.[1]

Spirit Lives and Can Be Felt in Dreams

Jung shares a prime example of how intimidating the spirit can be when experienced as an unseen presence in a dream. A Protestant theologian who was a patient of Jung's had this frequent dream:

> I stand on a mountain slope with a deep valley below covered with dense woods, and I know that in the middle of the woods is a dark lake. In this dream, I am aware that something has always prevented me from going there. But this time, I resolve to find the water. When I approach the lake, the atmosphere grows dark and uncanny. Suddenly a light gust of wind passes over the water's surface, which slightly ripples the water. I am seized by a panic fear and awake with a cry of terror.[2]

Jung reminded his client about the pool of Bethesda, which was stirred by a sudden breeze and then acquired curative powers when an angel descended and touched the water. Light wind is often a symbol for the spirit, perhaps even the Holy Spirit. Jung maintained that this breath of life taking wing across the dark waters is strange and mysterious like everything whose author is unknown. Something has given life to it, and it is obviously not our will. This spiritual force seems to live its own life. "The wind bloweth where it listeth, and thou hearest the sound thereof, but canst not tell whence it cometh, and whither it goeth: so is every one that is born of the Spirit" (John 3:8). This theologian trembled in its presence because he thought that spirit was something one read about in the Bible or heard at a Sunday sermon or discussed among fellow theologians. His reaction demonstrates that when spirit occurs naturally and unasked for, it can throw a naive mind into a panic.

Throw Your Kite into the Wind

I had moved from West to East for an early retirement. After a year and a half of golf, painting, and reading, my golden years took a sharp turn. A new friend who was the clinical director of the Rape Crisis Center persuaded me to give a dream seminar for the staff who worked at the center. After much resistance, I finally agreed. The seminar filled up fast because this subject attracted great interest but was a rare offering in this community. I had led many of these seminars in Los Angeles, but after my bout with cancer and the insights I had about myself during this illness, I pulled away from conducting them, because my heart wasn't in it anymore.

As the seminar date approached, I found myself stiffening with more and more resistance. About two weeks before the start date, I decided not to go through with it and plotted a withdrawal scheme that I hoped would satisfy my friend. I watched myself regress to adolescence as I concocted a fictitious story about being sick.

The night before I was going to call her with the bad news, a dream came to me that clarified the chasm between my ego and unconscious mind by contributing what was missing in my conscious attitude. The unconscious has its own agenda and can produce innovative thoughts and creative ideas.

I am standing on a sandy beach flying a kite out over the ocean. The summer day is magnificent with a clear blue sky and a favorable breeze for kite flying. Suddenly a great wind comes. It is not at my level but several hundred feet up, and I can feel the pull of the kite and the rustling of the paper covering. The tug is so strong, I get lifted into the air and fly with the kite. I don't struggle to hold on since my light grip is more than adequate. It's remarkable. So little effort is required of me to sail up into the blue sky. Below me is a panorama of ocean, earth, and distant mountains. Just as suddenly as the wind began, it stops.

I gently float down to the beach and land on the sand. The experience is so exhilarating that I want to go up again. But the wind is hundreds of feet above my head. How can I launch a paper kite that distance?

I try once unsuccessfully and then a second time. I consider tying a heavy cloth tail at the bottom to give the kite extra weight, but there is nothing to make it out of. Deciding to try one last time, I bend down very low, angle the kite, and thrust it upward. It zooms straight up and catches the wind. Off it goes, higher and higher. Then another great wind comes blowing out toward the ocean. Again I take off with the kite, only this time I go higher and further. What a remarkable panorama spreads out below me! Sky, earth, and sea broaden to distant horizons. Suddenly, I realize that the wind is not going to stop this time. I'm in for the journey of a lifetime. I awake exhilarated.

I know I was deeply moved in the dream, and when I awoke, a resurgence of energy, enthusiasm, and optimism gripped me. I decided to move with the wind of the spirit, and I have not looked back since.

Obviously, the dream experience and symbolism were urging me to give the seminar in spite of my resistance. Needless to say, I did, and it was a success. Two surprising benefits resulted from my efforts. First, I received a job offer to present my dream seminar all over the country. I considered this my "dream" job. With some astonishment, I discovered that the company provided all the necessary details and arrangements. My wife Sondra was even hired for on-site registration. We traveled all over the country and had many special adventures. Secondly, I met a book editor who was an attendee that day, and she suggested I use the material gathered from my dream study, teaching, and research to write a book. Dreams and experiences that

I collected from the seminars greatly aided the writing of this book. I realized that creating and conducting these dream seminars was my soul work, and each one was memorable and fulfilling. Paying attention to my dreams and following their guiding principles has made my life more complete.

This final piece continues the theme of my kite dream. It was written by a poet whose brother attended one of my dream seminars.

The Kite
by Gerry Stump

Blazing the trail of a brand new dream,
You race down the path to the hill.
The form with a tail on the length of a string,
Relentlessly follows your will.

Keep running and running as fast as you can;
Stay on your course—believe in your plan.
Hang on to the string and never lose sight
Of the dream you have of flying your kite.

Turning your head to glance around,
The kite gives a shudder and dips.
You tense with alarm as the tail drags the ground,
And a quiver begins on your lips.

All of a sudden the wind blows a gust;
You bolt with a certain knowing.
This is the moment you have to trust;
A kite has to go with the blowing.

Away you speed to the edge of town,
Undaunted by all you rush past.
Nothing now will slow you down,
Your kite is flying at last.

Out in the open, away from the trees,
The kite is caught by the blustery breeze.
Taking up string it soars to new height,
Tugging and pulling with all of its might.

While tugging at you from down deep inside,
Is the bursting you feel from the sense of pride
That comes with the rapture, joy and delight,
Of knowing you've launched your very first kite.

Keep running and running as fast as you can;
Stay on the course—believe in your plan.
Hang on to the string and never lose sight
Of the dream you have of flying your kite.

Live your life as if it really matters. Seek the answer to this basic question: What is my life's purpose? When you find your passion, throw your kite into the wind. Spirit is waiting to take you where you need to go. Don't ignore your dreams. Use them to protect your health, to grow, to glimpse the future, to create, to solve problems, to know your life's purpose, to mend relationships, to discover your potential, to keep you mentally alert, and to impact your community. Everyone needs something to believe in. It gives life power. Listen to the wind rustling within: it can take you to its source.

NOTES

Chapter 1: The Fog Clears: An Inner Landscape Appears

1. Gordon Zahn, *In Solitary Witness* (Springfield, IL: Templegate Publishing, 1986).
2. L. W. Rogers, *Dreams and Premonitions* (Whitefish, MT: Kessinger Publishing, 1998).
3. C. G. Jung, *Memories Dreams and Reflections* (New York: Random House, 1965), 175.
4. Mary Shelly, *Frankenstein* (Dover, DE: Prestwick House, Inc., 2006).
5. Jeremy Taylor, *Dream Work* (Ramsey, NJ: Paulist Press, 1983), 7.
6. Robert M. Utley, *The Lance and the Shield: The Life and Times of Sitting Bull* (New York: Henry Holt and Company, Inc., 1993).
7. Colours Art Publishers, Van Gogh Prints on Canvas, www.van-gogh-on-canvas.com.
8. C. G. Jung, *Psychological Reflections* (Princeton, NJ: Princeton University Press, 1970).
9. Dante Alleghieri, *The Divine Comedy* (New York: Alfred A. Knopf, 1995).
10. A term coined by Edgar Cayce. Henry Reed, *Edgar Cayce on Mysteries of the Mind* (New York: Warner Books, 1989), 54.
11. C. G. Jung, *Psychology and Alchemy* (Princeton, NJ: Princeton University Press, 1980).
12. Walt Kelly, *Pogo: We Have Met the Enemy and He Is Us* (New York: Simon and Schuster, 1972).
13. C. G Jung, *The Psychology of the Unconscious* (Princeton, NJ: Princeton University Press, 2001).

Chapter 2: God Has No Edges: A New/Old Vision

1. James Gannon, "Is God Dead in Europe? Many Signs Say Yes," *USA Today*, January 9, 2006, p. 11A

2. Stephen Prothero, "American Faith: A Work in Progress," *USA Today*, March 10, 2008, p. 11A.

3. C. G. Jung, *Memories, Dreams and Reflections* (New York: Random House, 1965), 39.

4. C. G. Jung, *Memories, Dreams and Reflections* (New York: Random House, 1965), 40.

5. C. G. Jung, *Psychological Reflections* (Princeton, NJ: Princeton University Press, 1970), 336–365.

6. David Hawkins, MD. *Power vs. Force* (Carlsbad, CA: Hay House, 2002), 183–186.

7. C. G. Jung, *Letters, Vol.2.* (Princeton, NJ: Princeton University Press, 1975).

8. A term used to describe interactions that are qualitatively different than normal ways of communicating with the world. These ways could include out-of-body experiences, clairvoyance, telepathy, psychokinesis (movement of physical objects by the mind), etc.

9. The Ramakrishna Mission Institute of Culture, Calcutta, Sri Ramakrishna, http://www.rkmathnagpur.org/sri_ramakrishna/teachings_sr.htm.

10. Thomas Keating, "Spirituality in America," *Newsweek*, Sept. 5, 2005.

11. Ibid.

12. Jerry Adler, "In Search of the Spiritual," *Newsweek,* Sept. 5, 2005

13. Michael Gelert, *The Still Good Hand of God* (York Beach, ME: Nicolas-Hayes, Inc., 1991), 37.

14. The Associated Press, "Three Former Professors Sue Oral Roberts University," *The Arizona Daily Star Newspaper*, Oct. 6, 2007.

Chapter 3: We Are All the Anointed Ones: The New Messiahs!

1. Sam Harris, *The End of Faith* (New York: WW Norton, 2005).

2. Christopher Hitchens, *God Is Not Great* (New York: Hachette Book Group, 2007).

3. C. G. Jung, *Civilization in Transition*, Collected Works of C. G. Jung, Vol. 10 (Princeton, NJ: Princeton University Press, 1970), 304.

4. G. A. Gaskell, *Dictionary of All Scriptures and Myths* (New York: The Julian Press, Inc., 1960), 280.

5. Isaac Meyer, *Qabbalah* (Whitefish, MT: Kessinger Publishing Co., 2003), 336.

6. Joel Covitz, *Visions of the Night* (Boston: Shambhala,1990), 7.

7. Rabbi Arthur Green, *Seek My Face, Speak My Name* (Woodstock, VT: Jewish Lights Publishing, 2003).

8. Nicholas Kristof, "Social Entrepreneurs, Not Politics, May Change the World," *The New York Times*, January 29, 2008.

9. Allan Luks, *The Healing Power of Doing Good* (New York: Ballantine Books, 1991).

10. Dr. Brian Weiss, *Many Masters—Many Lives* (New York: Simon & Shuster, A Fireside Book, 1988).

11. Christopher Hitchens, *God Is Not Great* (New York: Hachette Book Group, 2007).

12. Anne Lamott, *Thinkexist*, www.thinkexist.com.

13. Leonard Pitts, "Learning to Live Together," *The Miami Herald*, December 9, 2007.

14. Michael Talbot, *Holographic Universe* (New York: Harper Perennial, 1991), 83–118.

15. Bernie Sigel, *Love, Medicine and Miracles* (New York: Harper & Row, 1986).

16. Bruce McArthur, *Your Life* (Virginia Beach, VA: ARE Press, 1993).

Chapter 4: Is There a Doctor in Your House? Yes!

1. C. Kerenyi, *Asklepios* (New York, NY: Pantheon Books, 1959).

2. Sharon Sakson, *Paws & Effect: The Healing Power of Dogs* (New York: Alyson Books, 2007).

3. Edelstein and Edelstein, *Asklepios, A Collection and Interpretation of the Testimonies* (Baltimore, MD: Johns Hopkins University Press, 1998).

4. C. A. Meier, *Healing Dream and Ritual* (Einsiedeln, Switzerland: Daimon Verlag, CH, 1989).

5. Jeff Larson, "Moses Receives the 10 Commandments" cartoon, The Back Pew: Clean Humor & God's Truth, www.thebackpew.com.

6. Albert Schweitzer, *Out of My Life and Thought* (The Albert Schweitzer Library), (Baltimore, MD: The Johns Hopkins University Press, 1998).

7. C. G. Jung, *Memories, Dreams and Reflections* (New York: Random House, 1965), 353.

8. Lloyd Ostendorf, "President Lincoln at Prayer" original ink and wash by Lloyd Ostendorf, Abraham Lincoln Collectibles. Interactive Data Technologies. http://abelincoln.com/ostendorf_positives/sc-6.html

Chapter 5: Dream Incubation: Hatching Your Golden Egg

1. John Briggs, *Fire in the Crucible: Understanding the Process of Creative Genius* (Grand Rapids, MI: Phanes Press, 2000).
2. C. G. Jung, *The Structure and Dynamics of the Psyche*, Collected Works of C. G. Jung, Volume 8 (Princeton, NJ: Princeton University Press, 1970).
3. Gayle Delaney, *Living Your Dreams* (New York: Harper & Row, 1979), 20. The questions that I use in the initials stages of the incubation preparation have their origin in her work. They have been immeasurably helpful in getting the conscious mind to deeper levels of the incubation issue.
4. Henry Reed, "Dream Incubation Ritual," *Sundance Community Dream Journal* 2.1 (1977): 9.
5. Montague Ullman, *Working With Dream* (New York: Delacorte Press, 1979).
6. Claudia Wallis, "Faith and Healing," *Time*, June 24, 1996, 58–64.
7. R. Rosenthal and K. Fode, "The Effect of Experimenter Bias on Performance of the Albino Rat," *Behavioral Science* 8 (1963): 183–189.
8. R. Rosenthal and L. Jacobson, "Teachers' Expectancies Determinants of Pupils' IQ Gains," *Psychological Reports* 19 (1963): 115.
9. Gayle Delaney, *Living Your Dreams* (New York: Harper & Row, 1979), 22. This book stimulated the idea for the questioning technique.
10. The CD seems to have a very dramatic and dynamic effect on the subconscious mind's capacity to respond to the conscious need for problem resolution. The relaxation coupled with original music and the focus on the issue at hand brings about vivid and potent dreams. (See order form for ordering information.)
11. Mark Thurston, *Dream Interpretation Made Easy* (Virginia Beach, VA: ARE Press, 1986), 36.

Chapter 6: Unveiling the Mystery: Getting the Message

1. Strephon Kaplan Williams, *The Jungian—Senoi Dreamwork Manual* (Berkeley, CA: Journey Press, 1980), 90.
2. Mark Thurston, *How to Interpret Dreams* (Virginia Beach, VA: ARE Press, 1978), 58–69.
3. Dr. Bernie Siegel, *Peace, Love and Healing* (New York: Harper & Row, 1980)

4. Robert L. Van de Castle, PhD, *Our Dreaming Mind* (New York:Ballantine Books, 1994), 128

5. C. G. Jung, *Psychological Reflections* (Princeton, NJ: Princeton University Press, 1970), 53–77.

6. Ibid.

7. Ibid., 74.

8. C. G. Jung, *Memories, Dreams and Reflections* (New York: Random House, 1965), 133.

9. C. G. Jung, *Man and His Symbols* (New York: Doubleday & Company, Inc., 1969), 50.

10. Montague Ullman and Nan Zimmerman, *Working with Dreams* (New York: Delacorte Press, 1979).

11. Strephon Kaplan Williams, *The Jungian-Senoi Dreamwork Manual* (Berkeley, CA: Journey Press, 1980), 129–136.

12. Montague Ullman and Nan Zimmerman, *Working with Dreams* (New York: Delacorte Press, 1979), 208–209.

13. Ibid., 205.

14. Dr. Marcia Emery, *Intuition Workbook* (Englewood Cliffs, NJ: Prentice Hall, 1994), 9.

Chapter 7: Dreams Have No Boundaries: All Doors Open to the Dreaming Mind

1. Henry Reed, *Edgar Cayce on Mysteries of the Mind* (New York: Warner Books, Inc., 1989), 50–62.

2. Mark Thurston, *How to Interpret Your Dreams* (Virginia Beach, VA: ARE Press, 1978), 3–6.

3. Ward Hill Lamon, *Recollections of Abraham Lincoln, 1847–1865* (Whitefish, MT: Kessenger Publishing Co., 2007).

4. Charlotte Berad, *Third Reich of Dreams, The Nightmares of a Nation 1933–1939* (Wellingborough, Gr. Britain: The Aquarian Press, 1985), 79–80.

5. Elliot S Valenstein, *The War of the Soups and the Spark* (New York: Columbia University Press, 2006).

6. Raymond de Becker, *The Understanding of Dreams and Their Influence on the History of Man* (Chicago, IL: Bell Publishing Co., 1968), 82–102.

7. Dr. Gayle Delaney, *Breakthrough Dreaming* (New York: Bantam Books, 1991), 7.

8. Sandra Collier, *Wake Up to Your Dream* (New York: Scholastic Inc., 1996).

9. George Schindler, "Dreaming of Victory," *New Scientist*, May 31, 1997.

10. Deirdre Barrett, PhD, *The Committee of Sleep: How Artists, Scientists and Athletes Use Dreams for Problem-Solving—and How You Can Too* (New York: Crown Books, 2001).

11. David Harrison, "From Dream Lead to Invention," *Bristol Times*, November 26, 2002.

12. Deirdre Barrett, PhD, *The Committee of Sleep: How Artists, Scientists and Athletes Use Dreams for Problem-Solving—and How You Can Too* (New York: Crown Books, 2001).

13. Dr. Anjak Hazarika, *Daring To Dream: Cultivating Corporate Creativity through Dreamwork* (Thousand Oaks, CA: Sage Publications, 1998).

14. Kevin Todeschi, *Dream Interpretation Made Easy* (New York: Paraview Press, 2000), 116.

15. Raymond de Becker, *The Understanding of Dreams and Their Influence on the History of Man* (Chicago, IL: Bell Publishing Co., 1968), 80.

16. Doris Kearns Goodwin, *Lyndon Johnson and the American Dream* (New York: St. Martins Griffin, 1991).

17. Jeremy Taylor, *Where People Fly and Water Runs Uphill* (New York: Warner Books, 1992).

18. Mike Fish, "Manlius Remembers Max," *The Syracuse Herald Journal*, March 19, 2001.

19. Mark Thurston, *How to Interpret Your Dreams* (Virginia Beach, VA: ARE Press, 1978), 129.

20. Zak Martin, "The Man Who Dreamed of Horse Race Winners," UK Psychics, www.ukpsychics.com/luck2.html.

21. Walt Stover, *Dreams—My Lamp unto the Darkness* (Poughkeepsie, NY: Hudson House, 2007), 148.

22. Harmon Bro, *Dreams in the Life of Prayer and Meditation* (Virginia Beach, VA: Inner Vision, 1985), 86.

23. Edgar Cayce, *Dreams and Dreaming* Part I, ed. Marilyn Peterson (Virginia Beach, VA: ARE Press, 1976), 143.

24. Robert Frost, *Mountain Interval* (Whitefish, MT: Kessinger Publishing LLC, 2007).

25. Michael Talbot, *The Holographic Universe* (New York: Harper Collins Inc., 1991), 239–262, 268–273.

26. Plato, *The Symposium* (New York: Penguin Classics, 2003).
27. "Teilhard De Chardin's Quotes," Fun Shun, www.funshun.com/quotes/author-103.html.

Epilogue: Throw Your Kite into the Wind

1. C. G. Jung, *Memories, Dreams and Reflections* (New York: Random House, 1965), 140.
2. C. G. Jung, *The Archetypes of the Collective Unconscious* (Princeton, NJ: Princeton University Press, 1959), 17.

BIBLIOGRAPHY

Barasch, Marc Ian. *Healing Dreams: Exploring the Dreams That Can Transform Your Life.* New York: Riverhead Books, 2000.

Browne, Sylvia. *Sylvia Browne's Book of Dreams.* New York: Dutton Adult, 2002.

Delaney, Gayle M. *All About Dreams: Everything You Need to Know About *Why We Have Them *What They Mean *and How to Put Them to Work for You.* New York: HarperOne, 1998.

Delaney, Gayle M. *In Your Dreams: Falling, Flying and Other Dream Themes—A New Kind of Dream Dictionary.* New York: HarperOne, 1997.

Epel, Naomi. *Writers Dreaming: 26 Writers Talk about Their Dreams and the Creative Process.* New York: Vintage Books, 1994.

Faraday, Ann. *Dream Power.* New York: Berkeley Books, 1986.

Faraday, Ann. *The Dream Game.* New York: Harpercollins, 1990.

Garfield, Patricia, PhD. *Creative Dreaming.* New York: Ballantine Books, 1985.

Gendlin, Eugene. *Let Your Body Interpret Your Dreams.* New York: Chiron Publications, 1985.

Guiley, Rosemary Ellen. *Dreamwork for Soul.* New York: Berkley Trade, 1998.

Hall, James A. *Jungian Dream Interpretation: A Handbook of Theory and Practice.* Toronto, Canada: Inner City Books, 1983.

Hillman, James. *Dream & the Underworld.* New York: Harper Paperbacks, 1979.

Johnson, Robert A. *Inner Work: Using Dreams and Active Imagination for Personal Growth.* New York: HarperOne, 1989.

Jung, C. G. *Seminar on Dream Analysis.* Princeton, NJ: Princeton University Press, 1984.

Linn, Denise. *Hidden Power of Dreams.* New York: Wellspring/Ballantine, 1997.

Mellick, Jill. *The Art of Dreaming: Tools for Creative Dream Work.* Berkeley, CA: Conari Press, 2001.

Mindell, Arnold. *The Dreammaker's Apprentice: Using Heightened States of Consciousness to Interpret Dreams.* Charlottesville, VA: Hampton Roads Publishing Company, 2002.

Mattoon, Mary Ann. *Understanding Dreams.* New York: Continuum International Publishing Group, 1984.

Moss, Robert. *The Three "Only" Things: Tapping the Power of Dreams, Coincidence, and Imagination.* Novato, CA: New World Library, 2007.

Richmond, Cynthia. *Dream Power.* New York: Simon & Schuster, 2001.

Rock, Andrea. *The Mind at Night: The New Science of How and Why We Dream.* New York: Basic Books, 2005.

Sanford, John A. *Dreams: God's Forgotten Language.* New York: HarperOne, 1989.

Sanford, John A. *Dreams and Healing.* Mahwah, NJ: Paulist Press, 1988.

Savary, Louis. *Dreams and Spiritual Growth.* New York: Paulist Press, 1984.

Sechrist, Elsie. *Dreams: Your Magic Mirror: With Interpretations of Edgar Cayce.* Virginia Beach, VA: ARE Press, 1995.

Shainberg, Catherine. *Kabbalah and the Power of Dreaming: Awakening the Visionary Life.* Rochester, VT: Inner Traditions, 2005.

Sullivan, Kathleen. *Recurring Dreams: A Journey to Wholeness.* Freedom, CA: Crossing Press, 1998.

Tick, Edward. *The Practice of Dream Healing: Bringing Ancient Greek Mysteries into Modern Medicine.* Wheaton, IL: Quest Books, 2001.

Van de Castle, Robert, PhD. *Our Dreaming Mind.* New York: Ballantine Books, 1994.

Wray, T. J. *Grief Dreams: How They Help Us Heal After the Death of a Loved One.* San Francisco, CA: Jossey-Bass, 2005.

DREAMS: THE WISDOM IN SLEEP

Companion CDs by Arthur Bernard, PhD

Within each of us is a super-intelligence.
Its language is dreams: its subject is you.
C. G. Jung

By tapping into your dreaming mind, you can access more of your brain's capacity. These CDs will help you awaken your sleeping genius within.

CD 1: *Dreams for General Problem Solving* will help you induce dreams for solving most problems.

CD 2: *Dreams for Discovering Money-Making Abilties* will help you uncover new ways to increase financial abundance.

CD 3: *Dreams and Spiritual Progress* will help you create dreams to accelerate your spiritual growth.

CD 4: *Dreams for Health and Healing* will show you how to produce dreams that play an active role in your health care.

Send for these unique CDs and explore new dimensions in personal growth while you sleep.

SEE NEXT PAGE FOR ORDERING AND SPECIAL OFFER

ORDER FORM

Name_____

Address_____

City_____

State_____Zip_____

Tel. (   ) _____

Email_____

Please send me CD 1_____ CD 2_____ CD 3_____ CD 4_____
at $11.99 each plus $3 per CD for shipping and handling.

BUY THREE AND GET THE FOURTH FREE

Enclosed is a ____check or ____money order payable to:
Arthur Bernard, PO Box 502, Green Valley, AZ 85622

To pay by credit card, go to www.DreamTechniques.com or mail
this form to the PO box above.

Questions or comments?
Fax: 520-207-9236
E-mail: Dreemdoc@aol.com
Website: www.DreamTechniques.com

Printed in the United States
140471LV00004B/1/P